13th August 2017

To Helen,

EGYPT'S THOUSAND DAYS OF Revolution

A PARADE OF PRESIDENTS

On the occasion of your 90th Birthday, with much appreciation and affection for your long friendship with us all over the years!

BY

ALEXANDER MURRAY

Alex Murray

Printed in United Kingdom and United States

First Published 2015

ISBN 978-84-944274-0-4

Banana Books Europe
www.bananabooks.eu

All photos by Alexander Murray, except 7 July 2013 taken by Teleri Williams

Photo Editing by Iona Hodgson

Front Cover Photo: Arcade of Muhammad Ali Mosque, Cairo

Rear Cover Photo: View to Western Desert from Al Mokatam, Cairo

Contents

Many people have encouraged me on the journey to publish this book. I would like to acknowledge and thank, in particular, Teleri, Kathryn, Richard, Fernando, Dave, Ann, Evelyn and Catherine.

AM 2015

To my wife, mother and late father.

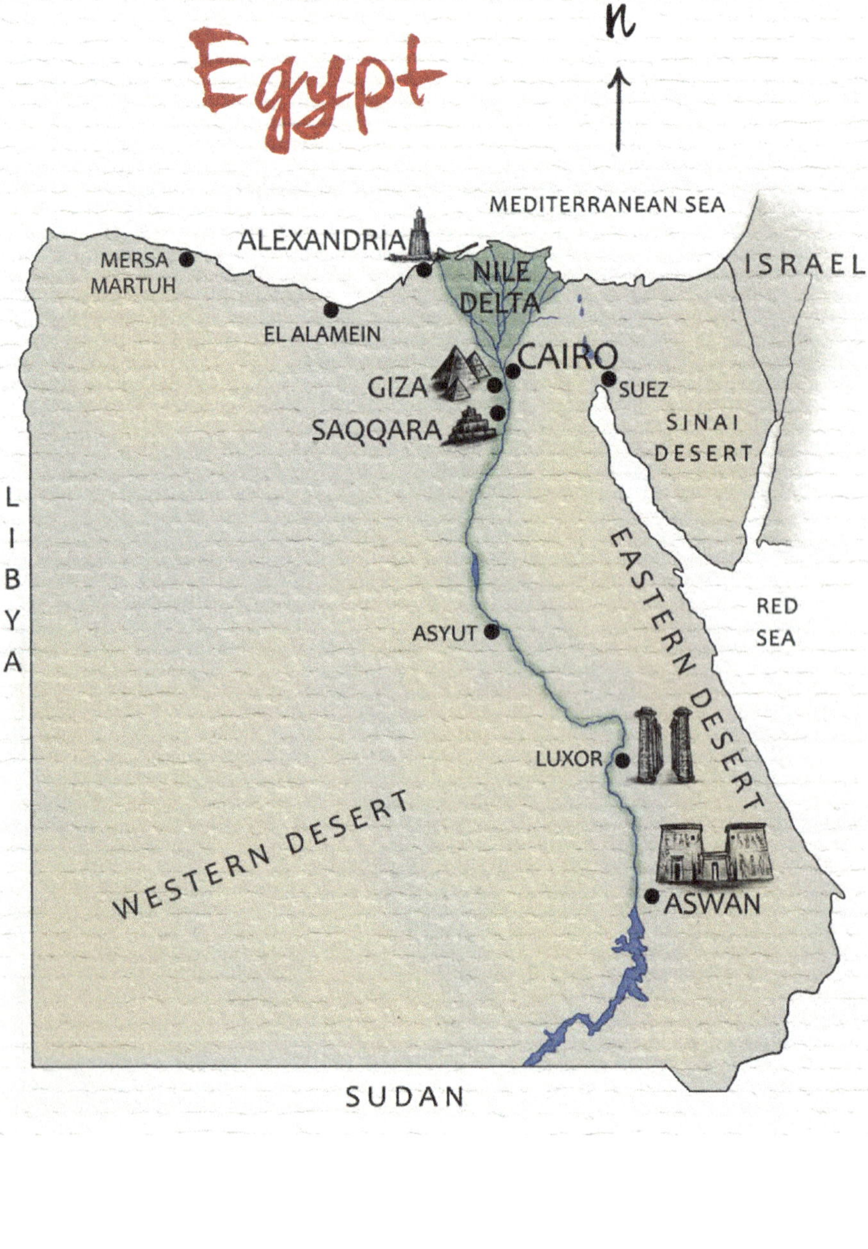

Egypt
n
MEDITERRANEAN SEA
ALEXANDRIA
MERSA
MARTUH
EL ALAMEIN
NILE
DELTA
ISRAEL
CAIRO
GIZA
SUEZ
SAQQARA
SINAI
DESERT
LIBYA
EASTERN DESERT
RED
SEA
ASYUT
LUXOR
WESTERN DESERT
ASWAN
SUDAN

Cairo

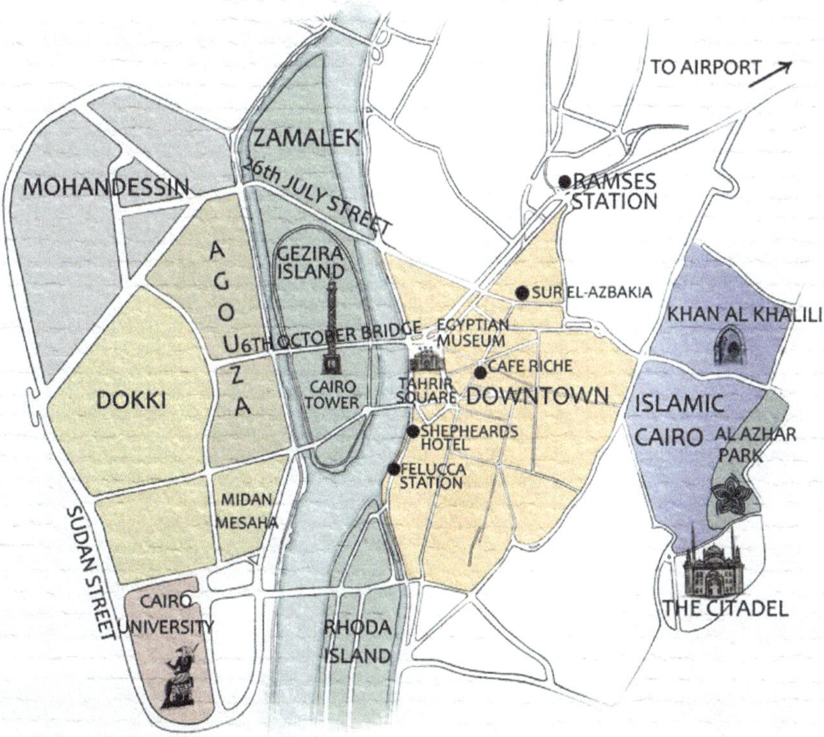
TO AIRPORT
ZAMALEK
MOHANDESSIN
26th JULY STREET
RAMSES STATION
AGOUZA
GEZIRA ISLAND
SUR EL-AZBAKIA
KHAN AL KHALILI
6TH OCTOBER BRIDGE
EGYPTIAN MUSEUM
CAFE RICHE
DOKKI
CAIRO TOWER
TAHRIR SQUARE
DOWNTOWN
ISLAMIC CAIRO
AL AZHAR PARK
SHEPHEARDS HOTEL
FELUCCA STATION
MIDAN MESAHA
SUDAN STREET
CAIRO UNIVERSITY
RHODA ISLAND
THE CITADEL

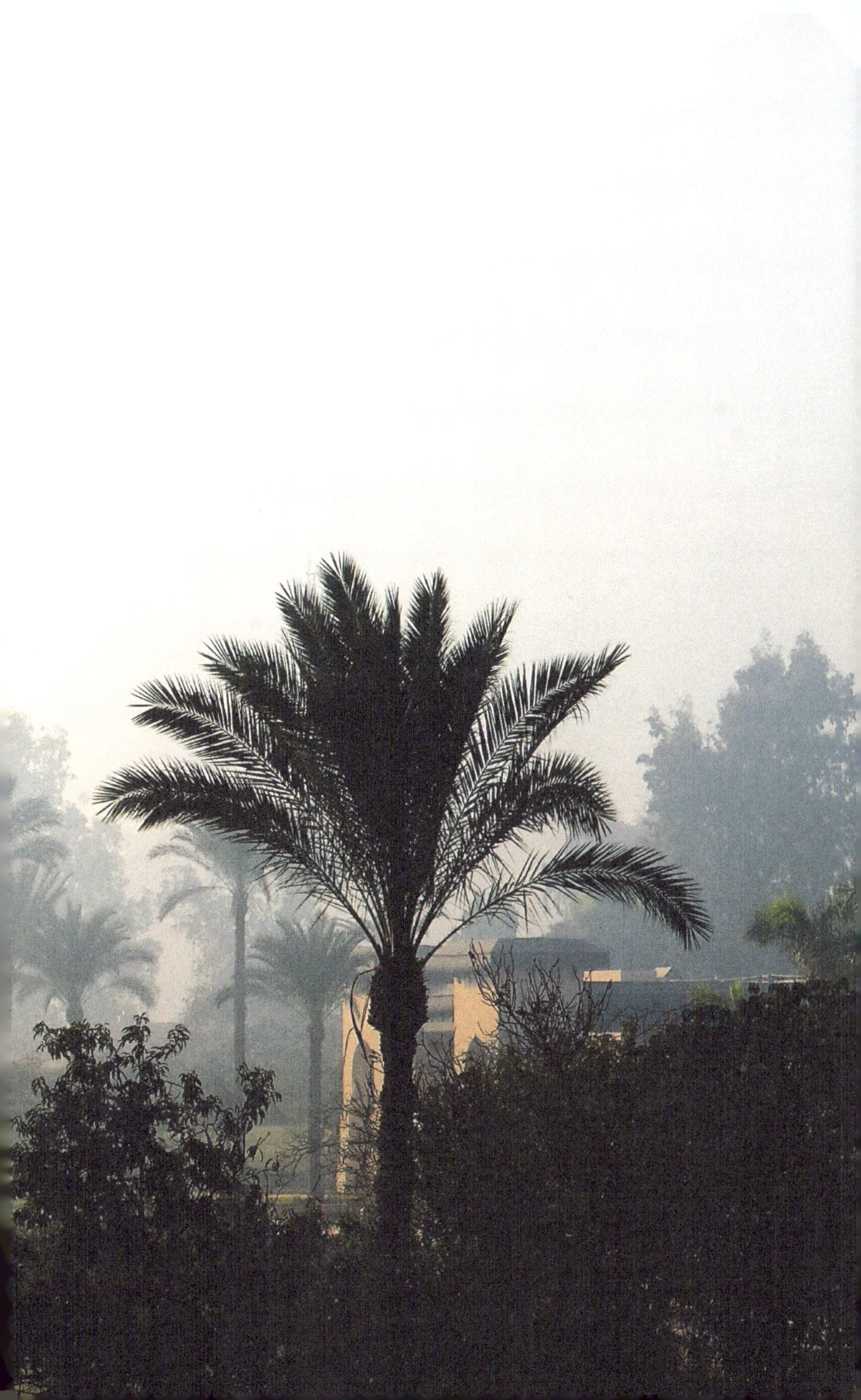

Prologue

Eshta Bel Avel – The Cream of the Milk

23 JUNE 2014

As I sit writing this prologue on a sunny June morning in Midan Mesaha near Cairo University, the scene of so much recent unrest and killing, I hear the news that three Al Jazeera journalists including the former BBC man, Peter Greste, have been jailed for seven years on trumped-up charges; the sentences are not only unjust but will be served in dire conditions.

As if on cue, police sirens are going off all around me as their vehicles chase round the square with blue lights flashing. Men stop and stare. Some are bewildered; some gesticulate and shout angrily.

I've wanted to visit Egypt since I was fourteen years old. I remember sitting in an art-appreciation class, transfixed by slides of the pyramids and ancient temples of the Nile, thinking, as the lights came up, 'They are so magical and far away, I'll never, ever get there.' It was a limiting belief I held until I was twenty years old and I can still picture that June morning in 1980 when it all changed.

I was in the law library of Edinburgh University, putting the finishing touches to my plan to follow in Laurie Lee's footsteps through Spain, inspired by his book *As I Walked Out One Midsummer Morning*. I should have had my head down in the constitutional law books piled high in front of me, preparing for exams, but, in my mind's eye, I was already treading sun-scorched tracks across the great Meseta plain of the Spanish peninsula. Travel, for me, has always been 'eshta bel avel'.

Across the aisle, a picture of the pyramids on the front page of a newspaper, being read by a fellow student, caught my eye. I thought suddenly, 'If I can get to Spain, I can also move the levers and pulleys of the world to arrive in that far-off, magical land of Egypt.'

I threw on my jacket, found a travel supplement in the newspaper rack beside the library's front desk, scanned the small ads, noted down a couple of telephone numbers, searched my pockets for change, and within minutes I was in a telephone box talking to a 'bucket shop' in London.

'Do you do flights to . . . Egypt?' I felt the world cracking open as I named the destination.

'Of course,' came the matter-of-fact reply.

'You do! Right, well . . . what's the cheapest you've got?'

'We have JAL at about £190 return, depending on your dates. When do you want to travel?'

'I need to save a bit first. I'll call you later.'

I did call them – a year later in 1981 – and I did fly JAL, without realising that I was going to witness the assassination of Anwar Sadat and have a personal brush with death. It would be thirty years before I visited the country again.

This book is essentially a journal, and like all journals it developed organically, day by day, dealing with a very personal and deeply felt re-encounter with a country that was pivotal in my own personal development but in which enormous political upheaval played an important part. That political turmoil became the main theme as the entries continued, and I returned to the country ten times in the following thousand days and was present at many of the key events in Egypt's recent history.

Those events have their roots in the overthrow of British rule in 1952 by the so-called Free Officers Movement, a group of disenfranchised lower- to middle-class Egyptian army officers. They ousted King Farouk, the nominal head of state, and went on to hold the presidency for the next sixty years. The populist General Gamal Nasser nationalised the Suez Canal in 1956, attempted to create a pan-Arabian alliance, constructed the Aswan High Dam and lost the Sinai Peninsula to Israel in the Six Day War of 1967. On his death in 1970, Anwar Sadat inherited a dispirited country. He launched the Yom Kippur War against Israel on 6 October 1973 to boost morale and retake the Sinai. He was successful in the first objective but failed in the second. The Sinai was only restored to Egypt through the 'land for peace' agreement of the Camp David Accords signed by Sadat in 1979. Most of the Arab world disapproved of Sadat's deal and it led to his assassination by Islamic fundamentalists in 1981. The new President Mubarak upheld the peace treaty but suppressed the fundamentalists and all other opponents by means of an Emergency Law under which any civilian could be detained indefinitely without charge. The country's population expanded, the economy continued its downward spiral and corruption spread. In 2010, the Arab Spring popular protests swept the Middle East. The region-wide call for freedom and social justice culminated in the Egyptian revolution of 25 January 2011 and Mubarak fell. The narrow Islamist agenda of his successor, the democratically elected President Mursi, along with the new president's failure to improve living conditions, led to his own overthrow on 3 July 2013. Adly Mansour led an interim presidency during which over 1,000 Mursi supporters died when they were ejected from their protest camps before General Abdel Fattah el-Sisi – the ouster of Mursi – was elected president earlier this month. Sisi continues the tough line against fundamentalists and calls on all citizens to work hard to restore the country's wealth.

My journey with Egypt has spanned the last thirty years of this period, from the Sadat assassination and my own near death and, much later, near arrest, through the revolutions of 25 January 2011 and 30 June 2013, to the parade of presidents comprising Mubarak, Mursi, Mansour and Sisi.

The golden thread of this journal is what it is to live in one of the poorest and most densely populated cities in the world; the reality beyond the headlines we read in the Western press or the TV bulletins we see delivered by reporters in bullet-proof vests.

The past thirty years under a military dictatorship have been unrelentingly harsh for the vast majority of the people in Egypt, now numbering nearly ninety million. No one can be confident that a better future lies in store for them – a future they long for and need and deserve, especially the 70% of the population under the age of twenty-five who brought so much energy, purpose and determination to the popular uprisings. Perhaps more than anything, seeing first-hand the youths' energy in every gesture, laugh and embrace has given me the greatest hope for the country but at the same time awakened the greatest dread: that by retaining control of the assets of physical force necessary to maintain absolute power, those presently ruling the country will continue to fulfil the age-old adage that 'absolute power corrupts absolutely'.

It continues to be a significant journey of discovery for me. Day by day, month by month, visit by visit and event by event, I've deepened, developed and often corrected my understanding of the forces and agendas at play, by talking and listening to a wide range of people from taxi drivers to lawyers and businessmen, all going about their daily lives in the midst of great happenings. This book brings my work on Egypt together for the first time, and my hope is that the photographs I took on the day of each respective entry intensify the street-level vision. Many people who have previewed the book have said that they feel they are standing beside me on the streets of Cairo, and I hope you will enjoy being there too.

Alexander Murray 2014

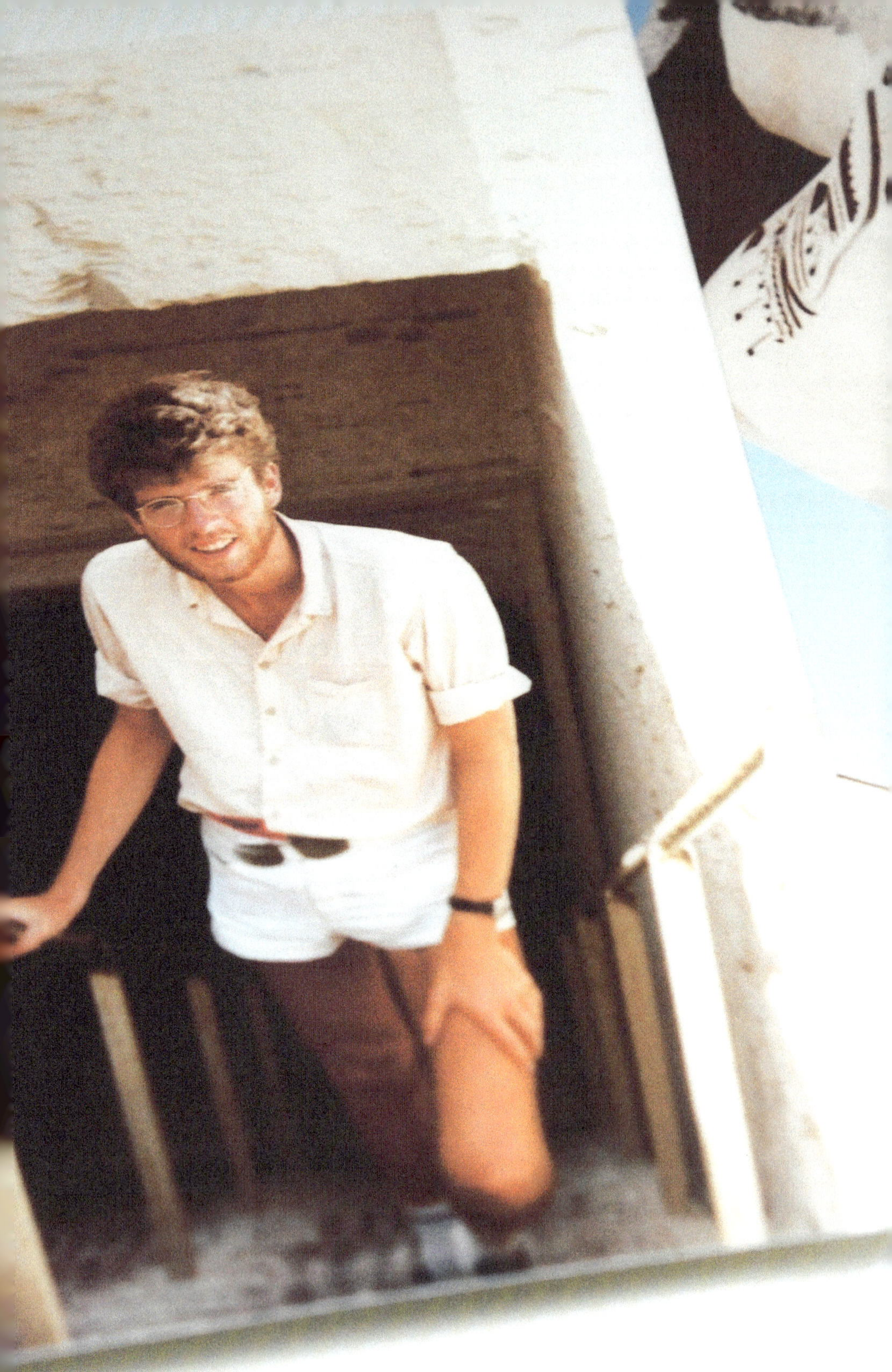

Chapter 1

Egypt Again

11 FEBRUARY 2011: MUBARAK FALLS

I was only a few kilometres from President Anwar Sadat when he was gunned down nearly thirty years ago in Cairo, and Hosni Mubarak began his period as military dictator of Egypt. That day I had rushed to the windows of the Islamic Museum to see the jets of the air-force display team scream overhead on their way to the stadium hosting the 6 October Victory Celebrations just down the road. It was under cover of the flypast that disenchanted Islamist troops, part of the president's Praetorian Guard, raised their machine guns and fired into the lines of dignitaries assembled on the tribune. Sadat was hit thirty-seven times and fatally injured, and Mubarak, beside him, lost a fingertip. Some say that it was truncated as he pointed out the president to the assassins.

The country made a mark on me physically. On my first day I was nearly killed by a bus; on the last, I ate a bad liver sandwich from a street stall that resulted in my own liver nearly packing in completely from a rampant inflammation of hepatitis A. I spent two weeks in hospital on my return home and then underwent a year-long recuperation, which meant I missed months of my final year of university.

It made a mark on me psychologically; it was the moment of realisation of my ability to be free as a young adult and determine my direction in life, as well as come to appreciate, viscerally, that many others on the planet were not so fortunate.

As a result, these recent days of revolution, which have led up to Mubarak's resignation today, have been absorbing to watch as the people wrestled free of his iron, self-styled 'father-of-the-nation' grip. I do hope that this latest stand for freedom will be successful.

In 1981, I said that I wouldn't return until significant change had occurred, and predicted a wait of thirty years. That period expires this year; maybe it's time for another visit.

The photo here shows me in September 1981 on the steps of Tutankhamen's Tomb in the Valley of the Kings, Luxor, set against photos of the statue which many say inspired Shelley's poem *Ozymandias* that I took at the same time. After all these years I can still recite it perfectly and, perhaps, the words ring especially true today.

OZYMANDIAS

I met a traveller from an antique land
Who said: Two vast and trunkless legs of stone
Stand in the desert. Near them, on the sand,
Half sunk, a shattered visage lies, whose frown
And wrinkled lip, and sneer of cold command
Tell that its sculptor well those passions read
Which yet survive, stamped on these lifeless things,
The hand that mocked them and the heart that fed.
And on the pedestal these words appear:
'My name is Ozymandias, king of kings:
Look on my works, ye Mighty, and despair!'
Nothing beside remains. Round the decay
Of that colossal wreck, boundless and bare
The lone and level sands stretch far away.

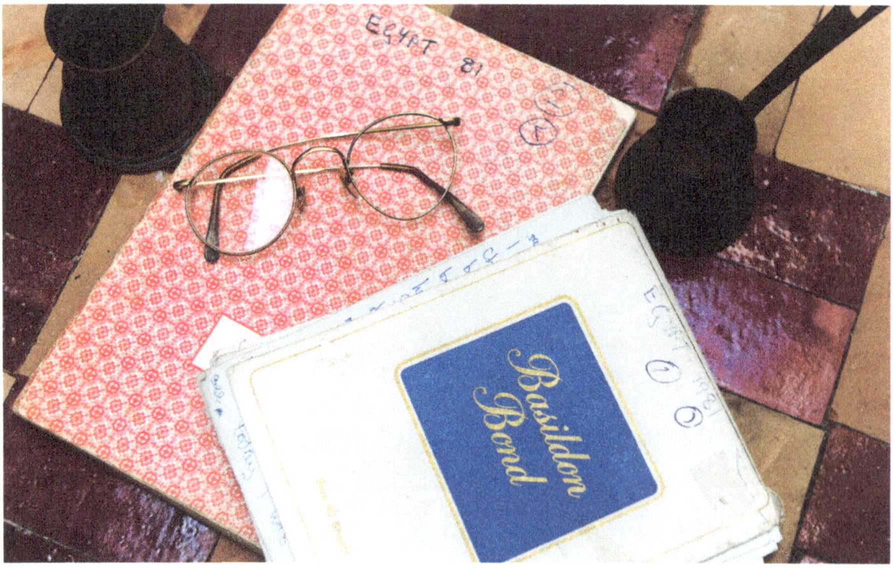
EGYPT 81
Basildon
Bond

12 JULY 2011: PREMONITION FULFILLED

I return to Cairo tomorrow. I feel something of the old thrill of travelling into the unknown, and yet it isn't the unknown. Here's the last entry of my 1981 Egyptian journal written on the day after President Sadat was assassinated.

> *Cairo, 7 October 1981*
>
> *And there below us, as the plane banks in the night, is a lie. Scattered like jewels on black velvet, rich, sparkling, beautiful, breathtaking . . . Cairo. Cairo, the city of dust, dirt, noise and teeming people.*
>
> *And I am deeply moved; I would like to cry. Those people down there are part of my world and yet I have hope and they have none. I can change my existence, they cannot. They are so desperately poor, so desperately over-crowded, so desperately depressed. It will need generations to change anything.*
>
> *I have learned many things on this trip. I know what it is like to be run over and feel as if I'm about to die, I know the thrill of discovery and I know what heat is, what dust is, what it's like to live in a cage, to feel the atmosphere when earth-shattering events well up all around. I know what Egypt is.*

I was twenty-one years old then and I predicted that thirty years would pass before my next visit. That time is up tomorrow, almost to the day.

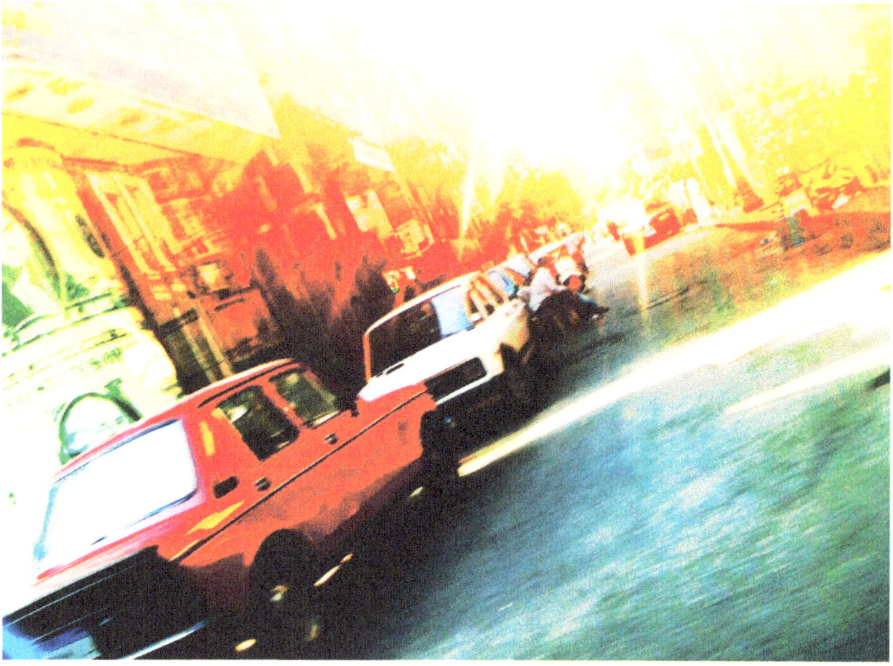

13 JULY 2011: CAIRO AGAIN

How can I describe coming back? A tingle ran down my back the moment I saw 'CAIRO' on the monitor above the departure gate at the airport. The features, complexions and robes of many of the Egyptians in the boarding queue stirred a sense of long-lost recognition. A vague apprehension fluttered in my stomach as people looked me up and down, soon to be the stranger again in a very foreign land.

I'm sitting now on a stool outside a bazaar in Zamalek, Cairo, with a glass of mint tea in front of me. Is this really happening? Am I really here again after all this time . . . here in this magical, terrifying land? Is it the same me that has returned? Do I think the same, feel the same, write the same?

I try to grasp my younger self, but it's like chasing a shadow through fog and my fingertips never quite touch his shoulder. They can, and do, touch my original journal in my bag beside me, which I re-read to discover a collage of images from that first arrival:

> *Cairo, 5 September 1981*
>
> *. . . banking high, leaning over a petrified city in the desert . . . engines reverse throttle, sand under the wings, I know what it is like to land on the moon . . . warm billowing air . . . 'This is Egypt,' I say, as I step from the plane . . . soldiers, buses, tarmac and atop the terminal building set on a trellis the name 'CAIRO' – oh, magic moment . . . crazy, skewing taxi, our driver hunched over the wheel, hungry for the road, flashing past a world of tumbled buildings, feeble donkeys, filthy children, tea places lit by cold fluorescent strips, crowds, robes . . . we pile drive into the heart of Cairo, rubble, dust, heat and life vital in the air.*

I experienced all these sensations in Cairo today. It's furnace hot, much hotter than the France I've just come from.

Here comes Shona, my wife, whose work in Egypt this month has been the catalyst for my unexpected return visit, although I firmly believe that a deeper synchronicity is at work.

She told the owner of the bazaar to look out for my arrival, which is why he called me over for tea the moment I got out of the taxi. He's just offered me 5,000 camels for her, but I declined, seeing that it's her birthday.

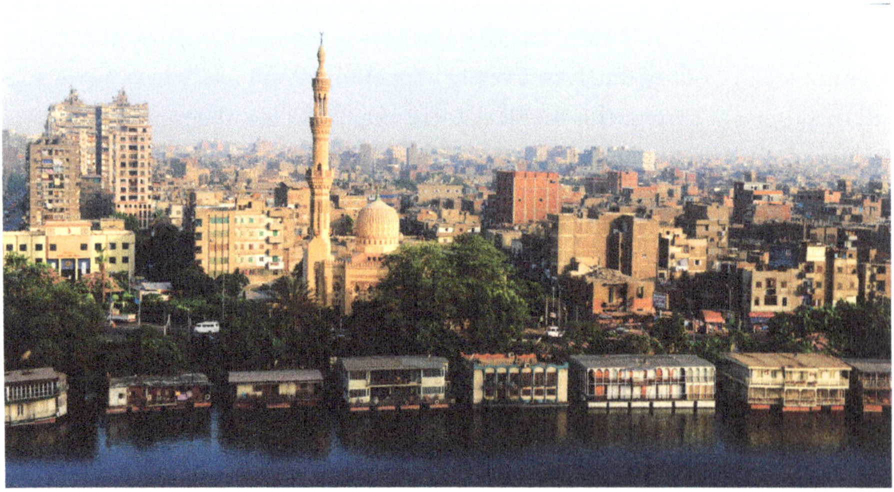

14 JULY 2011: ONTO THE STREET

I fall asleep fully clothed on my bed after breakfast and have to haul myself out of a deep pool of dreams. I listen to the constant honks of car horns in the street and study the sharp slants of sun as they strike the dusty facade of the building opposite. You need to summon your energies to enter the heat and fray of the Cairo streets.

I do gather myself and head out to cross traffic-congested roads, squeeze between tightly parked cars and navigate broken pavements to reach a tiny shop that sells SIM cards for phones. Shona pointed it out last night. From nowhere comes that slight disruption to expectations, which still typifies getting things done here.

'Come with me,' says the shopkeeper.

'Where to?'

'Please follow . . .'

I do, but wonder if everyone's thinking, 'Ah-ha, they've got another one.'

'Sit down' or 'Come with me' were the two most common responses whenever I tried to accomplish a task in 1981 and things don't seem to have changed. I notice I trust people more, even the guy who gives my passport to a boy and asks him to get it copied nearby. I think one's senses develop over the years with all of life's experiences and it's easier to go with the local flow.

My phone's set up and I stroll round the area. The distinguishing factors of Egypt emerge from behind its similarities with other very foreign countries I know like Brazil or India. It's in a hand movement, or a high step down from a pavement, or that particular smell of just-off fruit that wafts under your nose, as you seek your bearings on a street corner. Now it's back to the hotel to do some work and try to get the connections sorted out for a conference call with Miami tomorrow afternoon. Let's see how well I go with that flow.

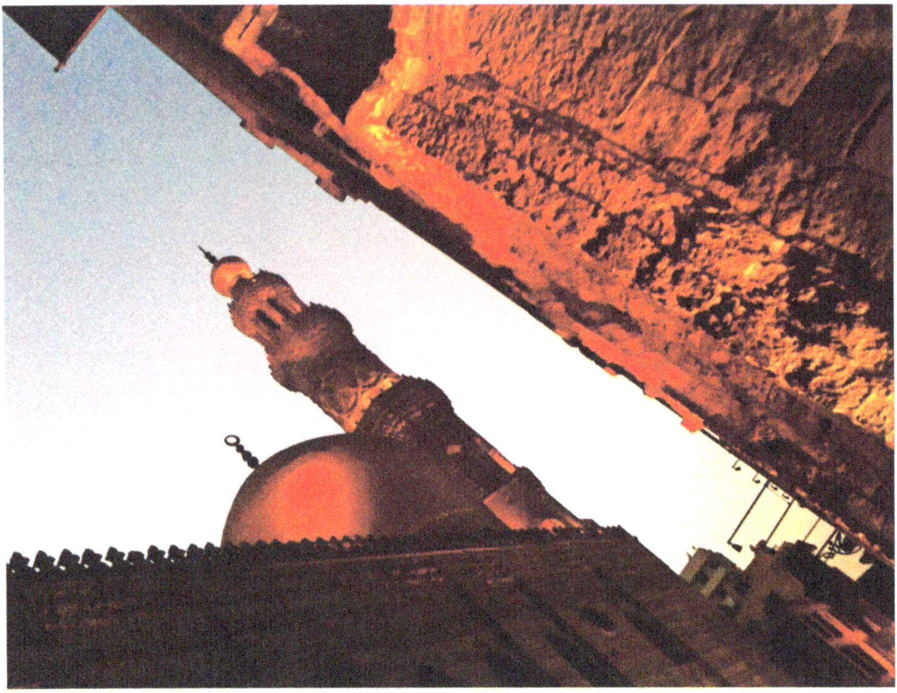

15 JULY 2011: KHAN AL-KHALILI

The night sky is indigo as we head to Islamic Cairo around Khan Al-Khalili and Sharia al-Muski. Our cab speeds across the Nile on 6 October Bridge, the scene of many battles during the revolution four months ago. The road turns into a rollercoaster and we soar high above squares teeming with people and brightly illuminated stalls. We whizz past bedroom windows in the cracked dun facades of apartment buildings and swoop down towards throngs of people at Khan Al-Khalili. They swarm around the cars and microbuses log-jammed on the road ahead and squeeze through gaps in the railings on the central divide of the road.

Our driver brakes late but we pull up safely at the drop-off point of Al Tarbeeaa Street. We step out of the taxi and it seems we've also stepped back seven centuries into a landscape unchanged in all that time.

Khan Al-Khalili was originally a large inn for Chinese merchants who arrived with their pack animals at the end of their journey along the Silk Road. You can imagine the weary camels, horses and mules as they stumbled into the central courtyard. They'd be tethered and given water, before tightly rolled bundles of silk and other goods were removed from their backs. The Chinese must have found their local hosts with their tobacco-coloured skin very different but were, no doubt, delighted and relieved to have reached Cairo after their long journey by sea and land, which would've taken up to a year to complete. That first meal by the light of flickering lanterns must have been welcome, before they retired exhausted to the dormitories above.

Next day they would display their offerings for sale: gold, silk, perfume, precious white porcelain, bronze ornaments, coral, amber, tea, rice, medicines, skins, varnish and asbestos. When everything was sold and they were rested, they would load up with Arabian glass and textiles for the trip home.

The original Khan is long gone. The stalls that replace it sell curios, many still made in China, to tourists, if they can find any. As one of a very few non-Egyptians in view we are very much in demand and the atmosphere is friendly.

'Back again! We've been waiting for you,' shout today's traders. Some are middle-aged and potbellied. They wear loose-fitting grey or fawn galabeyas with long cloths wrapped round their heads as they sit on small chairs at the entrance to their shops.

'Come in. Just lookey-lookey. It won't take a minute and you'll be on your way. No commitment,' they say.

Others in their late teens or early twenties run up to us, all smiles. Some have scarves displayed over their arms. This generation wear T-shirts and low-slung jeans with the colourful waistbands of their underwear visible. 'Mister. Good quality. Good price. Have a feel.' Or to Shona, 'Madame, smell our perfume. We have everything for you. Any combination . . . rose, jasmine, lavender, sandalwood, lotus flower, Nefertiti, Secret of the Desert. We grow our own flowers.'

Their business plummeted after a suicide bomb in the main alleyway killed twenty-two people in 2005. Another incident in 2009 killed two more and the uncertainty and unrest around the revolution still keeps tourists away.

Shona buys a few tops to wear for work and we take a Turkish coffee on a terrace before we head back.

My teleconference with Miami did go ahead at a reasonable cost after a couple of hours – going with the local flow – to get the connections sorted.

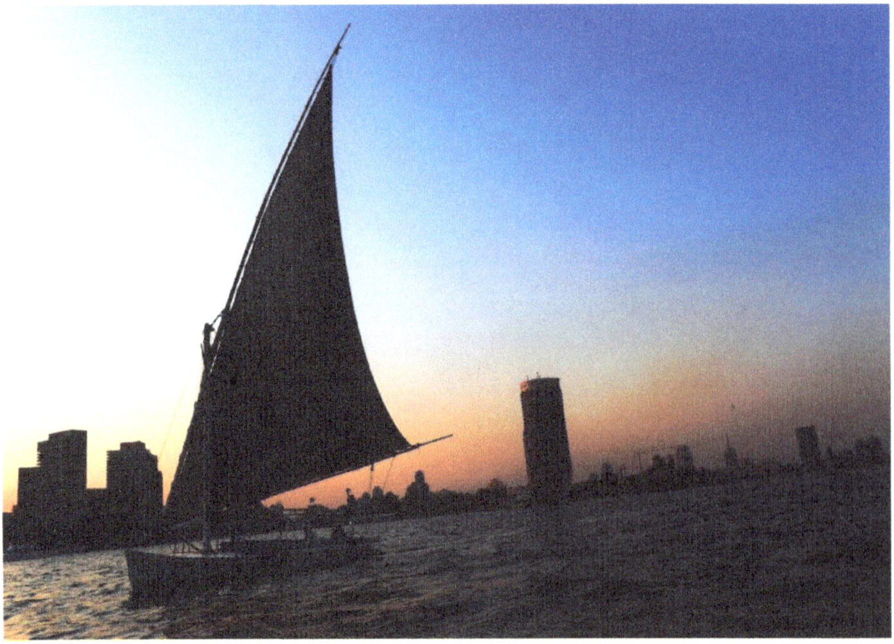

16 JULY 2011: OF CITADELS AND FELUCCAS

The taxi dumps us four kilometres from our destination. 'Muhammad Ali Citadel that way,' points the driver. 'One way . . . no go taxi.' With that we're on the street, a white dome and minarets just visible in the distance at the end of a very long road. What a walk it is. We pick our every step up and down broken pavements and around heaps of rubbish. Kittens play in gutters and children brush past as they chase each other under the stone arcades. We weave among stalls selling *fool* – the local bean stew – and others where falafel fritters sizzle in pans of hot oil. Backgammon players rattle dice around their boards and click-click their pieces into position. Shisha pipe smokers suck on their mouthpieces and the water in the glass bases splutters like a cappuccino machine. We hold hands and step into the paths of on-coming cars and buses, which is the only way to cross junctions filled with demon traffic. We pray their brakes work.

So, we traverse the furniture and musical-instrument making areas of Old Cairo, often tempted to flop into the enormous, brightly coloured armchairs and settees displayed for sale on the street. Shona has her big camera out. I'm at the rear with the bags and act as lookout out for any obstacles as she lines up her shots. She's very good with people and soon has young men posed in groups for photos; there's no lack of chairs on which to arrange them.

An hour and a half later, we've devoured the contents of two large water bottles and our clothes are plastered to our bodies as we reach the base camp for the final ascent to the mosque sat high on its dusty crag. A local guide asks us where we're going.

'There,' I point.

'Closed,' he replies.

My shoulders slump and I run my hand through my sodden hair.

It's either a long walk back through an alley into Islamic Cairo where we were last night or a taxi ride to the Nile. We choose the latter and the car inches its way along the street we've just walked, but the speed picks up as we hit the government and commercial areas; a heavy military presence in front of some buildings indicates the more sensitive ones. For a few minutes, we see the iconic white tarpaulins in Tahrir Square as we drive directly towards it, passing parked ambulances, before all traffic, including our taxi, is directed by police to make a sharp left turn.

In two more minutes we're at the felucca landing stage in front of the Four Seasons Hotel. A quick barter, a shaky step onto the prow, a rope untied and we glide out onto the Nile.

Whatever anyone has said about the relaxing escape of a felucca sail on the Nile at sunset in Cairo is true. The noise, heat and dust of the city fall away. You kick off your shoes and fall back on the cushioned seats. Captain Ahmed deftly moves to the mast, for all the world like Abdul, who captained the felucca on my three-day trip from Aswan to Luxor, thirty years ago . . .

The Nile, Upper Egypt, 26 September 1981

. . . back into midstream, Abdul lets the sail down, that beautiful swallow swoop, and we fly like a bird. It's exhilarating. The deck leans sharply. I lie on my back, propped up on my elbows, water racing by inches from my feet, a vast expanse of sparkling Nile, a jewelled Nile. This is living; the creaking of the hull and the mast, the snaking of the ropes, the jingling of little bells, the swing of the tiller. We race along on the lifeblood of Egypt; this very water, this blue swelling in the desert is Egypt and today I'm part of it, feeling its every surge in my veins . . . at night, I lie on my back as the deck rolls high and plunges deep. My hair blows in the wind with the Nile inches from my ear. Up above, the sail asserts its ancient shape against the darkening sky, everywhere are stars, wheying across the night . . . waking up, head poking from my blanket, everything's still, the sail is in, we've stopped somewhere. A canvas screen surrounds the sides of the boat. Up above, the stars are gone, the sky's opalescent, and an enormous silence pervades. I get to my feet . . . paradise. An island in the Nile, a stretch of sand, glass water, slender palms. A sweep of distance and time. It is everywhere. And this morning is the most beautiful of my life . . .

The sound of the shutter makes me turn. Shona lowers her camera and looks at me.

'Are you OK?'

'Yes . . . never finer.' I'm lying propped up on my elbows, the Nile inches from my feet.

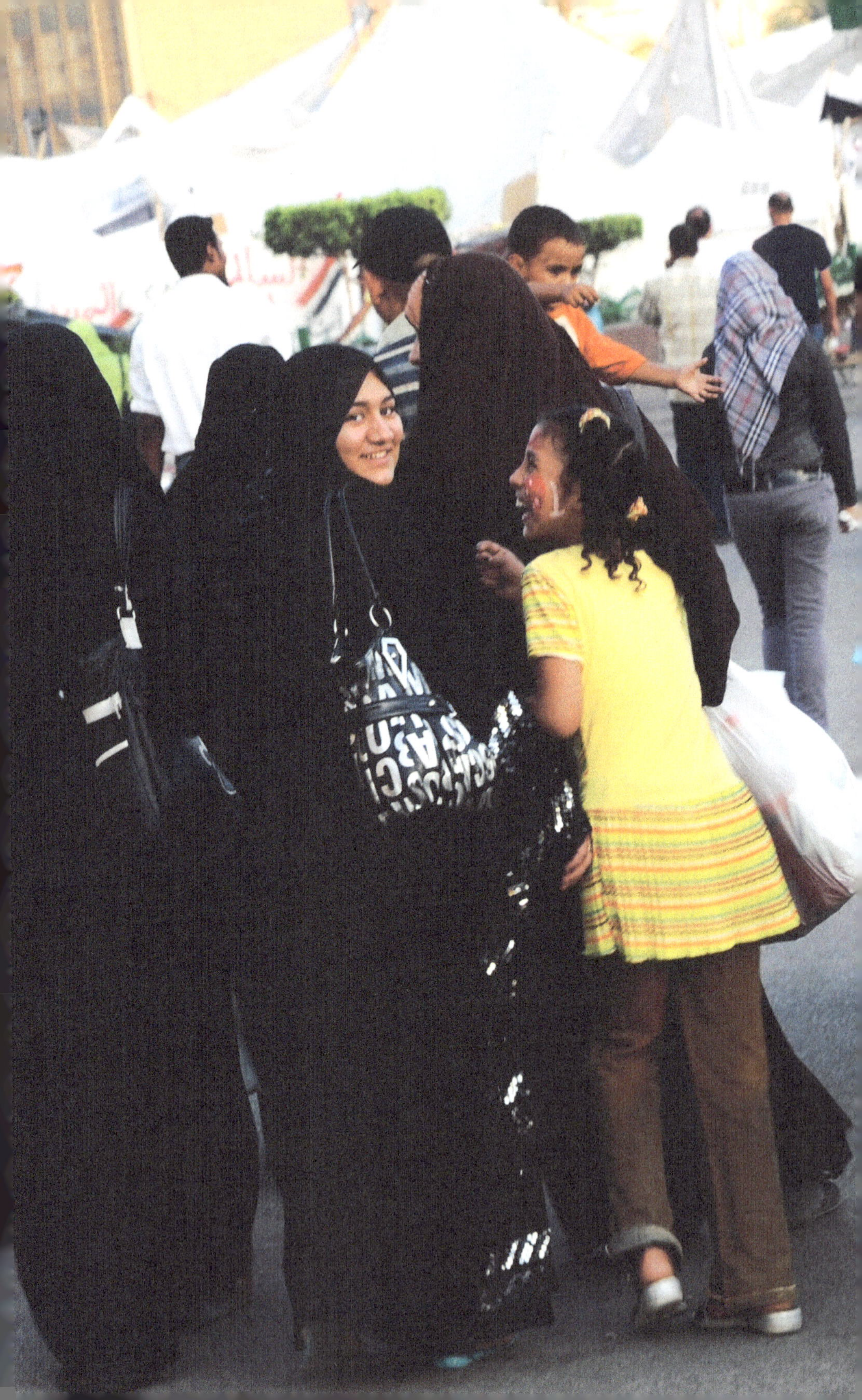

18 JULY 2011: HOPE IN TAHRIR SQUARE

As I approach Tahrir – Liberation – Square the advice of the British Embassy to stay away from it rings in my ears. I can almost hear a faint rustle of blood in my veins and remember how I had strolled into this spiritual heart of Cairo without a second thought thirty years ago.

'Does Egypt have a written constitution?' my travelling companion, Clara, asked me then.

'Yes,' I replied. 'One man, no vote.'

We laughed. It was pithy, witty and true and it's still true today. Shame on us for laughing, but we were young and had no idea what it would be like to endure the next three decades of tyranny, fear, and frustration.

'Passport.' I'm brought back to the present by the demand of a young, unshaven man in a black leather jacket at the first checkpoint to get into the square.

It's back in the hotel, but I pull out my credit-card wallet and produce my driving licence. 'Here.' I do my best to sound authoritative.

He studies it and I point to the letters 'UK'.

'OK,' he says.

I'm relieved to be moved along, first, for a body frisk and, then, to the next checkpoint, ten metres further on.

'Open bag,' orders another young man, who seems more highly strung than the last one.

My hands tremble a little as I unfasten the clips of my camera bag and unzip the main compartment. A few professional photographers have been detained in the last week and I wonder if I should've stayed away.

He lifts my heavy camera out and holds it in the air like a dumbbell as he shouts something in Arabic to one of his colleagues at another table. The other guy looks me up and down . . . and shrugs his shoulders. His expression indicates he doesn't care.

'OK,' says my man and thrusts the camera into my hands.

I'm through and look round with a new sense of the courage of the men and women who made their regime-toppling stand in this place. They took over the square to protest against Mubarak and demand bread, freedom and social justice four short months ago. The revolution exploded on 25 January with violent clashes around Tahrir and throughout Egypt. Hundreds died, but the protesters stood their ground and their numbers swelled night after night into February, with over a million people present demanding Mubarak's resignation. They shouted, 'Out! No more. We've had it with you. We will not leave until we have one man, one vote. Give it to us NOW!'

It was as simple but as daunting as that. The soft flesh of the people pitted against the hard physical assets controlled by the regime, including the enormous road and bridge infrastructure, the water and electricity supply lines, the broadcasting centres, the railroads and river barges, the defence and air-force ministries, the military barracks, parade grounds, weapons stores, helicopters, fighter planes and tanks. What a roar there must have been here when Mubarak resigned on 11 February this year!

A festive mood prevails beyond the security barriers. Bagel and balloon stalls line the perimeter of the area. Entire families savour the experience, eager to say in the future, 'We were there.' Kids paint their faces in the national colours and adults carry pennant flags. I take a few shots but think, enough's enough. As I walked from Ramses Station to Downtown, through the industrial tools area, the shoe market, the jeans market, the stationery market, and along the oil-smeared streets lined with car mechanics' workshops that lead to Tahrir, I haven't seen a single foreigner, not one. I feel many eyes on my camera and me. There's one heavily built, middle-aged man with a moustache and smart brown suit who's always behind me when I look round. I hear Shona's words of caution in my ears and know she'll be angry when I tell her where I've been. I don't want to become the next in the line of detained photographers. As I retrace my steps, many locals smile and give me the thumbs-up sign and, like them, I feel good to be here.

At the moment the country is under the control of Field Marshal Tantawi, who chairs the Supreme Armed Forces Council. It suspended both parliament and the constitution and promised to lift Mubarak's Emergency Law, which has been in force for thirty years, as well as hold free and democratic presidential elections. Neither promise has been fulfilled yet. Photographically, I missed the sun on the tarpaulins; let's hope that's not an omen for the revolution.

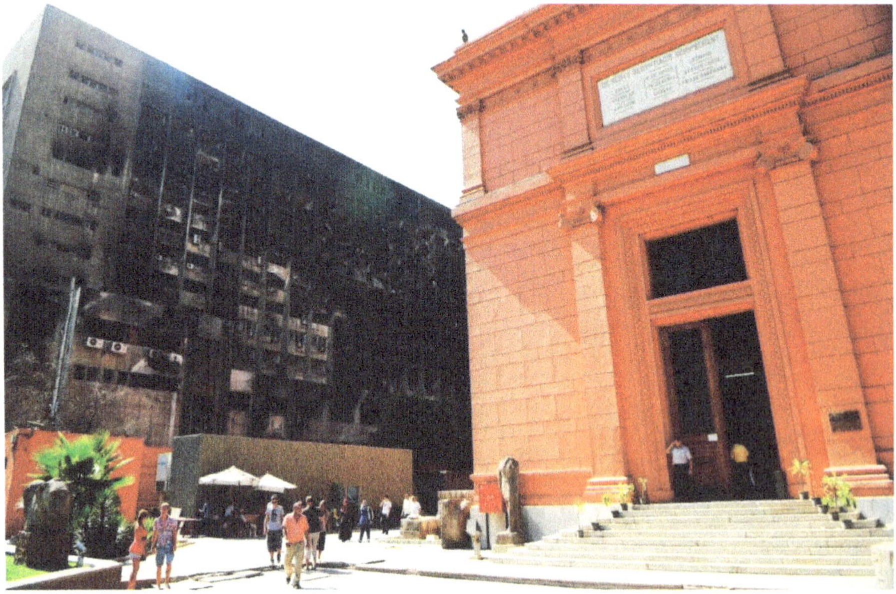

19 JULY 2011: A TALE OF TWO BUILDINGS

To the left is the former joint headquarters of Mubarak's National Democratic Party and the government-sponsored National Council for Women, which had a terrible record in the field of women's rights. The building was ransacked and torched during the height of the revolution on 28 January this year. To the right is the Egyptian Museum, still going strong. Both are close to Tahrir Square.

The museum opened in 1920 and looks like it's never been touched since. Dust hangs in the air under its central dome and discoloured paint peels from the walls. Large sandstone statues and granite sarcophagi dominate the main halls. I wonder how they were manoeuvred into place both at their original sites and here. Other exhibits are crammed into old glass cases and I need to lean close to read the original labels typed in Courier font on yellowed paper.

It's the smaller exhibits that catch my eye: a painting of geese, a child's coffin inlaid with coloured-glass hieroglyphics, the carved faces of wooden figures that stare at you from 3,000 years ago.

Tutankhamen's treasures occupy a room upstairs that has all the allure of a station waiting room. Air conditioning has been installed since my first visit in 1981, but the rest is the same. The contents are a feast to behold: the iconic mask, two large sarcophagi, a delicate forehead band, necklaces, brooches and rings. Such gold shining as new, such inlays of bright and subtle variations, such finesse and patience in their creation and such beauty in the result. They are timeless and seem to exist beyond the dimensions of their glass boxes.

I was alone in Tutankhamen's room for half an hour, apart from a security guard who was engrossed in his smartphone. I stood in front of the iconic mask and levelled my eyes with those of the young pharaoh, just the two of us. His face is beautiful and I felt very creased in comparison and so amateurish in the staring game. But we did connect, in our way. The mask's visage is said to be a true representation of the king's features, so that his soul would recognise the body as his own, in order to resurrect it. I suppose that was the question in my stare.

'Did you ever find yourself?'

'And, you, have you found yourself?' he seemed to reply.

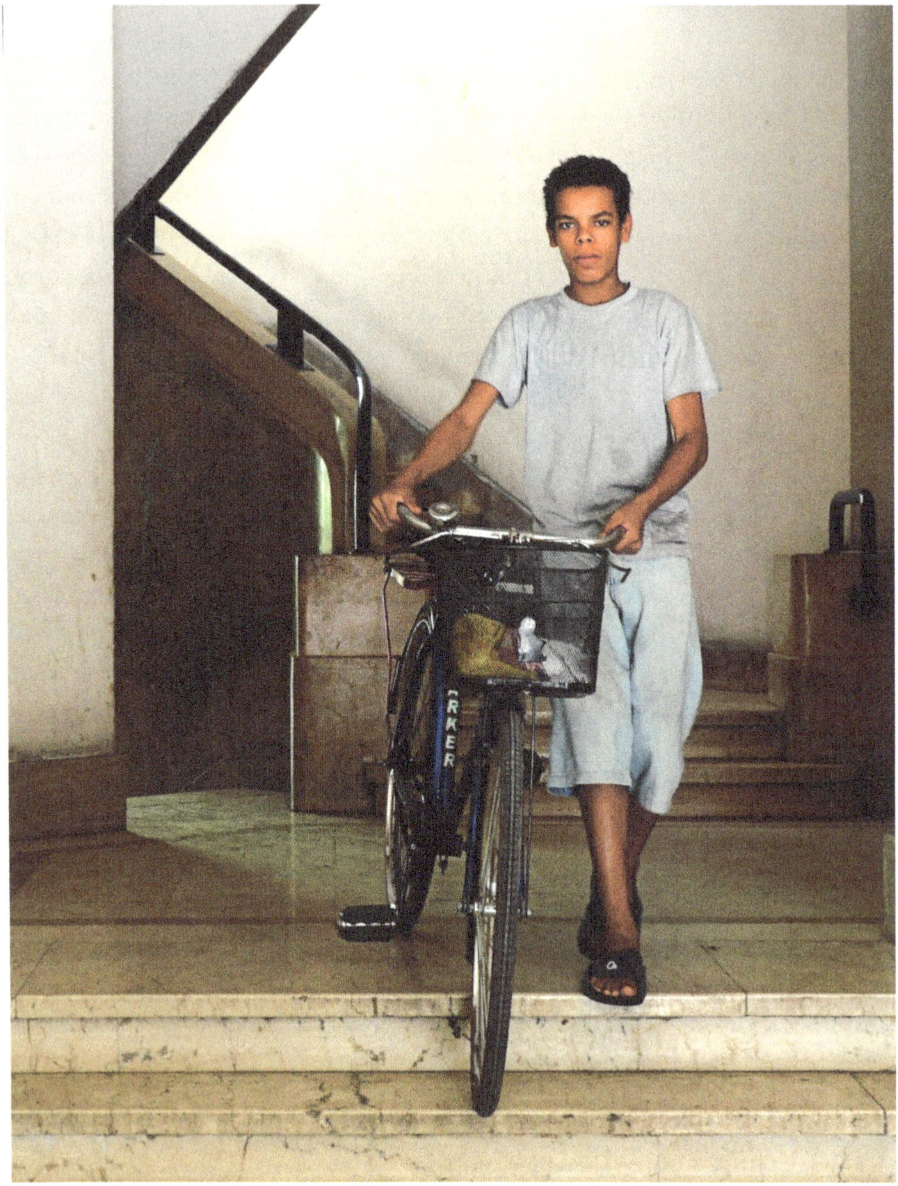

20 JULY 2011: THE FUTURE

This was my first photograph of the day and I like it for the sense it gives of 'Here comes the future'. The revolution and all the hopes that ride on it are for young people like this so they will not have to live under Mubarak's brutal regime with its disregard for dignity and development.

There were many other photos as well. It was one of those days when I felt bonded with the camera and that meant its bulk became an unnoticeable part of me. My fingers found a secure grip through sweat and suntan lotion and the camera's mass rested in the crook of my arm.

It took me back to blooding my Nikon F3 film camera in Cairo in 1981. It was my first real sortie with it and I disguised the fact that it was the top-of-the-range professional camera of the time – my twenty-first birthday present – by putting insulating tape over its logos. The pre-occupation with its safety clearly extended to my travelling companion, Clara . . .

Cairo, 6 September 1981

Today I was nearly killed in the cacophony of a Cairo afternoon . . . confusing sun, wrong-way traffic, a stupid step off the pavement looking the wrong way directly in front of a bus. I tense without seeing it. It holds me back by an inch and stops me from going under the wheels and being ripped in two. But the hard-ribbed side of the bus hits me. It corkscrews me into the air. I can't believe it, and in that instant feel the sickening twist of the end. Crack! The bus's mirror smashes into my head.

I land on my feet, somehow. Clara grabs my arms.

'What was that smash? Is your camera all right?'

'It was my head.' Blood pours down the side of my face and over my shirt . . .

I won't bore you with the hospital scenes but it was rudimentary, back-street stuff with flies, needles, iodine and stitches, nine of the latter. My head was swathed in bandages looping over my crown and under my chin so that I resembled a mummy. It lent some merriment to our visit to the pyramids the next day.

***

The big breakthrough of the trip so far is that I've worked out the reason for the frequent use of the car horn in Cairo; they don't tweet, here, but toot.

There's a toot for everything – one for 'Want a ride?', others for 'High-five!', 'Hey, look at me!', 'Who do you think you are?', 'Look out, I'm just behind you!', 'Thanks!', 'What the hell are you playing at?', 'Get out of my way!', 'See you later!', and also for 'You won't believe the crazy foreigner I've got beside me!' to name but a few.

For thousands of men behind the wheels of taxis and lorries and buses, it's their only form of social networking during long, long hours and days stuck in their cabins. Not effective enough to orchestrate a revolution but still the only means to have some sort of interaction, which is so vital to maintaining their sense of worth as human beings.

This may all seem fanciful but I swear it's true; you just need a practised ear to differentiate the toots.

Tomorrow to Alexandria.

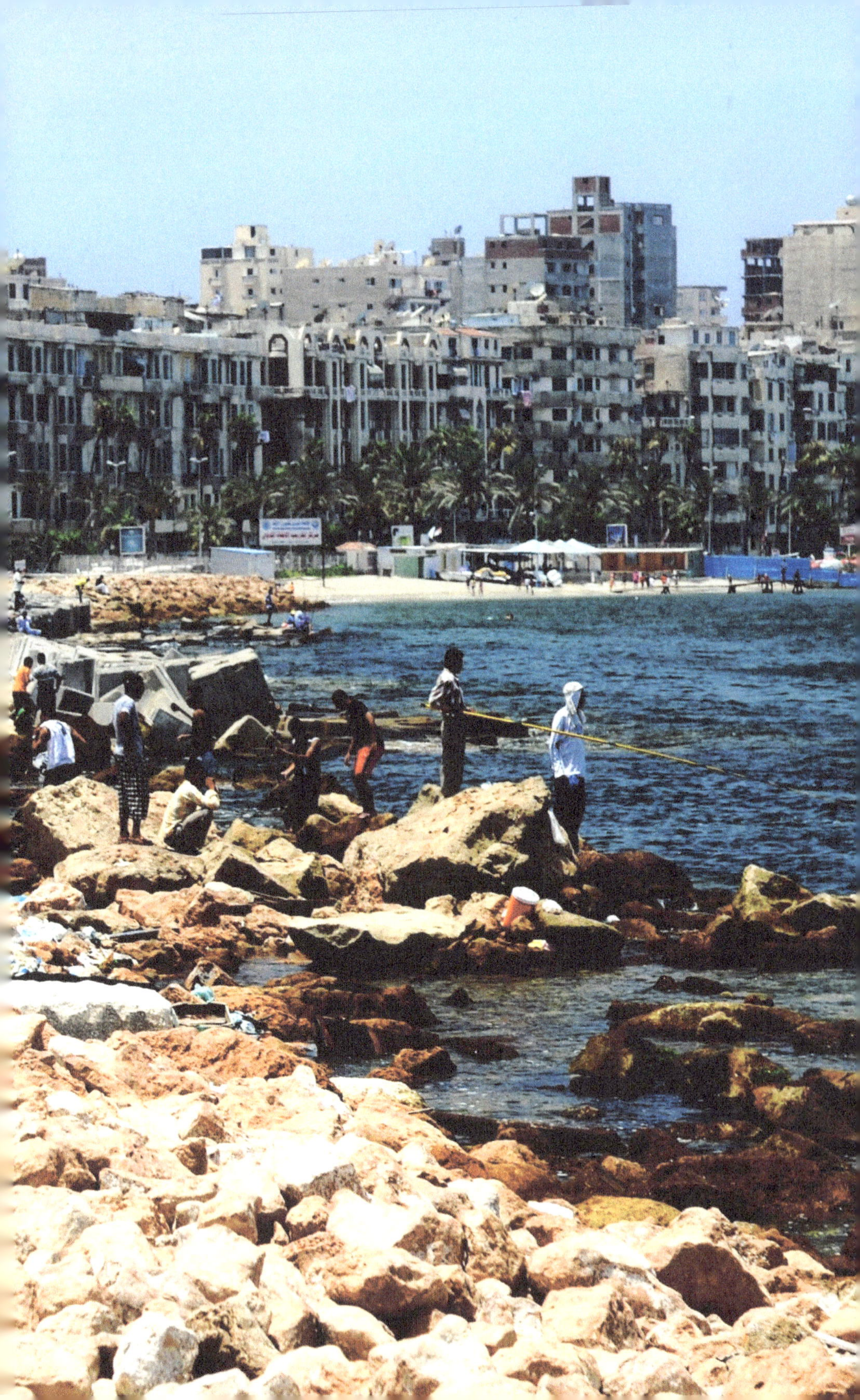

21 JULY 2011: TURQUOISE MORNING

From the Alex Desert Road . . . 10 am

It's all motorway to Alexandria now. Instead of donkeys, goats, sheep and carts it's Dandy Mega Mall, Smart Village, toll roads, and billboards: 'Samsung – Work it. Play it. Live it.' and 'Mobil 1 – Keeps engines performing like new', all in English.

It used to be unthinkable to hire a self-drive car for this trip, but it would be an option now if it weren't for the 120 kph squeeze-through manoeuvre that many drivers practise. That's the one where you spot a tiny gap between two cars ahead and accelerate towards it as fast as you can, hoping it will open up to let you through. I'm very glad I'm not behind the wheel today.

The desert's still here; the terrain that makes you more aware than any other of the miracle of H_2O and the need to have some close by. From the back of a car, you stare out and lose yourself in surreal strands of thinking. Alone in the deep desert with the air shimmering on the horizon you would lose your mind all together.

I'm typing live into my iPhone as we approach Alex. In these final forty kilometres, the motorway has broken down to become haphazard asphalt lined by mud-brick dovecotes with herds of goats loose on the earth verges. Vehicles make reckless U-turns across several lanes of traffic and people dodge between cars, trucks and buses to reach the other side. They stand still as one roars past, then spurt forward with a hand held out in a vain attempt to make the other drivers slow down.

Petroleum storage areas and military compounds are plentiful. The haze and dust seem as thick as in Cairo. Let's see what Alexandria, the Pearl of the Mediterranean, has to offer in the way of a turquoise morning today.

From the Cecil Hotel . . . 11 am

You can imagine Durrell and Churchill in the Cecil Hotel as soon as you walk through the revolving wood-and-glass door into the carpeted lobby with its wrought-iron lift cage and cream plaster walls. The grey marble floor in the café emits a sense of coolness in contrast to the heat outside. It puts me in the mood for a cold beer but the bar doesn't open for another seven hours. I order a Turkish coffee instead.

In 1981, it cost thirty-three Egyptian pounds per night to stay here. I know because I came in to ask then, but it was well out of my budget, which was in the two- to three-pound range. They've just quoted me 2,000 pounds for tonight, which shows the effects of inflation and devaluation. In 1981, the exchange rate was one to one with the British pound; now it's ten to one. The car for today, by the way, cost seven hundred Egyptian pounds.

I attempt to let the coffee settle but I've lost the knack of judging when to take the first sip; I'm too impatient for that explosion of flavour. My journal discloses that on arrival thirty years ago I went straight to the general hospital to find someone to remove the stitches from my head after the bus accident. I found a man in a white coat on the top floor eating a sandwich for lunch. He offered to help and I was impressed by his skill and efficiency. He refused point blank to take anything for his services. Only on my way out did I notice the sign 'Neurosurgeon' on his door.

Today, it will be straight onto the Corniche for a stroll and a photograph or two . . . damn, I'm still too quick with that first sip.

From the sea wall . . . 11.50 am

In one of my journal entries during that first visit, I described our breakfast of hot new bread and bananas taken on the sea wall. 'It was a turquoise morning,' I wrote. It still is.

There's something uplifting about the light and sweep of the Corniche, but gone is the time when Alexandria was the most beautiful, romantic, liberal and cosmopolitan place on the planet. I would have to spend a long time to get under the skin of the city now and not just rely on a vivid imagination to recall what it must have been like.

The turquoise-ness of the mornings made a real impact on me all those years ago, and I set a short story here. Fifty-one-year-old Henry Marsden of *The Times* was the main character in a tale of love and espionage. He fell in love with

Yasmeen, a beautiful young female revolutionary, who worked under the auspices of the Tourist Friends Association. A pivotal scene takes place on the sea wall where they sit breakfasting on hot bread and bananas. Yasmeen looks out at the sparkling sea and shares how her brother was arrested and tortured to death by the regime. The next banana that Henry opened was full of maggots and foretold his betrayal of Yasmeen. I left him retired in Salisbury, a broken man. I'm not sure if he's still alive. I should check and see if he needs to come back, too.

Where to now? I fancy going along to the fort but it's a long walk and the sun is high. I look around for a horse and buggy. There used to be hundreds of them and their drivers pestered us for a ride every minute of the day. Now, when I can afford and need one, they've vanished.

From the Cecil Hotel, again . . . 1.30 pm

Slightly self-conscious, I change my sodden T-shirt in the gents. The attendant hovers at my shoulder and passes me paper towel after paper towel to dry first my sunglasses, then my normal glasses, face and naked torso.

I recover sufficient equilibrium of temperature to put on my spare T-shirt without immediately soaking it and hand over a good five-pound tip. Boy, is this ice-cold Coca-Cola in the café going down well.

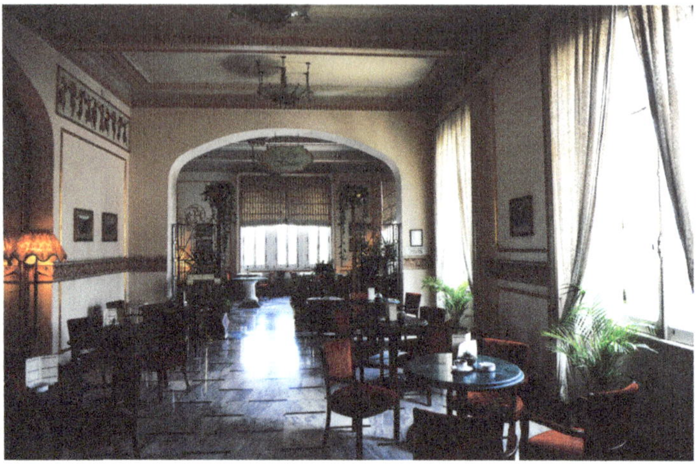

Café in the Cecil Hotel

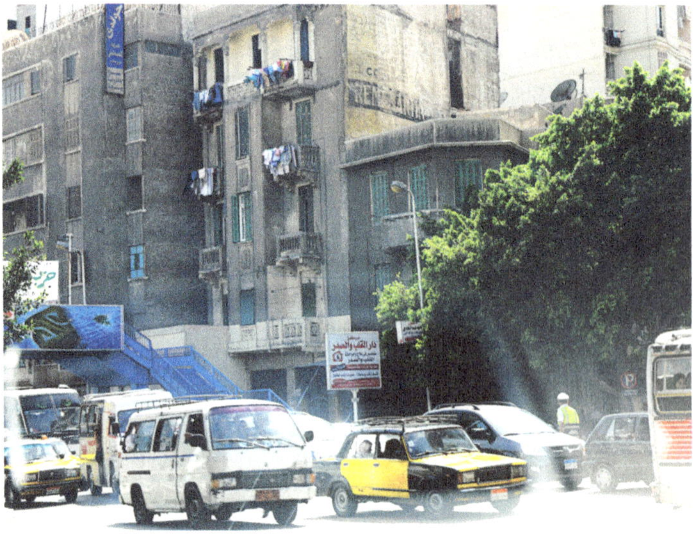

Mostafa Kamel Quarter Traffic

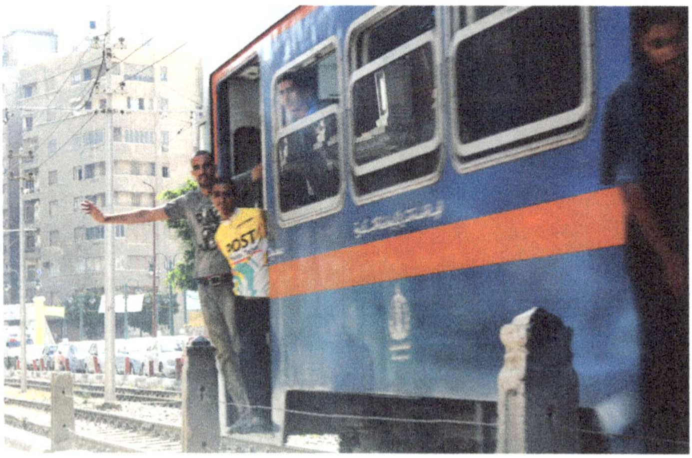

Bukeley Train

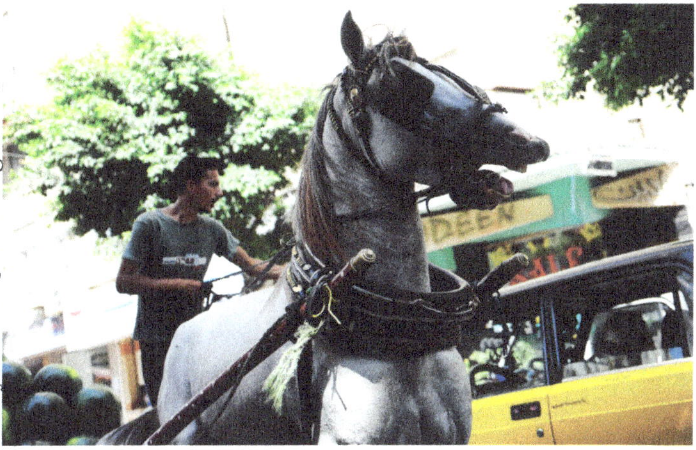

Mostafa Kamel Quarter Argument

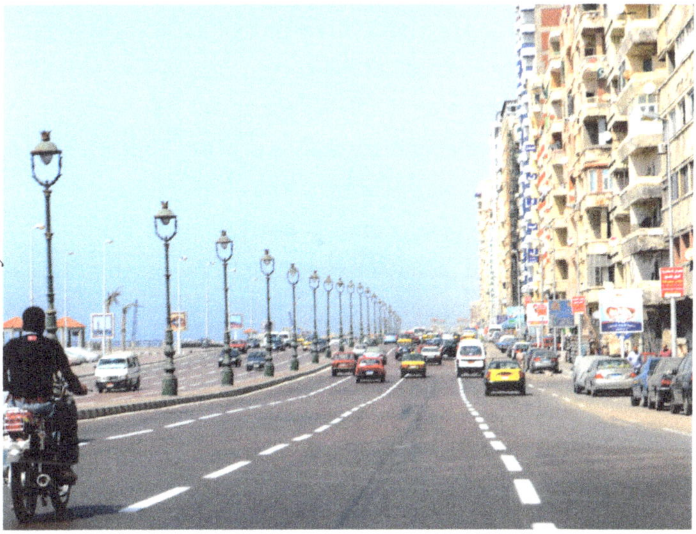

Corniche Towards Stanley Beach

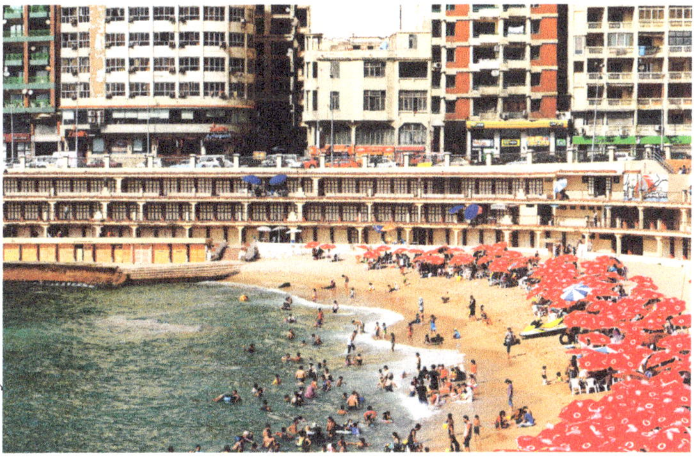

Stanley Beach

Mostafa Kamel Quarter . . . 2.15 pm

Without warning my Alexandria driver executes a U-turn in the middle of a busy thoroughfare as I struggle to type into my iPhone. You don't need to obey traffic laws here or it may be that there are no traffic laws to be obeyed. Everyone is very tolerant of the most mind-boggling manoeuvres. 'Allow what you wish to be allowed to you' seems to be the only norm.

I'm off the trail of my own back story to follow that of the fathers of two of my friends. One friend is the up-and-coming Brazilian photographer, Fernando Cohen, who specialises in street photography. I'm convinced he has an invisibility cloak as it's the only way to explain how he gets so close to his subjects without being noticed, especially with his head of unruly black hair. His father, Clemente, an Egyptian Jew denied the nationality, was forced to flee Egypt, first to Italy and then onto Brazil fifty-five years ago, not long after Nasser's revolution. He was part of a Jewish community that numbered almost 100,000 people; only twelve survive in Egypt today. His cousin, Eve Cohen, knew Lawrence Durrell and became his second wife. She is said to have been the basis for the character of Justine in his *Alexandria Quartet*.

My other friend is the poet and writer Teleri Williams. She lives in the south of France with her husband, after an exotic upbringing in various countries around the eastern Mediterranean and a period in her native Wales. Teleri is in her sixties, has rosy cheeks and sometimes wears her long brown hair in a bun. She tends to paganism, is a non-violent anarchist by nature and champions the downtrodden, women's rights and the indigenous languages of Welsh and Occitan. A wonderful poet, sensitive translator, preservationist, jazz lover, cook and market gardener, she's taught me a lot about writing, vernacular architecture, the preparation of paella over a wood fire, the use of indigo to dye cloth as well as the intricate designs of Catalan and Valencian floor tiles. More than anything I enjoy her conversation and wonderful sense of humour.

Her father, David Gwyn Williams, was Professor of English Literature in Alexandria and a close friend of Lawrence Durrell. He helped him elope with Eve Cohen and used to finish his account of it by saying, 'It didn't last, of course. Larry always married as a sort of parting gift.' Williams says in his autobiography that he became a writer in Alexandria – he later become prolific in the field of Welsh poetry. He and Teleri's mother met in Alex and were forced to flee at the time of the 1952 revolution with Teleri a seven-month infant in her mother's womb.

Williams, Durrell and Cohen met regularly in the bar of the Cecil Hotel, which I've just left on my mission to discover and photograph their and Clemente Cohen's old haunts of Bukeley and Stanley Beach. I'm doing my best to switch between my camera and iPhone notes in the front seat of the taxi that I took from the Cecil. I've taken some shots in the Bukeley area. I didn't find the local station although I did get one of a train on the track that cuts through the quarter. I think I may also have missed the school that Clemente attended as a boy, but maybe he'll recognise it somewhere in the shots I send.

Oh, and now we've got a fight between a cart driver with a cargo of melons and a taxi driver who is badly parked and refuses to move – the carthorse's head is nearly through my window. Phew, they've exhausted their shouting and we've managed to squeeze past. Now we track through back streets at a snail's pace on the way to Stanley Beach.

From Stanley Beach . . . 3.15 pm

We're here before I know it, a triple stack of bathing cabins, in a huge curve behind a beach of golden sand, which date from goodness knows when but certainly before 1952. I'm relieved that there'll be something for Clemente to recognise, as well as stir thoughts in Teleri. I know her father wrote about coming here by tram along the Corniche at the weekends and she feels she knows it herself from his accounts and reminiscences. We circle twice to find a safe place for me to get out for a shot without the need to dart across five lanes of traffic – not one of my strengths.

From the Cecil Hotel, a final time . . . 4 pm

I'm sitting now on the terrace of the Cecil Hotel. The 'Alexandria Beach' non-alcoholic cocktail listed on the menu card isn't available; the waiter has never heard of it. I've ordered another Coke instead.

It's nice to feel the air flutter about, cooling here and there. I need a little time to unwind after my wild ride around the Alexandrian block today. On the whole the place really hasn't changed in thirty years and I guess maybe not much in fifty-five years either, but that may be different for Clemente Cohen if he looks at the detail of the areas he knows at street level.

One thing that is different is that in a garden square fifty metres to my right, guarded by stern-looking revolutionaries, are the portraits of hundreds of martyrs of the revolution of 25 January 2011. They hang from tarpaulin lines or are wrapped round tree trunks. I half see my Yasmeen and her martyred brother among them. People stand and stare at the mostly young faces on the posters. I wonder what they're feeling or thinking. Sorrow for the loss of people they knew, perhaps a son or daughter? Admiration for the courage of the young? Perhaps, the thought: will it have been worth it, after all?

I'm going to close and breathe in the sea air a little more deeply before my return to Cairo.

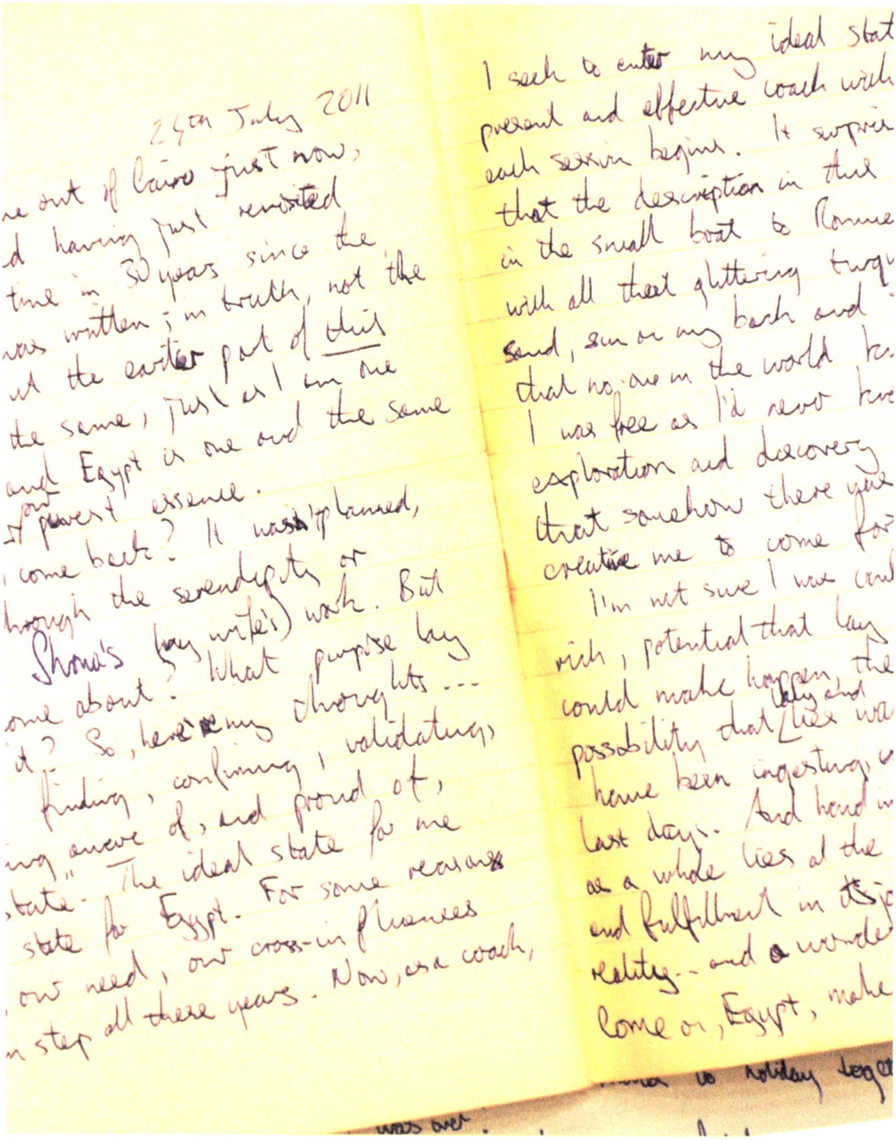
24th July 2011
e out of Cairo just now,
d having just revisited
time in 30 years since the
was written; in truth, not the
t the earlier part of this
the same, just as I am one
and Egypt is one and the same
t purest essence.
come back? It wasn't planned,
hrough the serendipity or
Shona's (my wife's) work. But
ome about? What purpose lay
it? So, here're my thoughts...
finding, confirming, validating,
ng aware of, and proud of,
tate". The ideal state for me
state for Egypt. For some reasons
our need, our cross-influences
n step all these years. Now, as a coach,
I seek to enter my ideal stat
present and effective coach with
each session begins. It surpri
that the description in this
in the small boat to Romme
with all that glittering turqu
sand, sun on my back and
that no one in the world kn
I was free as I'd never be
exploration and discovery
that somehow there yet
creative me to come for
I'm not sure I was con
rich, potential that lay
could make happen, the
possibility that truly and lies wa
have been ingesting
last days. And herein
as a whole lies at the
and fulfillment in its
reality -- and a wonde
Come on, Egypt, make

24 JULY 2011: THE JOURNAL CONTINUES

This evening I was sitting in my plane seat 35,000 feet above the eastern Mediterranean, trying to make some sense of my latest visit to Egypt. I reached for my iPhone to make some notes. The battery was dead. I reached into my trusty leather satchel for a pen. 'Now, where's some paper?'

I had a newspaper, a car magazine and the airline brochure, not a postage stamp of free space among them. Then I saw it, sitting there beside me, waiting as it had been during all these years, my Egyptian journal. Could I? Should I? There was no question – it was clear.

I picked up the second notebook and turned to the back. A short exhalation of breath escaped me . . . I smiled. There were six blank pages, just waiting.

You can see a photograph of what I wrote here but I don't expect you to decipher the raw script. The edited highlights are that this present journal and the 1981 journal are one and the same, as I am one and the same with my younger self and Egypt is too. The country and I are both on a journey to find and confirm our respective ideal states and have done that in step over the last thirty years.

My ideal state is all about exploration, discovery and possibilities. My trip in a small boat to Rommel's Beach at Mersa Matrouh in 1981 epitomises this and I recall the scene as if it was yesterday: sparkling sea ahead like diamonds cast on pale blue silk, pure white sand around, sun on my back, a feeling of freedom that not a single person in the world knew where I was and, as I surveyed the boundless horizon, the excitement that everything was possible.

As I progress to affirm my best self, then Egypt is doing the same as evidenced by the revolution earlier this year through which its people demanded their ideal state of 'bread, freedom and social justice'.

I close with an exhortation for us both to grasp our fullest opportunity. I hope it will happen. Inshallah.

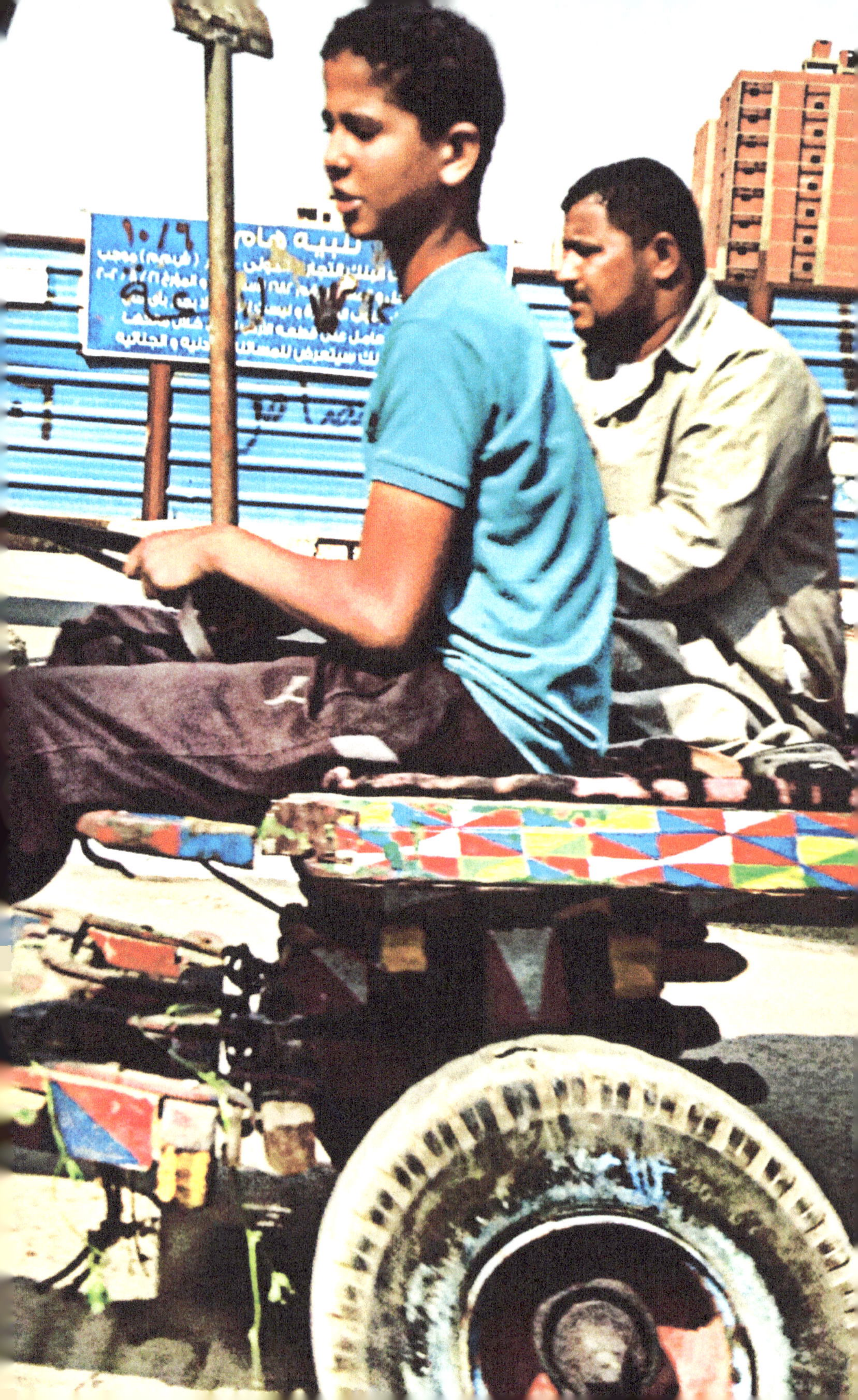

Chapter 2

First Elected President

14 JUNE 2012: A TALE OF TWO TAXIS

Every time we slow to a crawl in the Cairo traffic, the old Renault's engine takes a huge gulp of air and shudders as if it has turned its last. Mohammed, the taxi driver, jams the clutch in, feathers the throttle and the wreck vibrates as it somehow resurrects itself sufficiently to cover another fifty metres towards Downtown and the Nile. All under the tarmac-dissolving midday sun with me in the front seat behind a glasshouse windscreen and only a whimper of air coming from the vents.

'No good!' shouts Mohammed, as he lifts both hands from the wheel in frustration and elbows me in the side. 'Phufff!' he exhales. With that he turns off the air conditioning and presses the buttons of the electric windows. Each one judders down and the hot air and dust of Cairo rush in. Sweat stains spread across my shirt front and paste it to my body.

'How long to go?' I ask.

'One hour . . . maybe more.'

It was dark, early this morning, when I settled into the back seat of the E-Class Mercedes taxi in Paris. The seatbelt slipped home, the V6 engine was a distant murmur, and the car lifted and surged forward on the mirror-smooth surface of the silent streets.

'Is the temperature all right for you?' asked François, the driver.

'Very fine, thank you . . . and it's Terminal 1 today,' I replied, before leaning back to close my eyes in the gentle caress of the air.

'Air kaput!' Mohammed shakes his head.

'It's more than the air that's kaput,' I mutter, as we crawl past a yellow sign that warns we'll be fined if we exceed 60 kph. Before I can decide whether it's the car or the whole country I'm talking about, we pass a donkey and cart whose young driver and passenger show me how it's done. You don't get this in Paris, I think, as I raise the camera. That's why I'm here.

In more practical terms, I'm here to accompany Shona on her second work assignment. When we met twenty-five years ago in Scotland she was a marketing and public relations manager. The language barrier in France, which became our home in 1991, made it difficult for her to continue that line. She developed a second career in education. Now Shona advises universities with English-based curricula on developing a student-centred approach to their teaching practice. As a freelancer, she works in several countries each year, often returning at intervals. I try to be with her as much as my own freelance work allows.

Today I'm more than a little exhausted as I arrive after a trip covering South America, Europe and Africa in three days. A touch of airline food poisoning on top of my tiredness doesn't help, but it's lovely to be with Shona and an added bonus that we're in Egypt, with which I feel such affinity.

It's a historic time for the country. More than a year on from the fall of Mubarak, we are now in the middle of the first ever democratic elections for president long promised by the ruling Supreme Council of the Armed Forces or SCAF. No one had ever been allowed to genuinely challenge a sitting Free Officer Movement president and any parliamentary elections that did take place were a sham. The results were manipulated to suit the ruling party's political ends. All that is about to change.

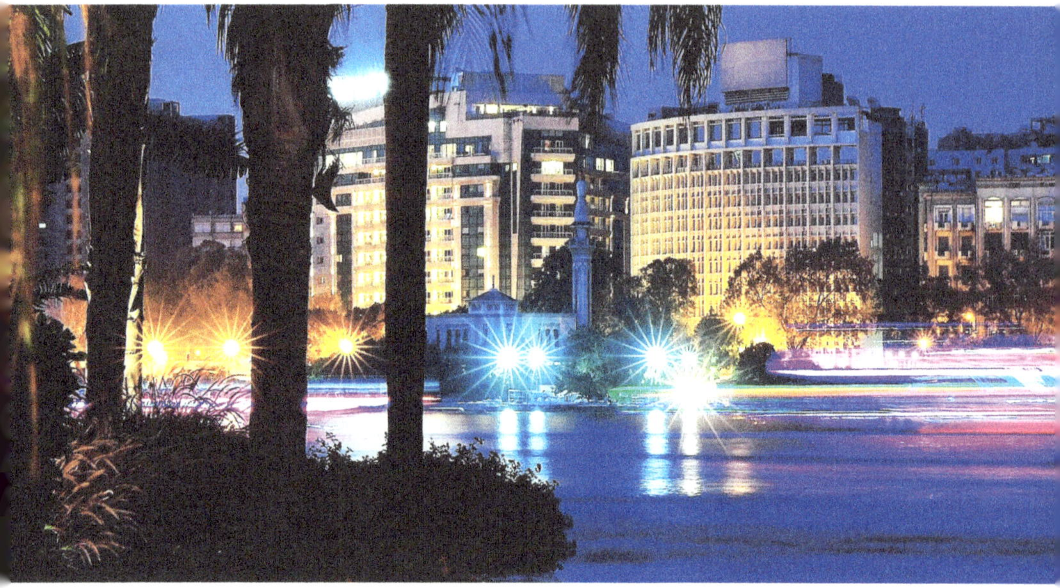

15 JUNE 2012: FRIDAY–SATURDAY WEEKENDS

Friday mornings are always beautifully quiet in Cairo, as far as that's possible in a city of twenty-three million people. It's the first day of the weekend and the main prayer day of the week, so the streets are practically deserted. A few shops open around 3 or 4 pm, after the midday prayers.

Saturday night is party night, before the return to work on Sunday morning. Nile pleasure craft dressed, as here, with gaily coloured lights embark with excited parties on board. Tables on café terraces fill with young people who smoke shisha pipes and nurse their Coca-Colas, waters and teas. Waiters weave between them with small charcoal stoves delivering embers to keep the tobacco alight. They suck air through the long shisha tubes to make sure that the pipes draw properly and then fit mouthpieces for their customers' use.

Smoking is the main recreational drug or stress reliever used on a massive scale given the widespread abstinence from alcohol. Shisha pipes are increasingly trendy, especially among young females. I don't think I saw any women drawing on pipes thirty years ago. Shisha tobacco blocks are worse for your health than cigarettes but no one seems to care too much. The social impact and cost to the health system of the ensuing tobacco-related illnesses is significant. Thirty per cent of Egypt's ninety million population are currently using tobacco products, with millions more exposed to second-hand smoking. According to the World

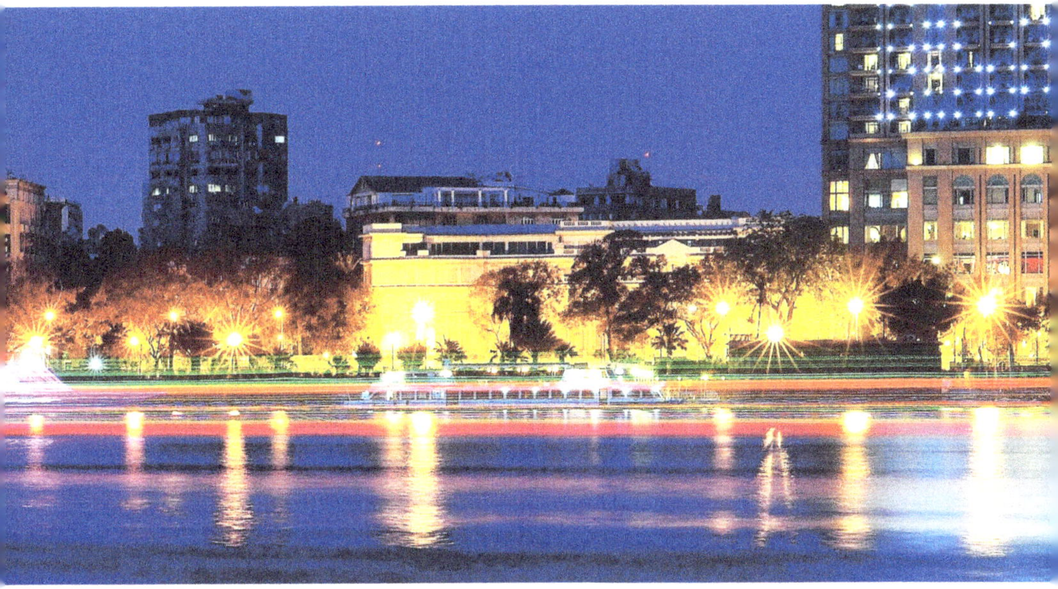

Health Organization in 2009, one third of cancer deaths in Egypt were related to tobacco consumption. In 2014, the number of deaths from lung cancer, heart disease and other non-infectious diseases had reached over 150,000 per year. More than nineteen billion cigarettes are smoked annually in Egypt, making it the largest market in the Arab world. Shisha pipes are claimed to spread tuberculosis. Experts say that while cafés often provide customers with new mouthpieces, bacteria can still reside in the shisha's tube, glass and water. In 2005, the healthcare cost of treating tobacco-related diseases was estimated at 3.4 billion Egyptian pounds or 616 million US dollars.

Shona, who has been here a month by herself, showed me around her block. I had heard a lot about it and it was nice to get so many warm welcomes as she introduced me to many of the locals she knows.

Groups of middle-aged men stood in earnest conversation, presumably discussing the presidential elections, which conclude this week. It's the second and final round and two candidates are left standing. One is Ahmed Safiq, seen as a representative of the discredited Mubarak regime, and the other is Mohammed Mursi, the 'leader' of the Muslim Brotherhood – fundamentalists who have a history of being persecuted politically for their views. It was Islamist soldiers who gunned down Sadat and there had been Islamist unrest up and down Egypt in Luxor, Asyut and Helwan, which I witnessed first-hand, in the lead-up to his assassination.

I put 'leader' in quotation marks because the low-profile Mursi is a last-minute stand-in candidate for the Brotherhood after their preferred candidate, Khairat Al Shater, was disqualified due to a previous conviction for a political offence. Mursi is guided by the Brotherhood's supreme and deputy spiritual guides, as in Iran.

The Brotherhood played a canny game before and during the revolution last year. They withheld public support for it until three days after the revolution started, but when they did declare themselves in favour it was a factor in Mubarak's resignation two weeks later on 11 February 2011. Tomorrow will tell if their strategy will carry them to the ultimate prize.

The more liberal and younger revolutionaries supported the left-leaning Hamoud Sabahy, but he was narrowly defeated in the first round and therefore eliminated from this second round.

I ask a smart young friend of ours who he'll vote for.

'There's no choice for me, so I'm boycotting them,' he says. 'I'm ambitious for my country and these two candidates do not offer hope of any progress. I cannot bring myself to vote for either of them as they will not honour the aims of the revolution.'

'But isn't it better to make a choice, even if it's a hard one, or at least spoil your ballot paper?' I ask.

He was adamant about the lack of appeal of both candidates and as for spoiling the ballot paper added, 'We don't do that here.'

Maybe it is a concept too far, given the lack of democratic sophistication in the country where even a free vote is a novelty. We ended the day by taking a felucca sail after sunset. The Nile looked very black, in keeping with the mood of the frustrated young liberals.

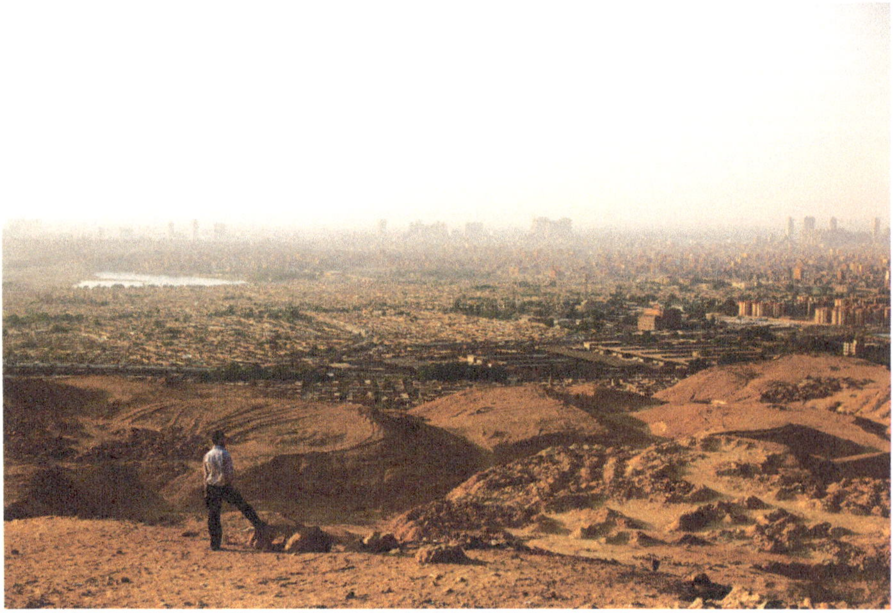

16 JUNE 2012: ONE MAN, ONE VOTE

We drove up past the Citadel under high sandstone rock faces to the viewpoint of Al Mokatam in order to enjoy a panorama of the city on this historic election day. We looked out across the city to the Western Desert through a haze that was more smog than heat haze. I wonder what the young man in the photograph was thinking as he contemplated this sweeping vista, today of all days. The election? His vote? His forebears? His future? The pollution?

Later, we walked around our area. Everything was very quiet with no queues whatsoever at the two polling stations we came across. The boycott has been effective and resulted in a low turnout. We were shooed away from both stations by armed policemen when they saw our cameras. I mistook the hand signal of one of them as a 'Come on in' invitation, but when I went forward to accept with my best attempt at a relaxed smile, I realised I had misread it as he barred the gateway with his body.

In the evening, I spoke to a young lady about the choice between the boycott approach or a spoilt vote. She was adamant that a low turnout figure was difficult to hide whereas the percentage of spoiled papers would be lost without trace. It looks like the eventual winner may be elected with a low percentage of votes from the total population eligible to vote.

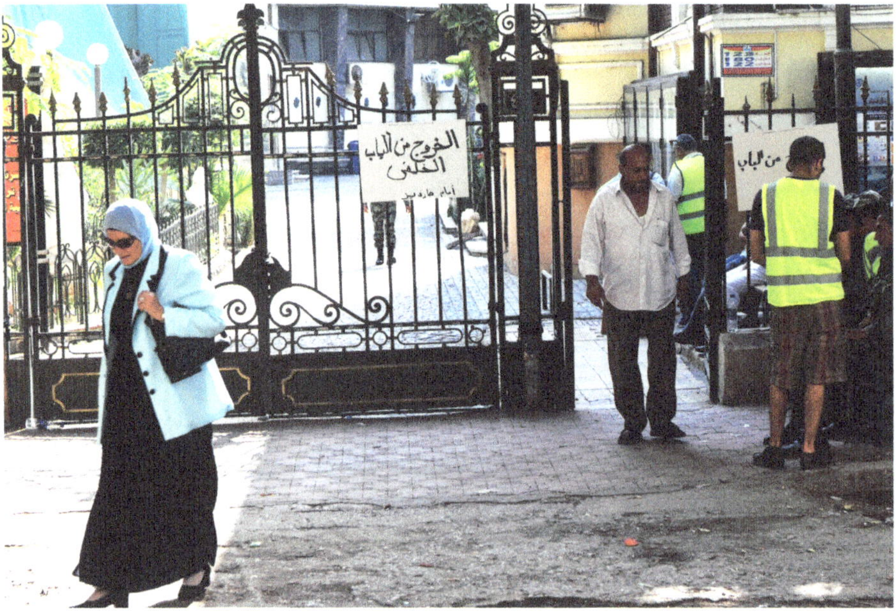
الخروج من الباب
الخلفى
أمام هارديز
من الباب

17 JUNE 2012: (EXTRA)ORDINARY

A very ordinary photograph but it still represents an extraordinary day in the history of Egypt; a well-dressed woman leaves a non-descript polling station in the final hours of voting in the election process to determine the country's first ever democratically elected head of state in 5,000 years.

No matter what you think about the hard choice or absence of choice for the people in this second round of presidential voting, the fact remains that someone may occupy the presidency before the week is out who has no support from the military dictatorship that has dominated Egypt for more than sixty years.

You can argue the electoral system favoured some parties over others, or that behind-the-scenes machinations have amounted to nothing less than a counter-revolution, or that the new president will have a mandate from only 20% of the electorate but, at least, the people will have spoken. You may also, in the words of one losing American senator, say, 'Damn them!' but their verdict should be accepted as a first step on the path to the country establishing a democratic process.

A president with a 20% mandate would be unwise not to seek to appeal to the other 80% before his term of office is out, and the voters of the moderate middle should be better organised and politically savvy next time, which is in five years, not 5,000 years.

This scene is where I was turned away yesterday. It was even quieter today and I took the photograph from the spot where the TV cameras and satellite dishes had been. The pavement was empty and no one took a blind bit of notice of me. There's talk of demonstrations in Tahrir Square tonight by the boycott movement and the military are rumoured to be working behind the scenes to restrict the powers granted to the new president in a reframed constitution.

The British historian Arnold Toynbee asserted that 'history is one damned thing after another'. That appears to hold true for the history of Egypt.

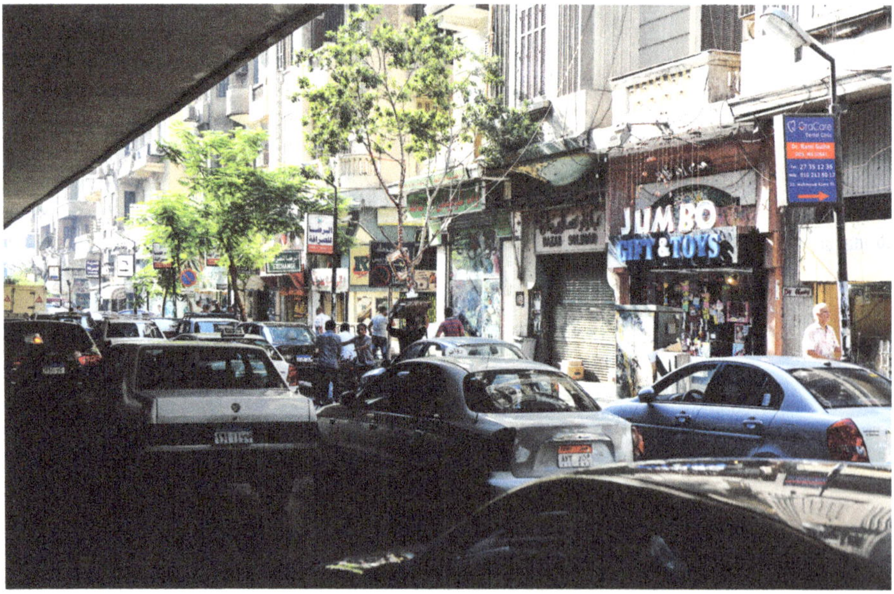
JUMBO
GIFT&TOYS

18 JUNE 2012: 26 JULY STREET

I switch off the BBC World News programme as I leave our hotel room. The election in Egypt was the lead story, which will have been seen by many people around the world. Do I understand more by being on the ground? I wonder. If so, it must be through the things I experience first-hand. Here's a selection from today.

The hair-dryer heat as I step out onto dirty pavements and pick my way over broken slabs and around open drains. The three robed women who scream and rush at me as I line up a shot of the street corner where they wait for a bus. The old man in his galabeya at a café table with his Turkish coffee, shisha pipe and pink smartphone. The live pictures on the TV screens behind him of huge crowds in Tahrir Square, with on-screen comments from Facebook users. A man in his parked car below the flyover, fiddling with his car radio as rumours circulate about what the army is up to today. The *Daily Mail*s and *Telegraph*s, dried, dusty and date-expired, clipped to tinder-dry newsstands. Boys perched on top of delivery trucks that buck over humps and plunge into potholes in the road. A cool eighteen-year-old dude who admires his Ray-Ban, cap and T-shirt combination in the window of a Coffee Bean & Tea Leaf outlet. A lad from the local laundry who holds aloft freshly ironed white shirts that billow like a schooner's sails as he delivers them along the street. A group of men huddled in deep discussion at one street corner, while two enraged men scream and punch each other at another. A white-uniformed tourist policeman on his way home for lunch who slips a newly bought bunch of coriander into his semi-transparent carrier bag containing rondals of unleavened bread.

All this took place on 26 July Street, named for the date on which King Farouk left the country at the time of the 1952 revolution. I wonder if any of the political developments this week will result in it being renamed for today's date of 18 June. If so, we'll know what happened here today, in the shadow of these momentous events.

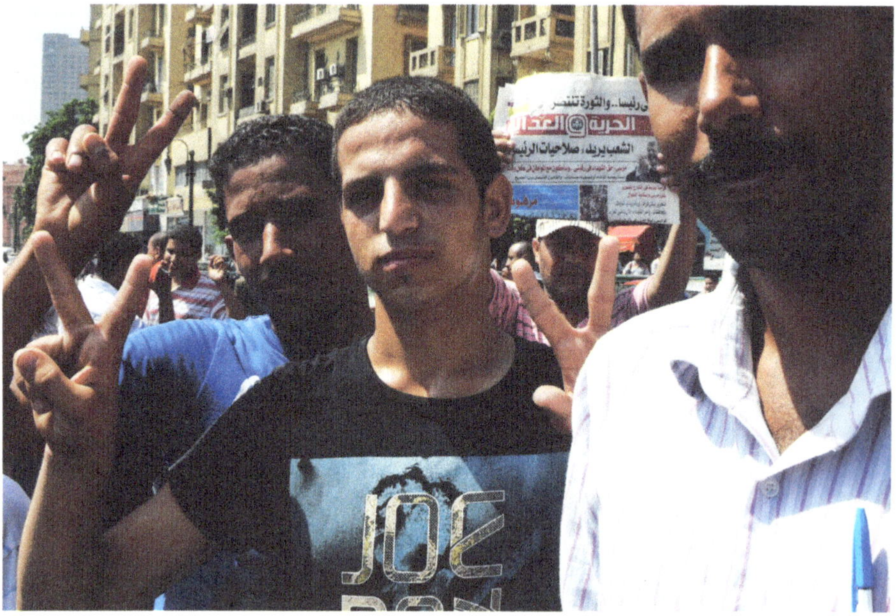
والثورة
الحرية
الشعب يريد
JOE

19 JUNE 2012: THE HEART OF TAHRIR SQUARE

I skirt round barb-wire barriers and stand at the heart of Tahrir Square, which is still the epicentre of the revolution of 25 January 2011. Locals prepare for either celebrations or protests this week, depending on their political persuasions. Some speak to television crews surrounded by an admiring group, proud of their countryman's command of English. Others help to set up the speakers' platform for tonight's speeches. There's a tangible sense of anticipation and, somehow, a confidence and calm. I don't detect any anger or friction.

The supporters of the Muslim Brotherhood, often indicated by their robes and beards, are prevalent in the crowd. I think it will be their show over the next few days. It'll be interesting to see if the moderate/liberal revolutionaries rally round in this famous place too. I like the shot here, as 'Joe' seems in tune with that group and was very keen to be photographed. I hope his V for Victory sign doesn't wither.

I drop off the back of the square to rediscover my own block of Cairo around Mohammed Mahmoud Street, where I first stayed over thirty years ago. The alleys are home to small glassmaking and engineering workshops. Herds of goats and flocks of guinea fowl wander unrestrained. Basic restaurants with tiled floors and marble-topped tables serve cold, battered fish kept stacked against their street windows. Suited and robed men draw on shisha pipes seated at teahouses whose chairs spill onto the pavements.

I feel I am finally home in Cairo, despite last year's visit. This is where I first ate and slept, where I nursed my split head after my encounter with the bus and also nursed my friend, Clara, through five-days of gastroenteritis. She had eaten cold battered fish that had stood too long unprotected from flies, probably in the restaurant I saw earlier. Would you believe that when I set off in search of a doctor for her, I found a fat, perspiring, red-haired, blue-eyed Egyptian who had a Scottish grandmother and had studied at Edinburgh University? Clara recovered but not before I had spent days exploring every inch of the streets around this block. Home, indeed.

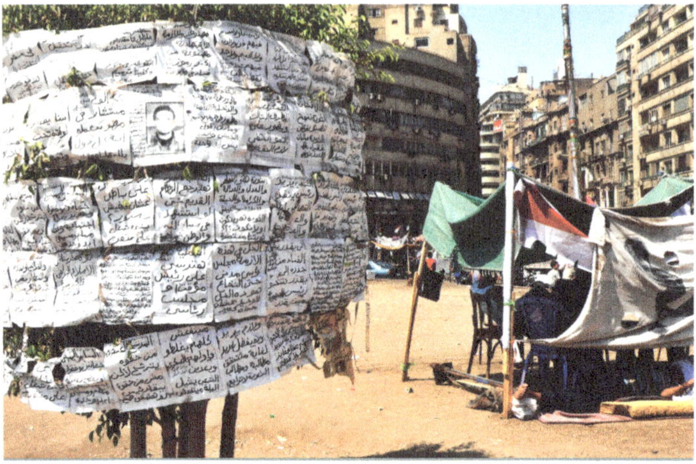

Remembering the Tahrir Martyrs

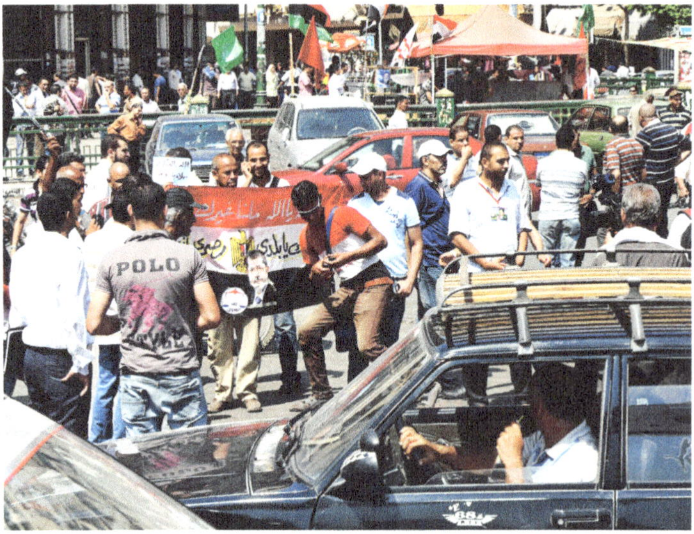

A Sense of Anticipation

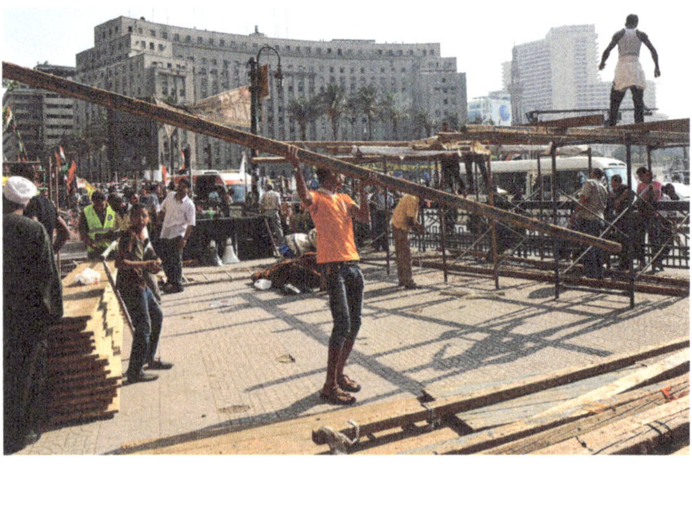

Setting up the Speakers' Platform

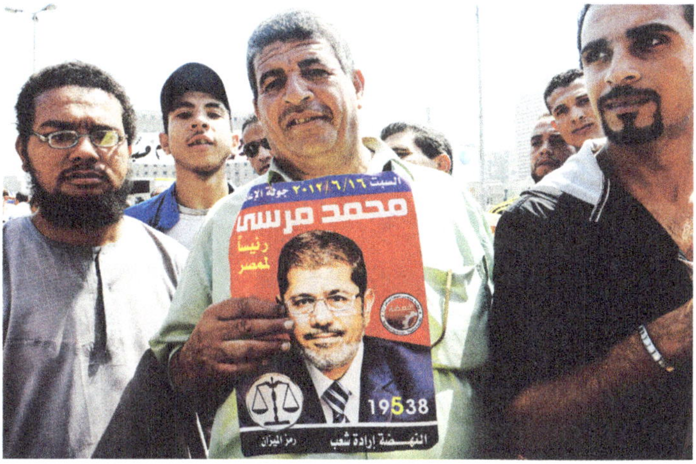

Mursi Poster

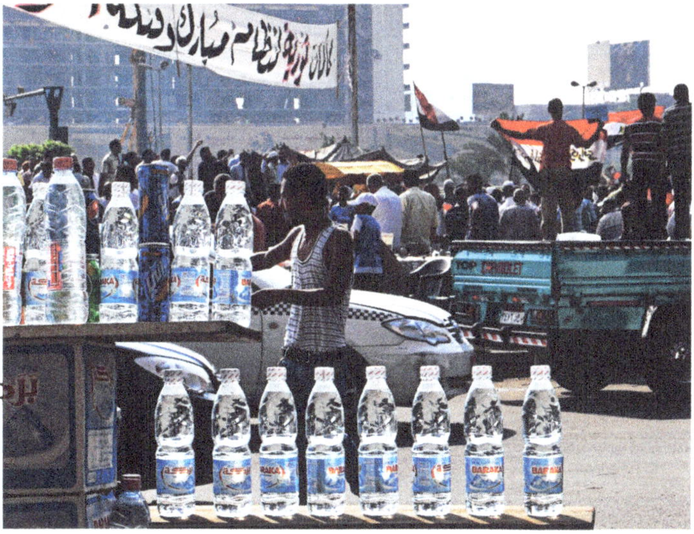

Essential Supplies

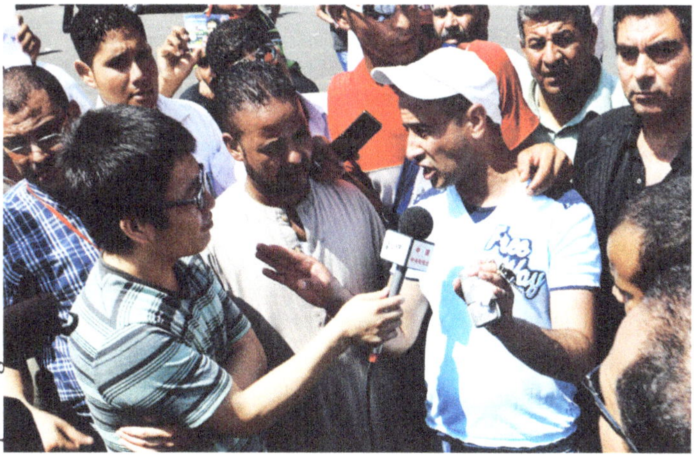

Speaking to Television Crews

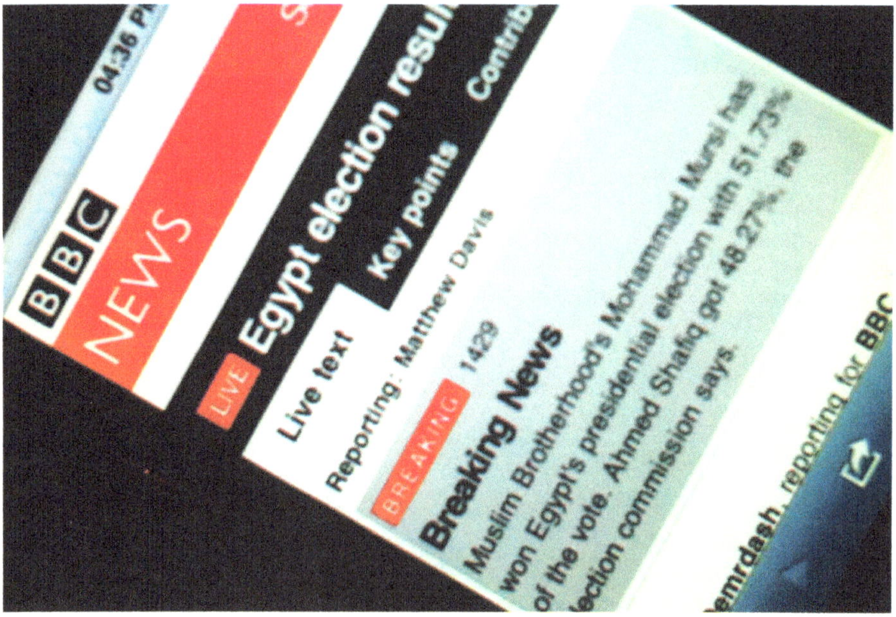
BBC
NEWS
LIVE Egypt election
Key points
Live text
Reporting: Matthew Davis
BREAKING 1429
Breaking News
Muslim Brotherhood's Mohammad Mursi has won Egypt's presidential election with 51.73% of the vote. Ahmed Shafiq got 48.27%, the election commission says.
reporting for BBC

24 JUNE 2012: BREAKING NEWS

There it is. A Muslim Brotherhood member, Mohammed Mursi, has been declared president of Egypt, an event unthinkable eighteen months ago or at any time during the last thirty or even eighty years. I remember Anwar Sadat railed against the Brotherhood every night during his three-hour television addresses in September 1981. It was not enough for him to avoid the hail of bullets that came his way on 6 October that same year. Some say Mubarak was behind the assassination and his motive was Sadat's failure to sufficiently suppress the Muslim Brotherhood. Mubarak did a good job on all suppression fronts during the subsequent three decades and it is the supreme irony that his own successor will be from the Brotherhood.

We wait to see what powers the army allows the new president. The Americans may have to tighten the military-aid purse strings in the next few days to influence that outcome; 'There must be no back sliding from democracy,' said the US secretary of state.

Good luck to the brave people of Egypt in this next phase, so full of jeopardy but also possibility.

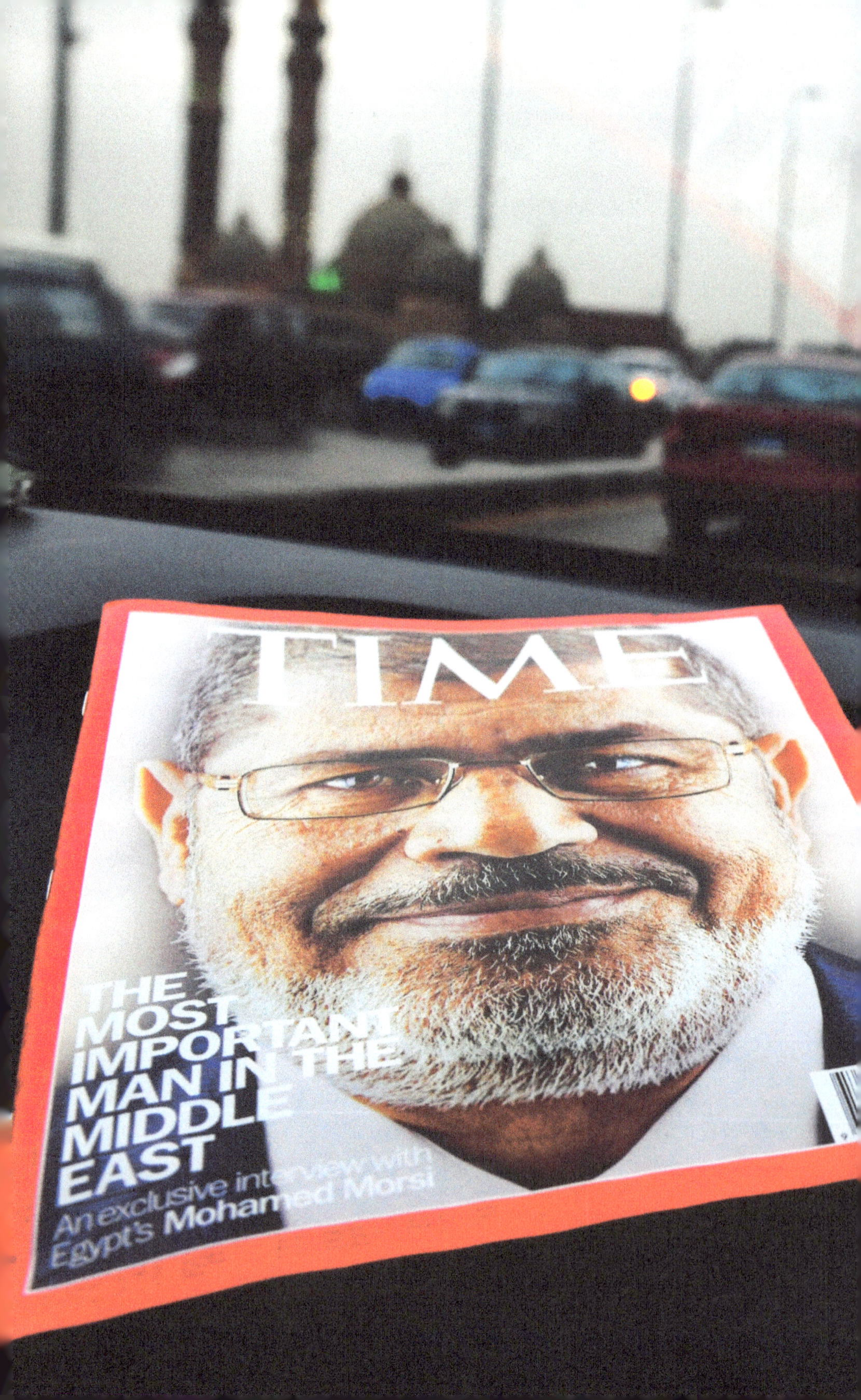
TIME
THE MOST IMPORTANT MAN IN THE MIDDLE EAST
An exclusive interview with Egypt's Mohamed Morsi

Chapter 3

A New Constitution

4 DECEMBER 2012: THE MOST IMPORTANT MAN IN THE MIDDLE EAST

I ask Ahmed, my driver today, if it's safe to take photos on the way in from Cairo airport. Almost six months have passed since my last visit when President Mursi came to power and I don't want any trouble.

'No problem. That's freedom, dear!' he replies.

We laugh and I lay out on the dashboard the edition of *TIME* with Mursi's portrait on the cover that I bought in Paris early this morning. I planned the shot from the moment I saw it on the newsstand.

I take some practice shots and wait for us to reach the stretch of road that runs by the El-Noor Mosque, visible in the background here. I wonder what's in store for the country and those of us in it over the next days as the country prepares to vote in eleven days' time in a referendum on the new constitution.

Mursi is the most important man in the Middle East just as Sadat and Mubarak, his two predecessors, were during their dictatorships. The big question is: which style is Mursi adopting, democratic president or autocratic ruler? At the moment it seems to be the latter. He issued a decree two weeks ago that gave himself full executive and decree-making powers, unchallengeable by the courts of the land. The proposed constitution has been drafted by a committee dominated by Mursi supporters and is biased to his own party's agenda rather than the wishes of the whole people as expressed through the revolution. There's been no national dialogue on its contents and a lot of protests.

'Do you trust him?' I ask Ahmed.

'Yes, we have to. He's like a doctor doing a small operation. The patient will get better soon.'

The last Islamist operation here was the shooting of Anwar Sadat; that patient never recovered.

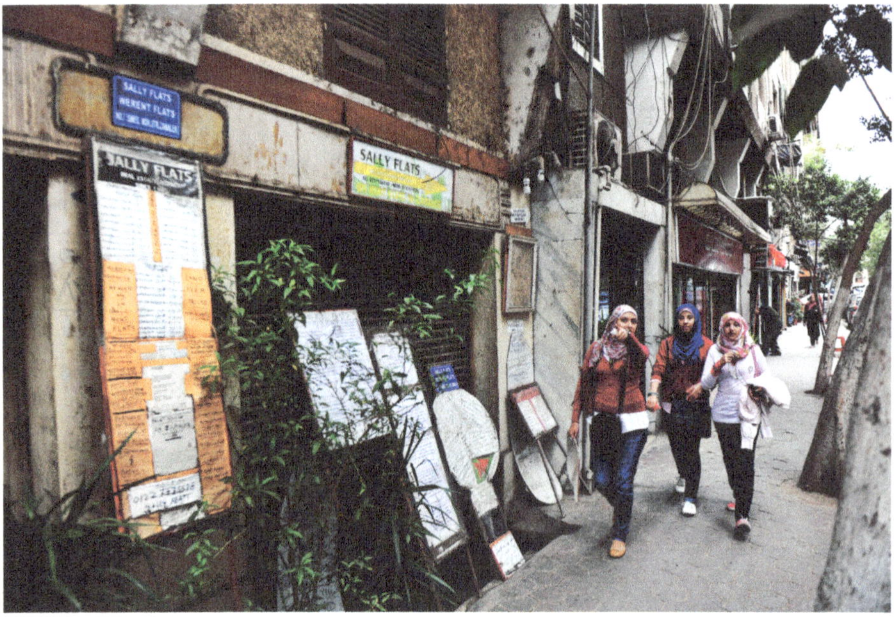
SALLY FLATS
SALLY FLATS
SALLY FLATS

5 DECEMBER 2012: MOVING FORWARD

These are the words of President Mursi, taken from his recent interview in *TIME*. On President Obama:

> *I can say, really, that his deeds coincide with his intentions . . . he's been very helpful.*

On Palestine:

> *Democracy is better for the whole world. If there is a place where you have dictatorship, where people are not free, people are not satisfied . . . this is a dangerous spot for the whole world.*

On whether the Muslim Brotherhood is democratic:

> *This is a big yes, sure. This stems from Islamic belief – freedom for everyone, freedom of belief, freedom of expressing their opinion, equality, stability, human rights . . . equal rights for men and women, for Muslim, Christians, for whoever is carrying an opinion.*

On the post-revolution:

> *What I see now is, the Egyptians are free. They are raising their voices when they are opposing the president and when they are opposing what's going on . . . but, I see things more than they do. We're learning how to debate, how to differ.*

On his decree taking all power to himself:

> *I know what it is perfectly to have a separation between the three powers – executive power, legislative power and judiciary. I hope, when we have a constitution, what I have issued will stop immediately.*

On the protests:

> *Peacefully expressing opposition is very healthy. But not violently. That's what's different. And violence is related to, as I said, to the old regime. It's not easy to lead [the new phase] now but it's OK. Inshallah.*

Actions speak louder than words, Mr President. Police sirens fill the air as I sit writing this beside the Nile, a few kilometres from the Presidential Palace. Last night, many Egyptians voiced their concerns there at Mursi's actions so far. He fled the building. Never a good sign.

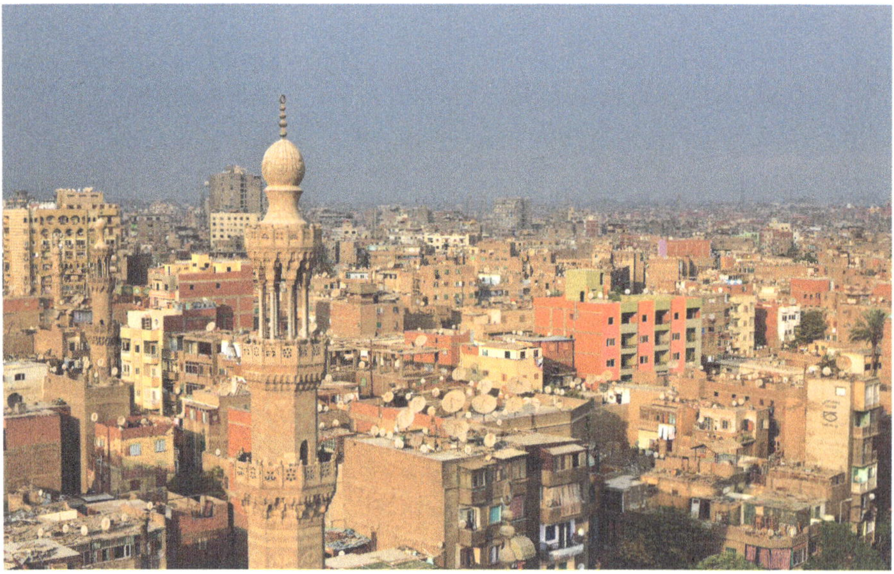

6 DECEMBER 2012: MOTHER CAIRO BEREAVED

Five people who would have seen this view, or one like it, every day of their lives did not wake up this morning to share the dawn. They died in disturbances outside the Presidential Palace on a December night in the second decade of the twenty-first century in Cairo, Africa and the Middle East's largest and most influential city.

In a Zamalek coffee shop, when the sun is higher, I talk to a young liberal Muslim about the situation.

'Have you been to the palace?' I ask.

'No,' he says. 'I don't know why. Two years ago, I couldn't have told you the name of any politician other than that of the president. I wasn't interested . . . my family was doing well . . . I never thought about politics. Now I want to go and be involved but I don't . . . maybe it's fear.'

'What about the new constitution?'

'It's not legal. We don't want to vote for it. Last time we had no choice between Mursi and the old regime and so we didn't vote. Now they present something illegal and we don't want to recognise it either.'

'What will Egypt be like in five years' time?'

'Do you mean what I *want* it to be like?'

'No, what do you think it *will* be like?'

He stares into his cup. 'Just like today or worse. My brother's an army officer . . . they're just waiting.' He looks me straight in the eye. 'Worst case, we'll have civil war.'

My coffee's gone cold.

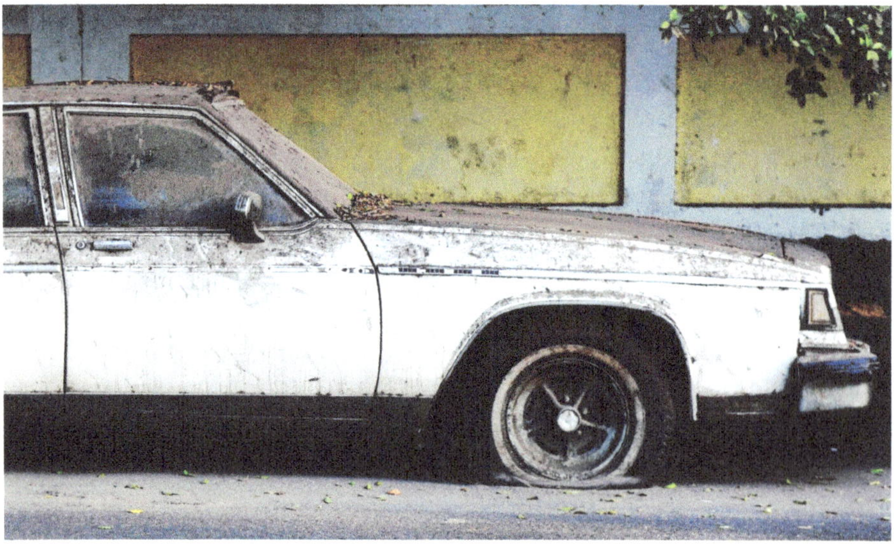

7 DECEMBER 2012: BETTER DAYS?

The atmosphere grows more tense in the city and it's clear better days are a long way off. There's a state of high alert this Friday prayer day following the recent violence and deaths. Long sermons are broadcast through loudspeakers across the street and river. On national TV, we see huge crowds pour from the mosques where the most radical clerics preach. Many in the crowd chant angrily and point skyward. An equal number hold smart phones aloft to film the scene. A writers' conference featuring authors from Edinburgh has been cancelled due to safety concerns and one of Shona's new colleagues has delayed the start of her assignment. Businesses near the Presidential Palace are closed. Dialogue proposals with the opposition on the twin issues of the president's power-grab decree and biased draft constitution flounder. Protesters breach the palace perimeter once more.

We've kept a low profile today, the first day of Shona's weekend. We crossed the river to the Swiss Club for their Christmas Fayre. Later, we strolled in Zamalek and captured a few scenes. At the river bank, crews readied the pleasure boats with their gaudy lights for this evening's birthday cruises on the Nile. Life goes on.

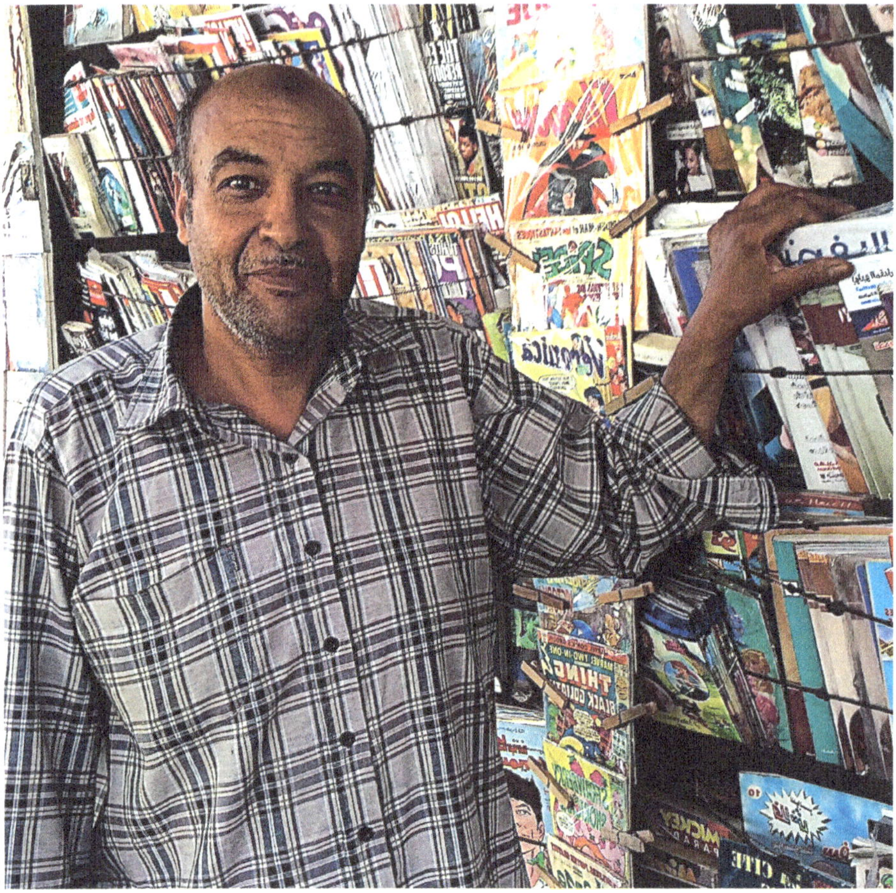
MARVEL TWO-IN-ONE
THING
BLACK GOLIATH
MICKEY

8 DECEMBER 2011: READ ALL ABOUT IT!

Hamoud, this newsseller, has a variety of English-speaking newspapers on his stand. The degree of crispness of their front pages depends on their date of publication. Today he has a hot-off-the-press copy of the *International Herald Tribune* dated 8–9 December 2012. He folds the paper in three and smacks it against his hand to displace the dust that has accumulated on it. I hand him his money through the ensuing cloud.

An elderly, Western-suited Egyptian gentleman is buying a national daily paper next to me. He asks where I'm from.

'Scotland,' I say, wondering if a scam is coming. I shouldn't have doubted him.

'I thought you were American,' he said, nodding at the paper. 'Are you a journalist?'

'No, but I follow events closely.'

He smiles and I decide to ask him what he thinks of the current situation.

'We're in a mist,' he says. 'No one knows what's going to happen. President Mursi is doing his best and, you know, without a constitution in place he has supreme power anyway.'

'You mean his recent decree is irrelevant?'

'Yes, and putting a new constitution in place quickly, by its very nature, will establish the separation of powers again.'

'So, you don't think he's an autocrat.'

'No. And let's not forget, he is the elected president of the country.'

Overall, we've had a very quiet Sunday type of a day on this the second day of the weekend; a long lie, some reading, a stroll along the business-as-usual 26 July Street, a beer on the terrace of the Marriot where the BBC reporters spend their free time, followed by an early dinner in an Italian restaurant owned by Omar Sharif's son.

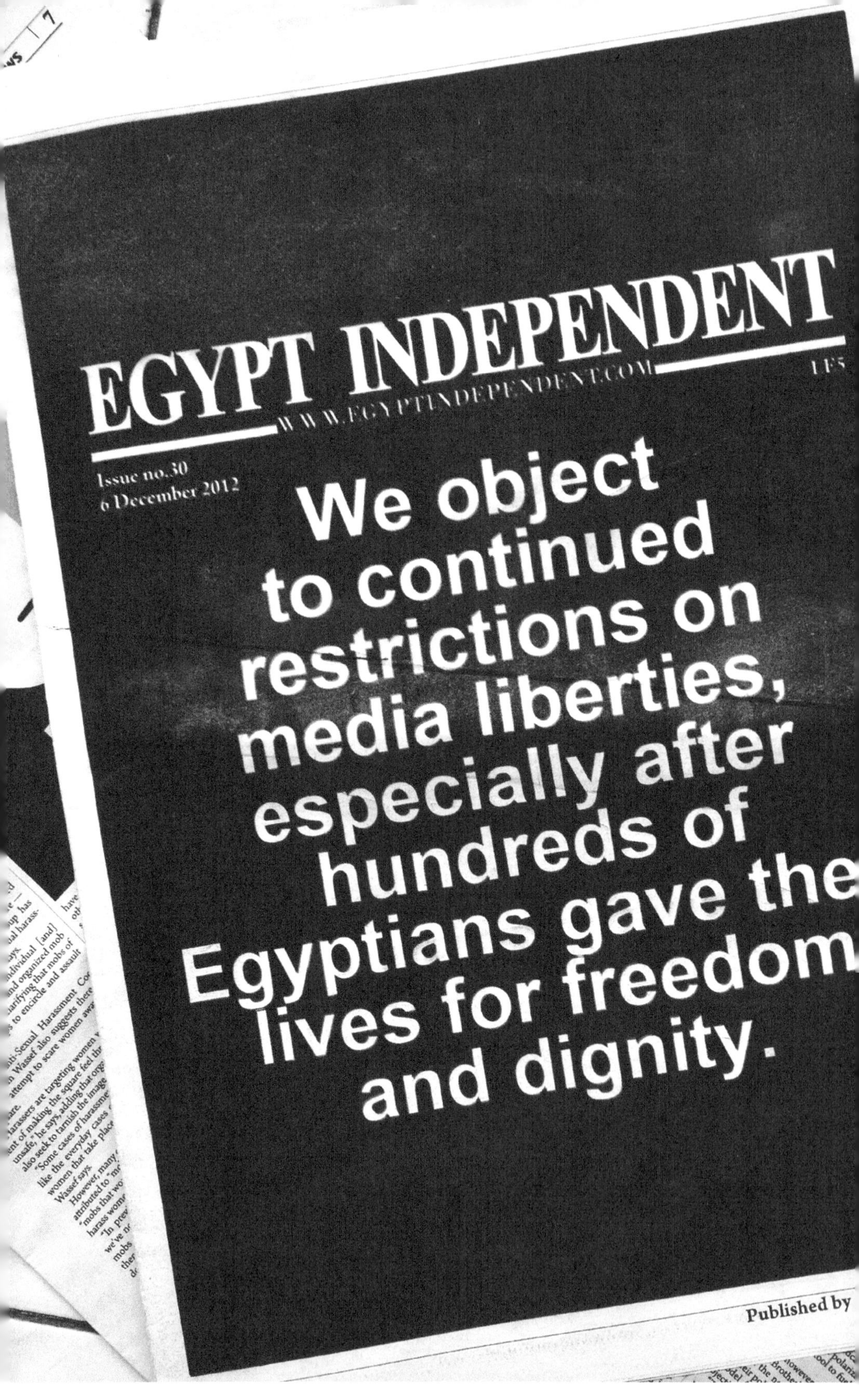

EGYPT INDEPENDENT

WWW.EGYPTINDEPENDENT.COM

LE5

Issue no.30
6 December 2012

We object to continued restrictions on media liberties, especially after hundreds of Egyptians gave the lives for freedom and dignity.

Published by

9 DECEMBER 2012: BLACK AND WHITE

Elements of the independent press in Cairo highlight a number of important issues today.

The lead story is President Mursi's decree that gives his office total and unchallengeable power, although it appears the decree was revoked this morning after the papers went to press. The second story is the upcoming referendum on the new constitution. The latest protests are a result of Mursi's apparent determination to rush through the constitution without national debate.

Two other stories feature prominently. One is the executive's alleged interference with the programming of private TV channels and their choices of talk-show guests. It is also unhappy with criticism and insults directed towards the president by the presenters. The Head of State Television resigned yesterday. He claimed interference in his work is far in excess of that by the Mubarak regime.

The other is the work of anti-sexual harassment units set up to protect women who enter Tahrir Square from sexual assault and rape at the hands of paid harassment squads. The accounts relate how even mature women in full body-covering Islamic dress are stripped and raped with fingers and objects in broad daylight.

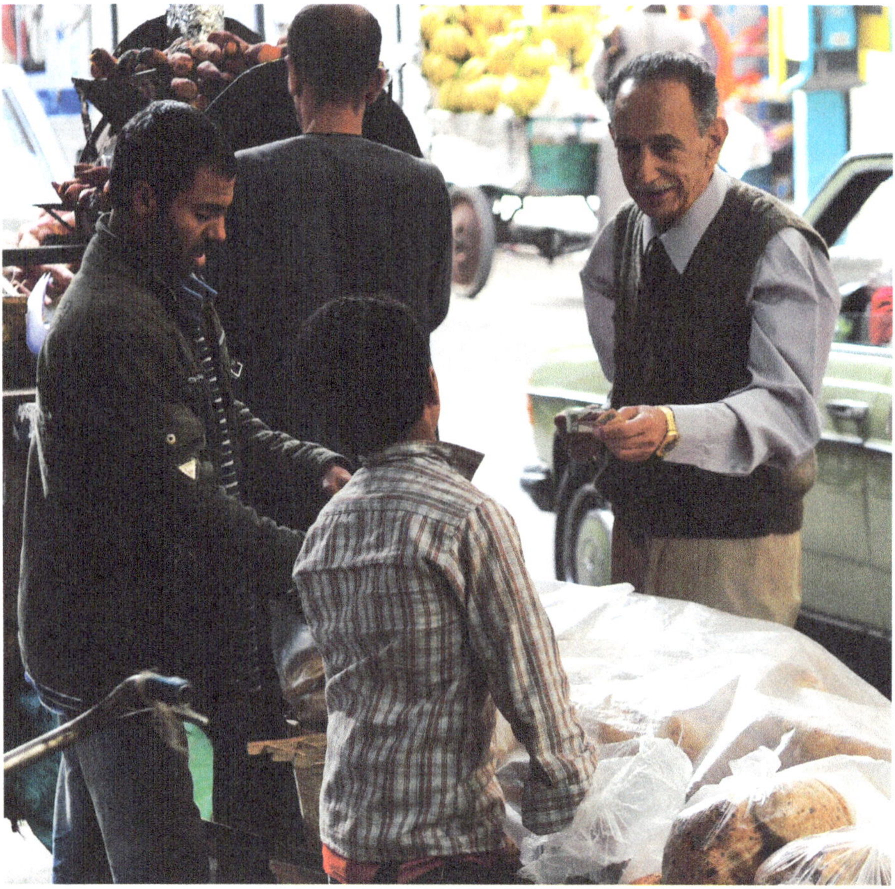

10 DECEMBER 2012: THE WIND'S UP

The wind was up on the banks of the Nile today. It swirled dust into eyes, and filled shoes with grit. People turned their heads with their scarves pulled up high to mitigate the effects. In the back streets it was less strong and people went about their normal tasks. An elderly man bought unleavened bread. Roasted sweet potatoes and bananas were also available at the junction shown in the photo here.

The president has empowered the army to arrest people as the country prepares for the referendum on the new constitution on Saturday. Does that make him a democrat or autocrat? On TV, I saw blocks of concrete being lifted into place around the palace, but in this area there's no sense of unrest in the air and the pavements have enough obstacles to navigate without the need for more. Must get on with writing the Christmas Letter.

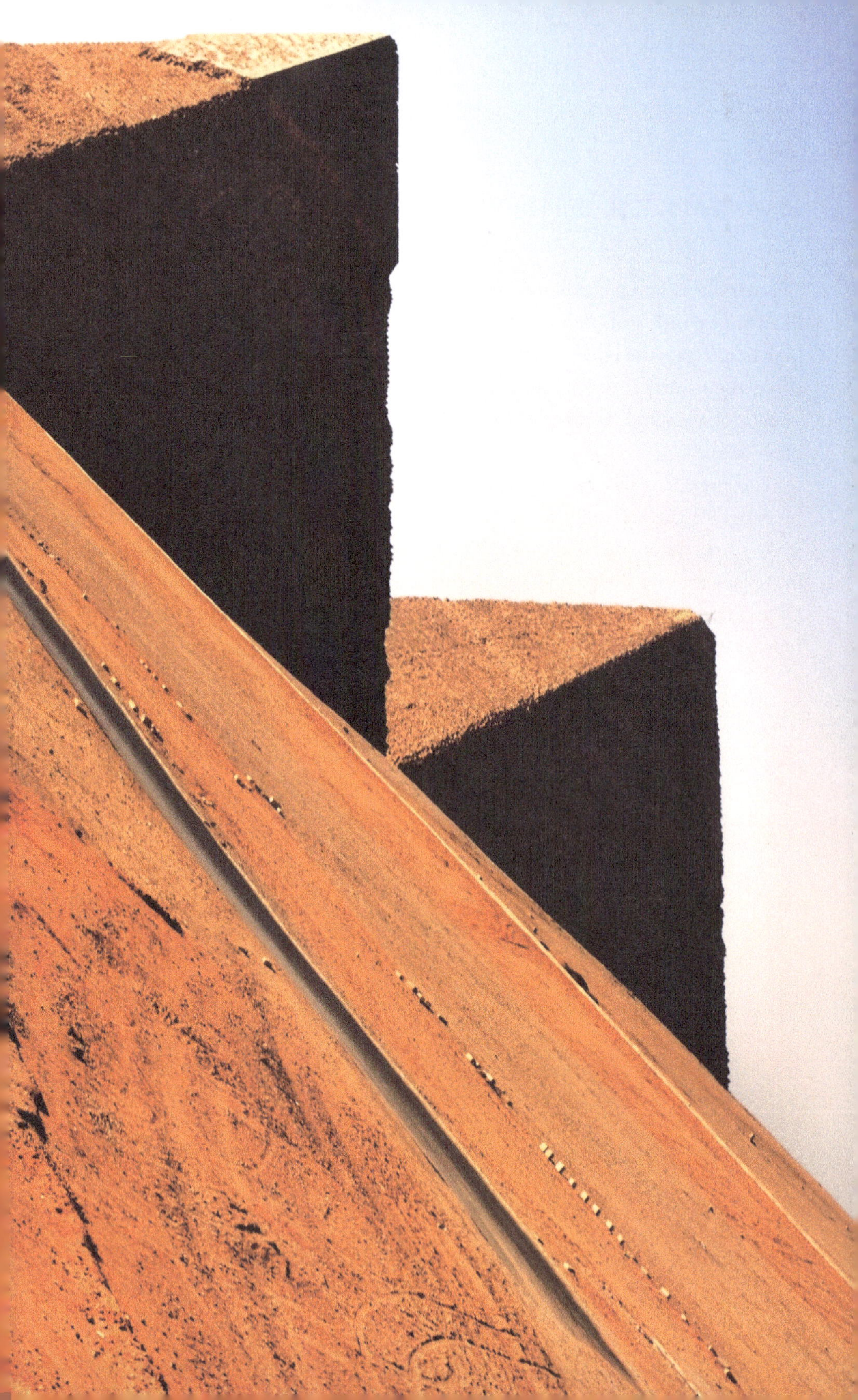

11 DECEMBER 2012: 'AH, YOU'RE A SERIOUS SNAPPER!'

That's what my Egyptian guide tells me as I finish today's shoot with some low angle shots at the Son et Lumière seating area in front of the Sphinx. Today I reached a personal landmark, having taken 1,000 consecutive daily photographs; that's almost four years' worth. I decided to change my work routine and celebrate by going to the most iconic site in the world.

My 1,000 shots seem a lot until I contemplate the monuments around me and calculate that if each consecutive pharaoh had done the same, using their contemporary technological equivalent, all the way down the line to the first elected president in office today, they would have notched up over 1.6 million daily records. Just think if they had kept a journal of their days too. Maybe they did and we just haven't found them yet. I must go back and ask my friend, King Tut.

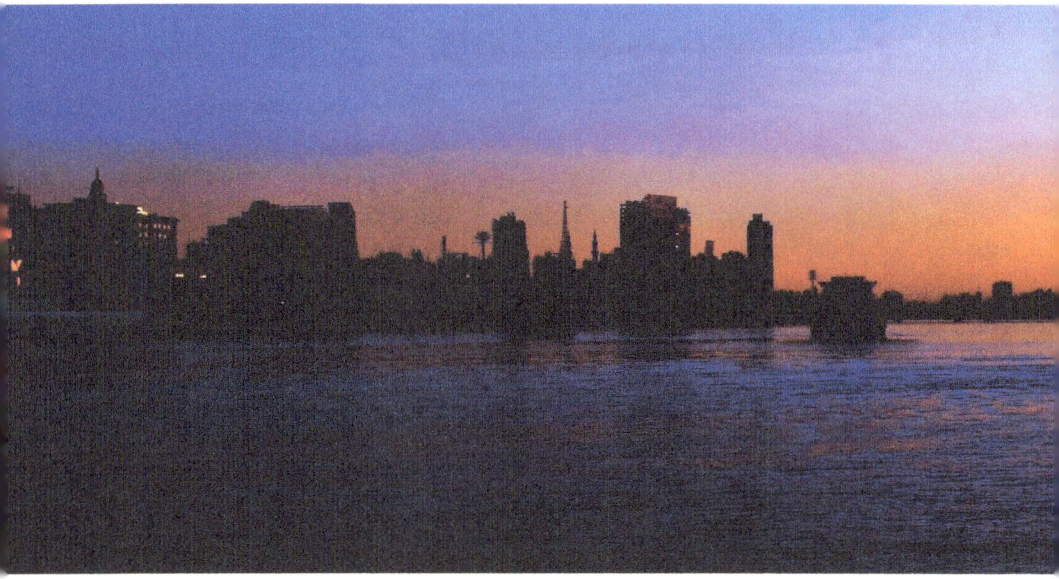

12 DECEMBER 2012: WHEN THE EVENING IS SPREAD OUT AGAINST THE SKY

The colours of the sunset that closed my afternoon beside the Nile in Cairo show a palette that goes well with today's date – 12/12/12 – which is said to bring luck and harmony. The number twelve is perceived as a unit of completeness and has found resonance in religion, the twelve apostles, and our daily lives, twelve hours on our clock faces. It is also perfectly divisible by more numbers than most: one, two, three, four, six and twelve to be exact.

The next such date lies eighty-eight years ahead on 1 January 2101 – 01/01/01. Any bets on what we would find in Cairo then? Perhaps someone will write about it with this book in hand, open at today's page.

If my view was uplifting, then my taxi driver was all gloom on the way home. He's in the camp that predicts that 01/01/01 will bring more of the same.

'It's very obscure,' said Mohammed. 'We're in the hands of a gang. The Muslim Brotherhood are worse than the Mafia. At least with them you know what you're getting . . . it's all very honest; drugs, arms, and extortion. *This* gang deal in minds; it's very dangerous.'

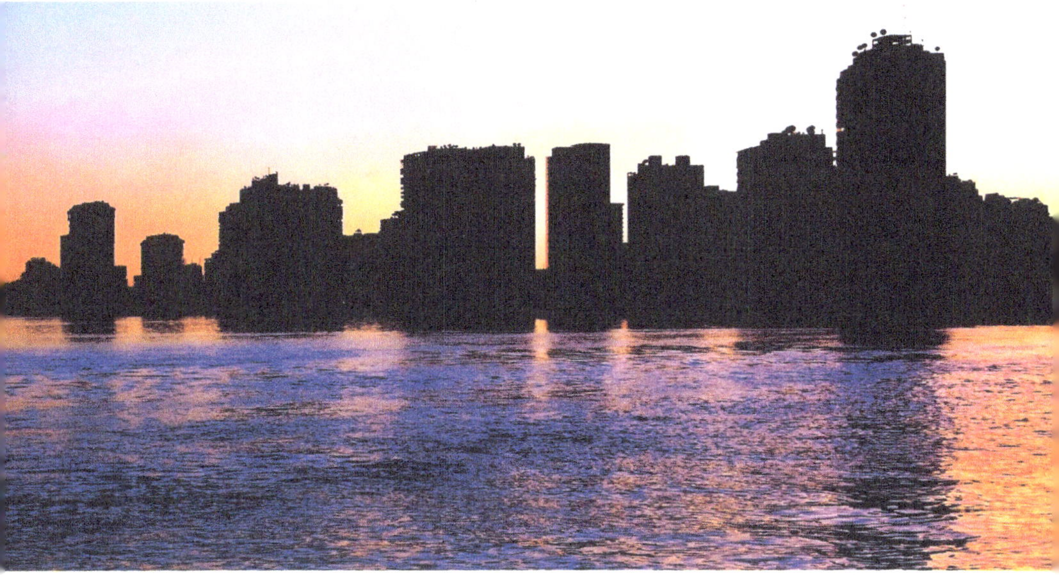

A sense of trepidation prevails as the country prepares to go to the polls on the proposed new constitution. The opposition are making noises about mounting a 'No' campaign, which would seem to be a good use of the ballot box, as long as the vote isn't rigged. They've left it a bit late, as usual. Let's see what happens.

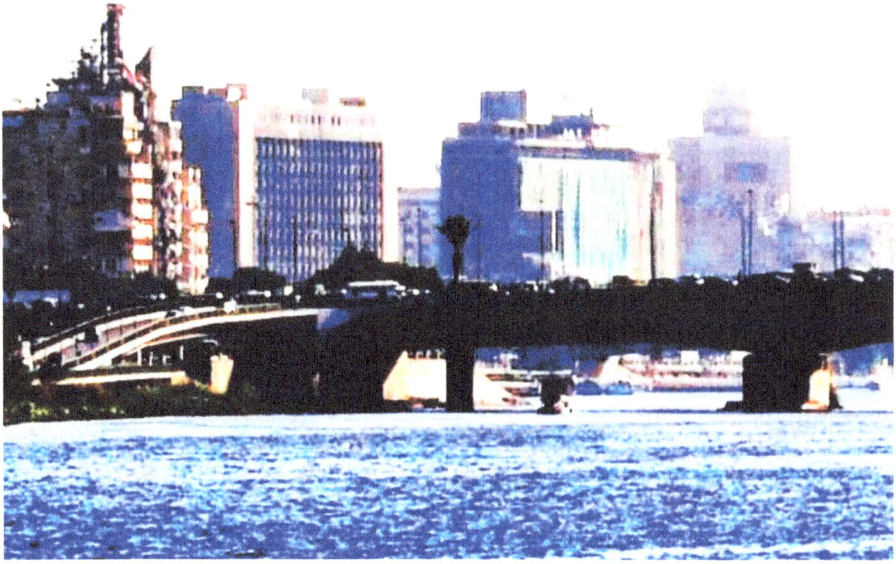

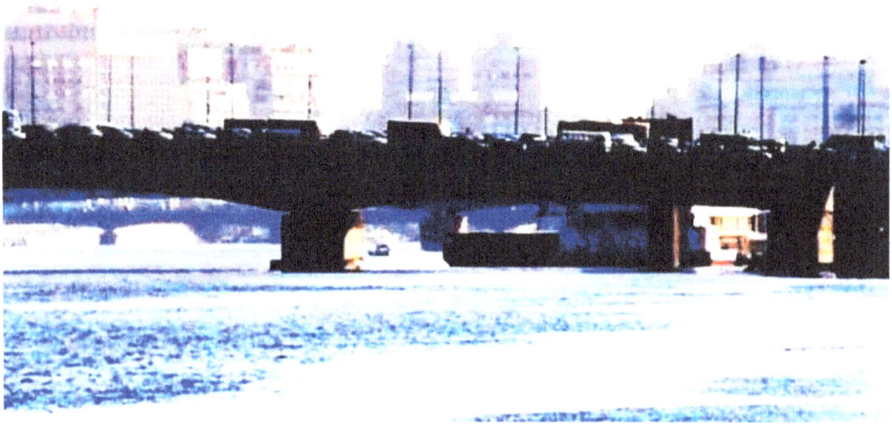

13 DECEMBER 2012: TAHRIR BACKLOG

Tahrir Square is closed to traffic today, as the weekend vote approaches, leading to all sorts of congestion elsewhere. Here you can see the 15 May Bridge a few minutes' drive from the square, with a huge backlog of traffic on it. My taxi driver is less fluent in English today.

'See this hair?' Amir takes both hands from the wheel and holds them in front of his face to simulate a beard before continuing, 'No good. Mursi has hair like this. Means he makes no decisions. Only Grand Sheikh makes decisions, like Khomeini. Here soon will be Libya . . . and I'm a Muslim!'

I ask him if I can take his picture.

He laughs and wags his finger. 'No, No.'

'New constitution . . . Saturday . . . you vote?' I ask, using my thumbometre to gauge his opinion.

'Vote NO!' He thumps the wheel and throws back his head with a great roar of laughter.

When we arrive at my drop-off point, I notice that the handler, whose dog sniffs for explosives around the wheels of our car and inside the boot, has the legend K.9 on his uniform. All's not lost.

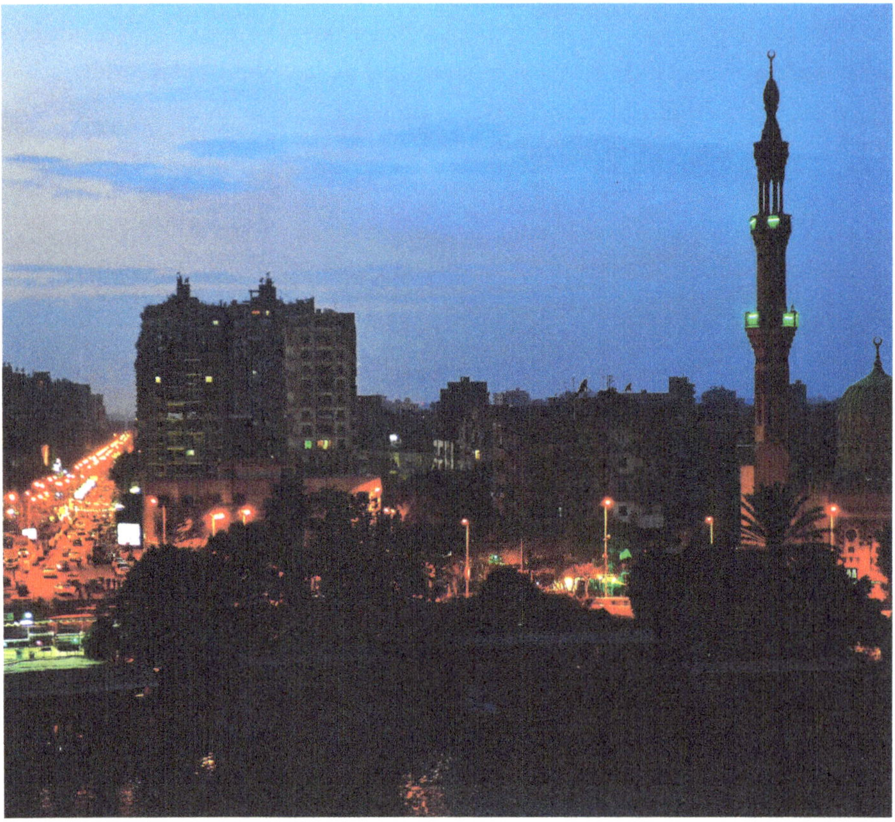

14 DECEMBER 2012: CALL TO PRAYER

Allah is the almighty (intoned four times)

I testify that there is no deity other than God (intoned twice)

I testify that Muhammad is the Messenger of God (intoned twice)

Come to prayer (intoned twice)

Come to Salvation (intoned twice)

God is almighty (intoned twice)

There is no deity other than God (intoned once)

Adhan, the call to prayer, is heard from the minarets across the city five times every twenty-four hours, Friday being the most important prayer day of all. Originally, the minarets were purely functional and supported an elevated platform on which the muezzin sat. He would project his voice across the nearby streets to alert the faithful that the doors of heaven were opening at that moment and remind them that it was a propitious time to pray.

Over time, the minarets became taller and more ornate as tastes developed and status factors became a consideration. The live human voice was enhanced by electronic amplification or replaced by a recording. Cairo has perhaps the greatest range of minarets of any Islamic city and they form a significant part of the city's heritage.

In the *Diwan* bookshop on 26 July Street, a popular meeting place for Westerners and Egyptian intellectuals alike, 'Have Yourself a Merry Little Christmas' was playing quietly in the background.

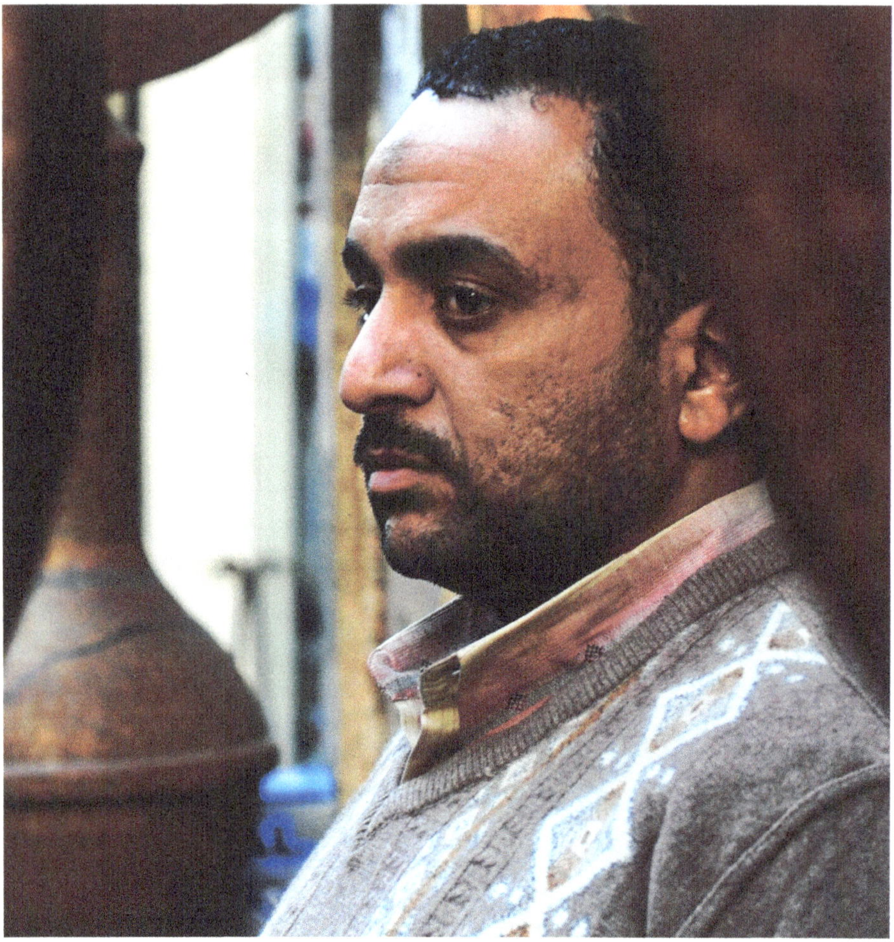

15 DECEMBER 2012: A PENNY FOR YOUR VOTE

I wonder which way this unshaven and gloomy-looking trader in Islamic Cairo voted today, if at all, in the referendum on the draft constitution. The 'No' campaign seems to have mobilised itself quite well, with a higher than normal overall turnout reported. A liberal Egyptian friend of ours posted excitedly on Facebook that he was in the queue at the polling station and had been for four hours.

We visited several mosques and minarets in the afternoon and then went to Downtown, the former glory of the city in its belle époque era in the first half of the twentieth century. Cairo became the most cosmopolitan city in the world, drawing heavily on English and French influences, and its intellectual and cultural life flowered. We strolled past the Grand Hotel and Claridge's, as well as the Cafés L'Americaine, Excelsior, Groppi and Riche.

Finally, we covered the final two hundred metres that brought us to Tahrir Square, our first visit together, and felt emboldened enough to each take a few shots to mark our visit there on this historic referendum day.

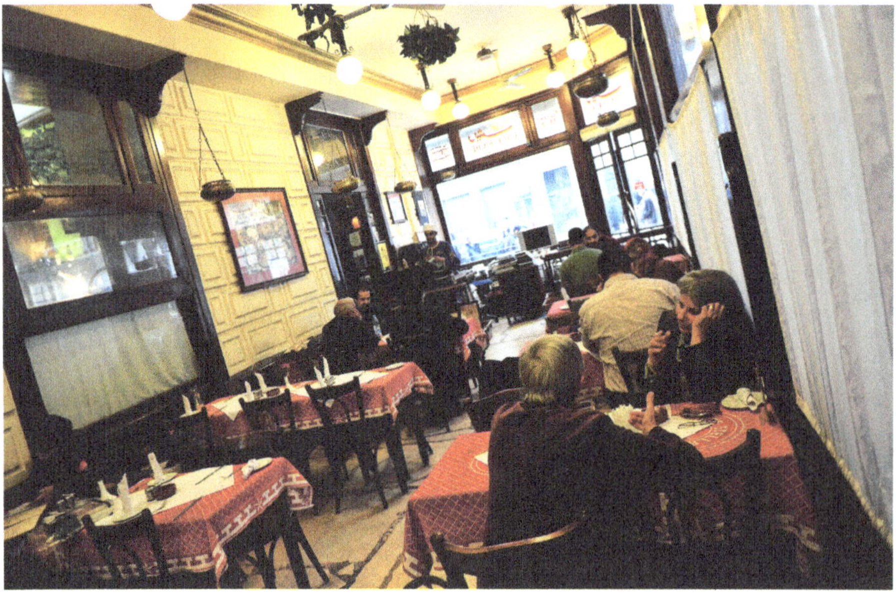

16 DECEMBER 2012: CAFÉ RICHE

Last night became a little fiery in Tahrir Square after we left. Here are snippets of the conversations I heard today in Café Riche, a traditional haunt of journalists and writers.

> *There were firecrackers and Molotov cocktails but it was hard to say who had organised what . . . It's incredible how the Muslim Brotherhood have burned their bridges and become so unpopular in only one year . . . The upper- and middle-class 'No' queues moved more slowly, the women's queues too . . . It's good the 'No' vote has come out so the Brotherhood don't think the country belongs to them . . . The opposition need a charismatic young leader . . . The constitution is not the be-all and end-all. It somehow reflects the current balance of power, and will change over time, like the French one has done.*

The café is situated just off Tahrir Square and has been on the go for a hundred and four years, so has seen it all. Around the wall of the inner dining room hang large black-and-white photographic portraits of all the Egyptian journalists of note who have followed the country's development during all that time, with pride of place given to Naguib Mahfouz, the Egyptian Nobel laureate for literature.

We popped in for a lunch of lentil soup with cumin and lemon juice, stuffed vine leaves, baba ganoush and hot unleavened bread. Because Shona had a day off we had taken a rare trip round the city together, visiting the Muhammad Ali Mosque and the Egyptian Museum. King Tut was silent on the subject of hidden pharaonic journals when I asked him, although I think he was just being coy. Time will tell.

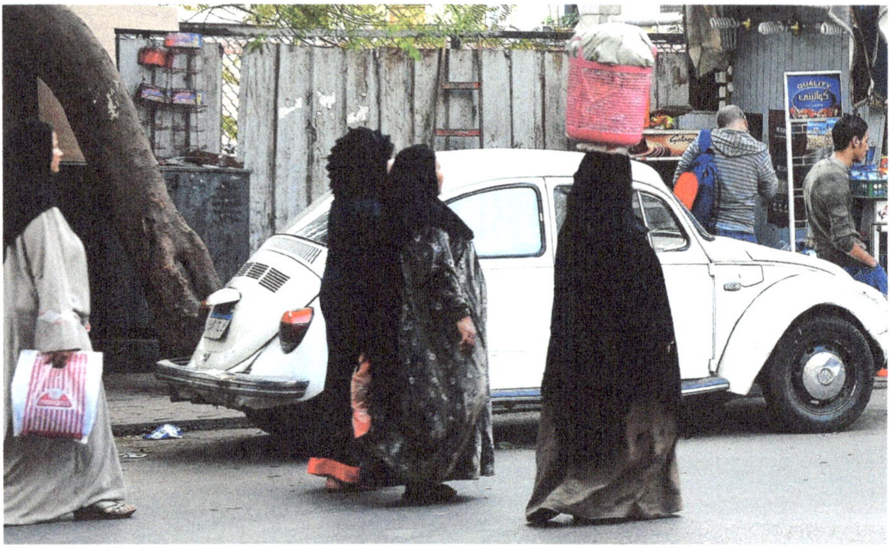

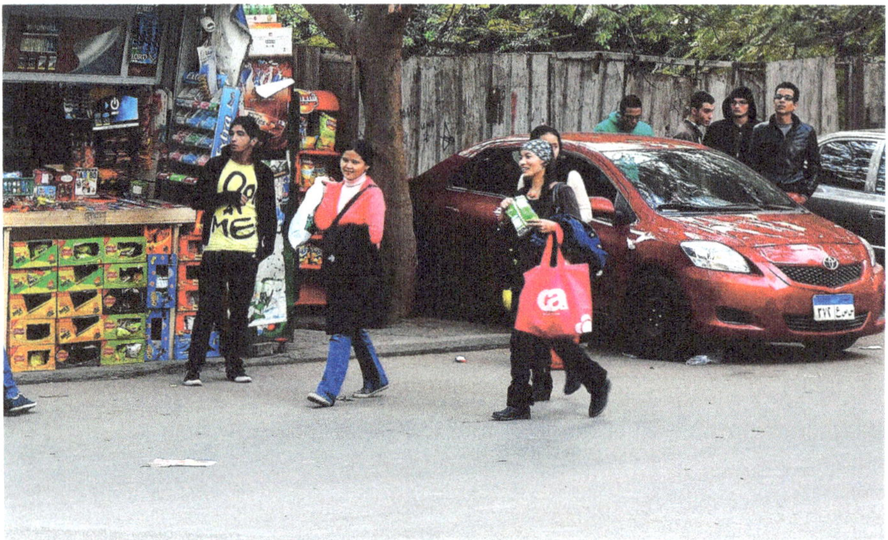

17 DECEMBER 2012: UNITED COLOURS OF CAIRO

Pink's in on the streets of Cairo. But it's the only sign of unity from these people of very different persuasions who are clearly still headed in opposing directions.

Only 33% of those eligible to vote turned out to do so in the poll on the constitution on Saturday. So, the 57% majority in favour of it, as claimed by the Muslim Brotherhood, is still a very small percentage of the total number of voters at about 19%.

The 66% of those eligible to vote who stayed at home did so for a variety of reasons including apathy, fear, and ignorance. There's a need for greater organisation by all parties, effective steps to reduce intimidation, and education on the power of each and every single vote. Until then the true voice of the Egyptian people, the source of sovereign power, will continue to be unknown and unrepresented, at least through the ballot box. Taking to the streets is another matter.

Learning democracy needs to be done the hard way and it may take years, but the risk is that the often insidious and increasingly overt influence of the Muslim Brotherhood will restrict freedom of speech and inhibit cultural expression to such an extent that there may not be a free election in four years' time. What then the revolution?

Time to make votes count.

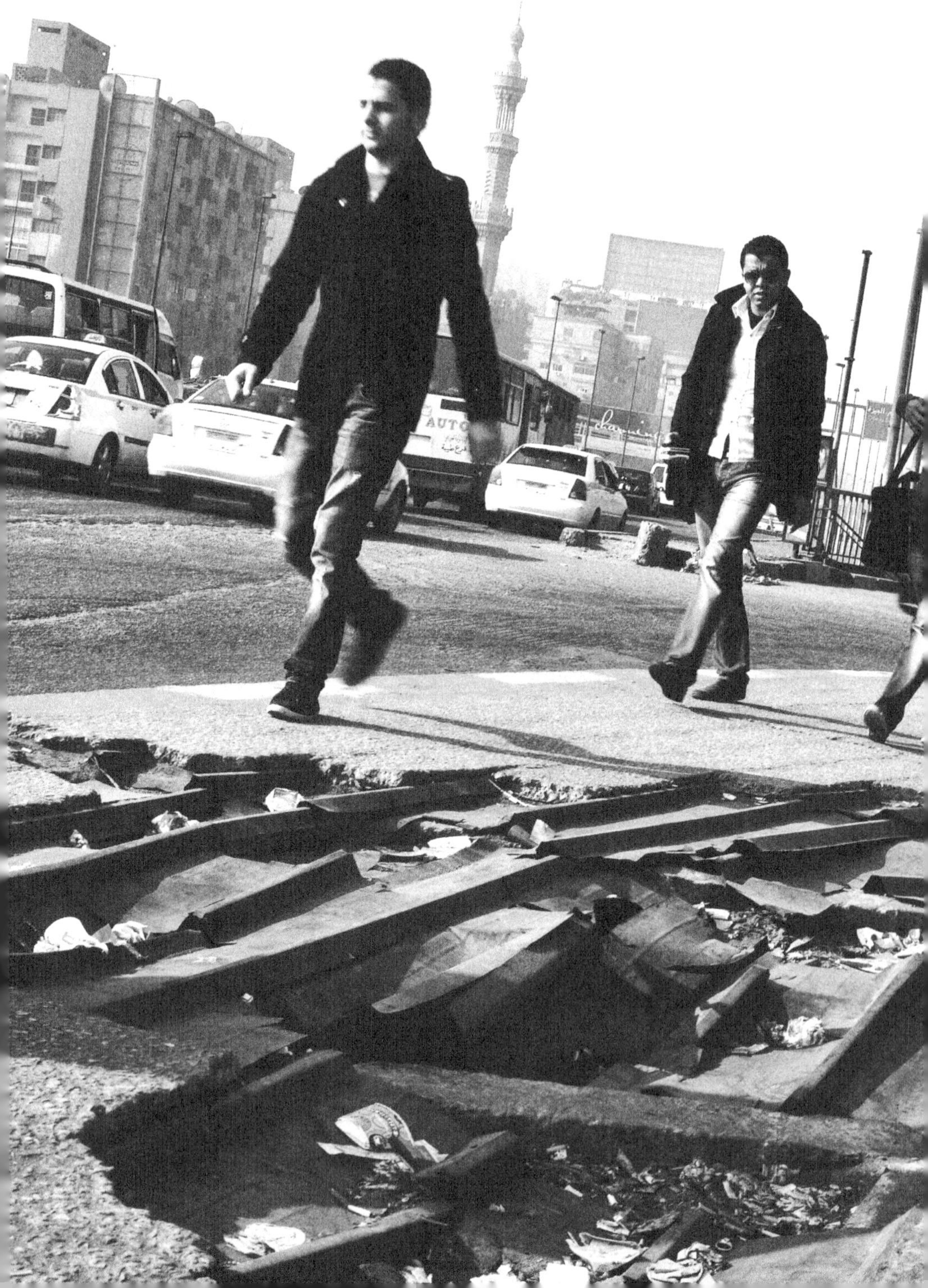
AUTO

18 DECEMBER 2012: PARADISE LOST

On 7 October 1981, when I was leaving Cairo the day after Anwar Sadat's assassination, I wrote that Egypt was 'so desperately poor, so desperately overcrowded, so desperately depressed'. Today, as I leave again, I can report that nothing has changed, except for the worse.

The purchasing power of the vast majority of people has reduced hugely due to the effects of devaluation and inflation. The average income is still a pittance at around $2 per day. The population has increased by nearly 90% from forty-four million in 1981 to approaching ninety million now. All live in the same narrow strip of land along the banks of the Nile, which constitutes 4% of the total land area of the country. Greater Cairo is among the largest and most densely populated cities in the world, with a population of almost twenty-three million people.

Beyond the numbers, what have I seen? I've seen vacant and worried expressions on people's faces in the street. Black-robed women scavenging on stinking rubbish heaps. Large, glassless apartment blocks built on protected fertile land. Congested, littered and dusty streets lined with mounds of debris from illicit building sites. Groups of children on their way to and from hot-desks at school where they receive a politically biased curriculum from exhausted teachers. Plumes of blue smoke rising from the exhausts of over-revved tuk-tuks as they bounce along rutted roads in search of scarce passengers. Workers looking hollow-eyed through dirty windows from their cramped seats in microbuses, as more people squeeze on board at pick-up points beside motorway slip roads. Donkeys with sacks piled high on their backs receiving sharp cracks on their necks from their minders as they urge them on under the midday sun. Above all this, the call to prayer drifts through the air and the doors to paradise open once again.

It is perhaps no coincidence that the felucca I sailed on all those years ago from Aswan to Luxor was captained by a scoundrel who had accidentally misnamed his boat *Parodies*; he had intended to paint 'Paradise' on the prow. His hand was certainly the wrong one on the rudder of that particular vessel and it's a valid metaphor for the great ship of Egypt steered with such ruthlessness by President Mubarak during his thirty years in power. Is it still relevant to describe the ship of state under President Mursi? A few weeks ago, I would have been tempted to say that the jury's out. But that was before this self-styled democrat eliminated the jurors, making himself the supreme commander on the bridge.

Parodies? Seems appropriate.

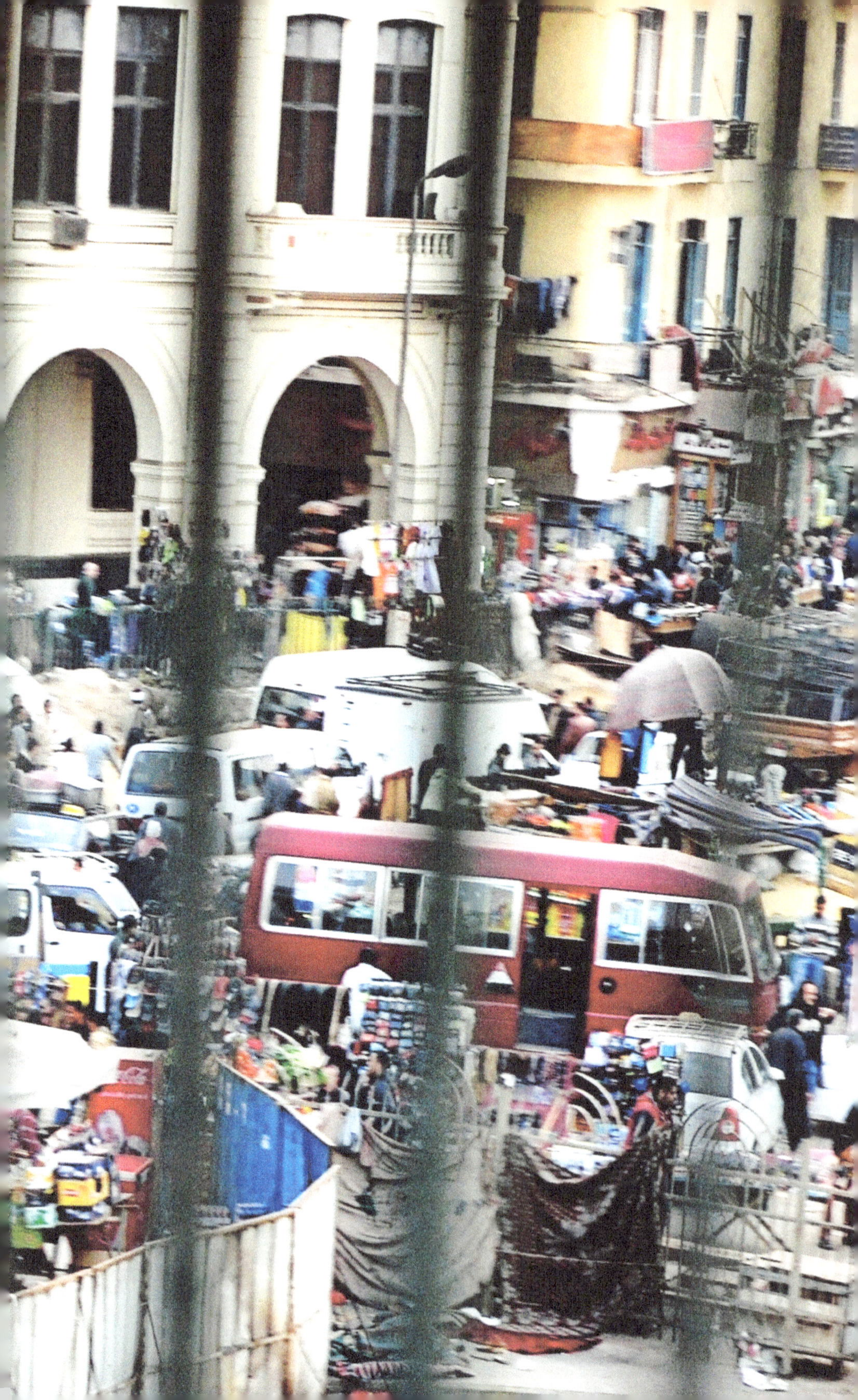

Chapter 4

Daily Life

12 FEBRUARY 2013: PICKING UP?

The smartly dressed Egyptian man across the aisle of the plane bends down and pulls a white galabeya gown from his bag. He takes off his jacket and slips the garment over his head. Several silk-worm convulsions later and his shirt emerges on the floor, shortly followed by his trousers. A few more wriggles and his hands emerge from the sleeves. He bends to put on his shoes again. Just as well we're in the emergency-exit row with extra leg room.

After folding his Western clothes away, he's ready for his return to Cairo, and I look out of the window to get ready for my own. The cloud clears to a haze and the great dun expanse of the country appears, studded with deeply shadowed apartment blocks like headstones in a cemetery.

There have been over sixty deaths in recent troubles stretching from Cairo north to Alexandria and across to Port Said where President Mursi has imposed a state of emergency and curfews. He's getting well practised in his trade and the jury seems to be back in with a thumbs-down verdict. At least according to Ahmed my driver, who sixty days ago on my last visit had given him the benefit of the doubt, saying 'the Egyptian patient' would soon recover. Now he's changed his tune.

'No one trusts him,' he says. 'He's not got the experience a president needs, and just looks after his own party. We need a strong parliament to ensure the nation's interests are looked after. People want the economy to pick up. That's all that matters.'

Down below in Ramses Square, site of the main railway station for Alexandria and the Nile Delta, there's nothing picking up except buses to take people home to their hovels.

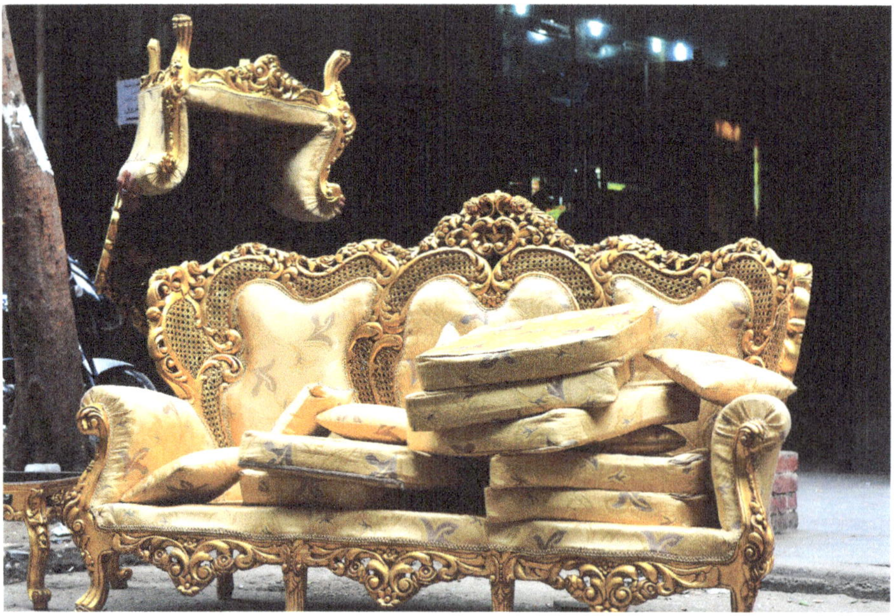

13 FEBRUARY 2013: OUT WITH THE OLD, IN WITH THE NEW

It's taken me a little while to work out if this street scene represents a removal or a delivery; I think it's the former. The furniture represents power and privilege, which is beyond the reach of the Cairene sitting atop the crates on the local delivery truck.

I'm not sure if anything new is being delivered here in Cairo, after all, and that 'all' includes the 25 January 2011 Revolution. The political situation continues to confuse, with calls for the president, his cabinet and the current parliament to be changed in order to properly prepare for fresh and fair parliamentary, as opposed to presidential, elections this coming April.

All opposition parties agree with these calls, albeit for different reasons. President Mursi has been advised by a prominent columnist to rise to the challenge of being a great statesman or decide to be a dictator, before he's washed down the drain of history without trace. Let's see what this latest round of musical sofas brings.

It's lovely to be reunited with Shona. We've negotiated the rate of the hotel back to that of the last visit, but the internet connection continues to come and go as often as the ladies in Prufrock's room.

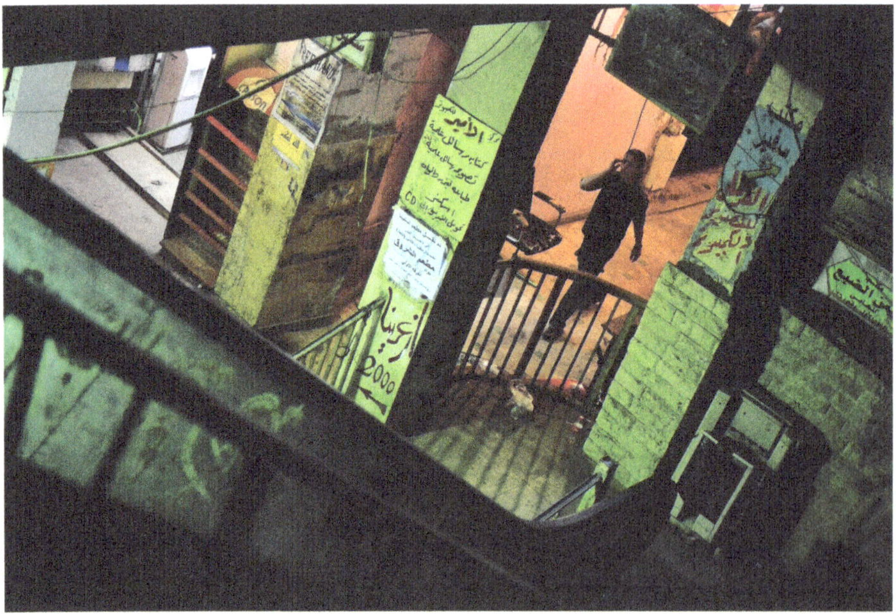
2000

18 FEBRUARY 2012: HOPE AMIDST DECAY

The escalator says it all. Installed when the building was erected in the 1970s, it looks as if it fell into disuse not long after. It connects, in a manner of speaking, the ground and first floors of this decrepit fifteen-storey building. The escalator's side panels keel over so that its mechanical guts are exposed and rubber straps poke out like hernias. Its steps are filthy and haven't been swept in years. The whole thing screeches and moans like the hull of a sinking ship about to burst.

To ascend it feels like an above-water exploration of the *Titanic*; finely powdered dust substituting the all-covering barnacles of the deep. Just as rainbows of fish flitted into that colossal wreck to give it new life, so here art material shops, their employees and customers having arrived to populate the first floor. Young men stretch canvases, others rub varnish into frames, and women hold up sheets of coloured paper to check their varied hues. Only I seem to notice with my unaccustomed eyes the decay stretching all around.

Maybe, all's not lost.

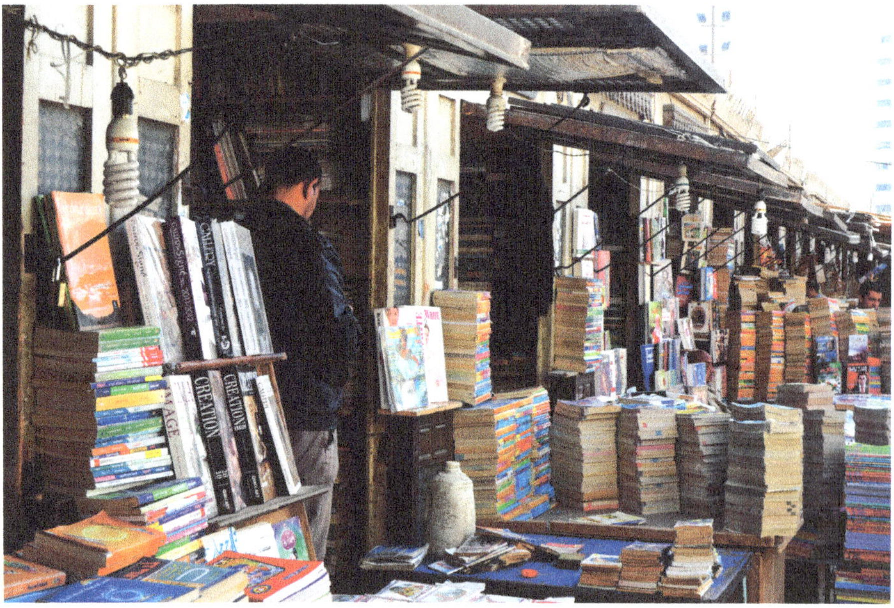
CREATION
CREATION

20 FEBRUARY 2012: THE BOOKSTALLS

'Reading habits have changed,' says the article in a local newspaper. 'There's now a huge interest in books on the revolution, and not just this one, but every revolution that Egypt has had. And it's the young who are buying . . . they've never been interested in politics before.'

I take a break this afternoon to head off to the Sur el-Azbakia area to see for myself. Apparently, there are one hundred and thirty-two second-hand bookstalls there.

'Yes, yes, yes. Books, many books,' says Sayed, my driver, as he pulls up on the edge of a large square in front of the decayed former Continental Hotel. It's taken an hour in congested traffic to get here.

'Over there,' he points. 'But not now.'

'What do you mean "not now"?'

'I mean not now. Now only cheap watches, bags. Too much Alibaba.'

'But I'm not looking for Alibaba. I'm looking for books.'

He shrugs.

'Please wait here,' I half-grumble as I push the door open and set off.

I pass the shoe stalls, tailors' stalls, sports bag stalls, CD stalls, tutu stalls and the, well, Alibaba stalls until I stand in the centre of a wide spread of tarmac surrounded by tea-making stalls. Now what? I wonder.

Sayed appears from nowhere.

'You were right,' I say. 'Alibaba everywhere.'

'Wait a minute,' Sayed says. He heads off to one of the tea makers, chats, scans the square and then signals me to follow him, even deeper into Alibaba land.

Ghetto blasters assault us with their noise. Some people wag their fingers and shout me down if I raise my camera from my hip. Others cry, 'Me, me, me!' if I don't. Eventually, under a hot sun, we reach an oasis of calm . . . the bookstalls. All one hundred and thirty-two stalls are present, correct and numbered. Sayed shrugs.

'Meet you back at the car?' he asks.

'No,' I put my hand firmly on his shoulder. 'You wait here . . . but thank you.'

One of the booksellers spots me trying to stay cool in the shade with my camera nestling in the crook of my arm. 'You want photo?' he asks. 'Photo away.

Go ahead. Don't worry. That man over there is married – he doesn't mind. And that's a good photo there with the gentleman browsing.'

'And what about you?' I ask.

'Me? No, not today,' he laughs. 'My wife wouldn't approve!'

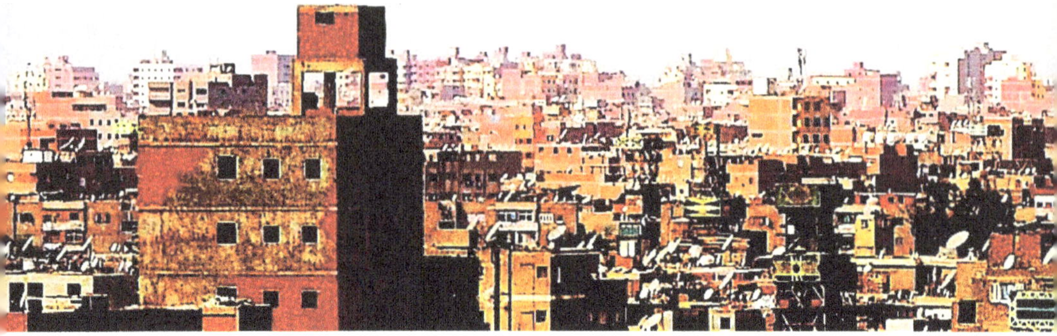

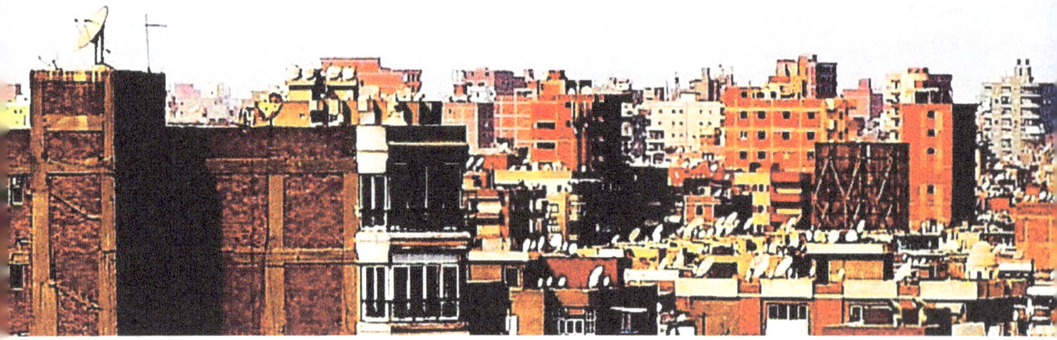

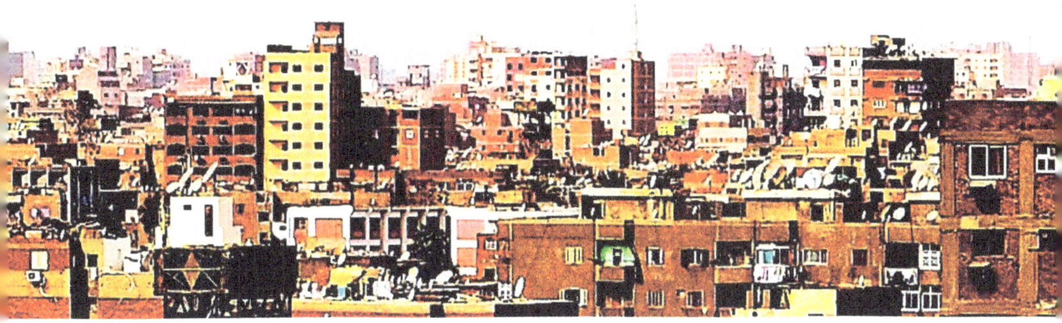

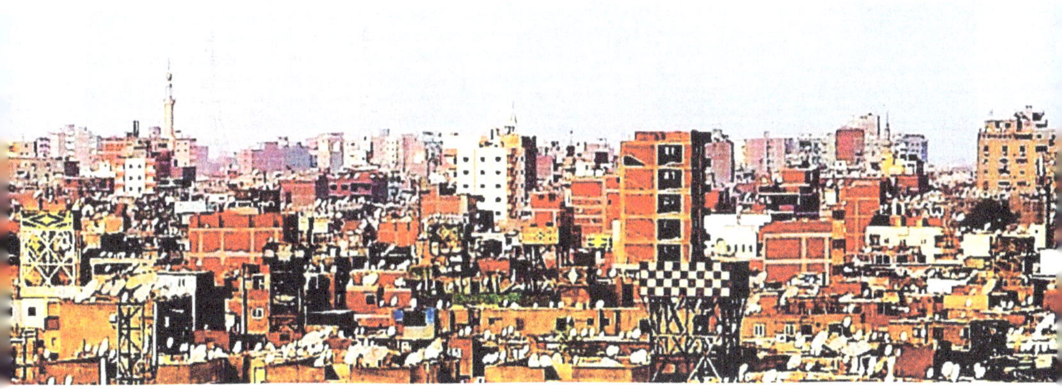

21 FEBRUARY 2012: OPALESCENT SKY

Out there under an opalescent sky lies Cairo and its people; twenty-three million impoverished, uneducated, frustrated, disillusioned and disheartened people, without a hope in hell that any one of these adjectives will fly off soon. They crowd the streets and alleyways, surviving as best they can with their futile dreams of one day acquiring a place of their own or maybe just some glass for their windows. Dreams that will never be fulfilled because others have misappropriated their country's wealth and trodden on their self-respect during the last thirty years. There is no one to turn to; not the police, not the courts, not the government nor the president. Make no mistake, it's one almighty mess, out there under the opalescent sky.

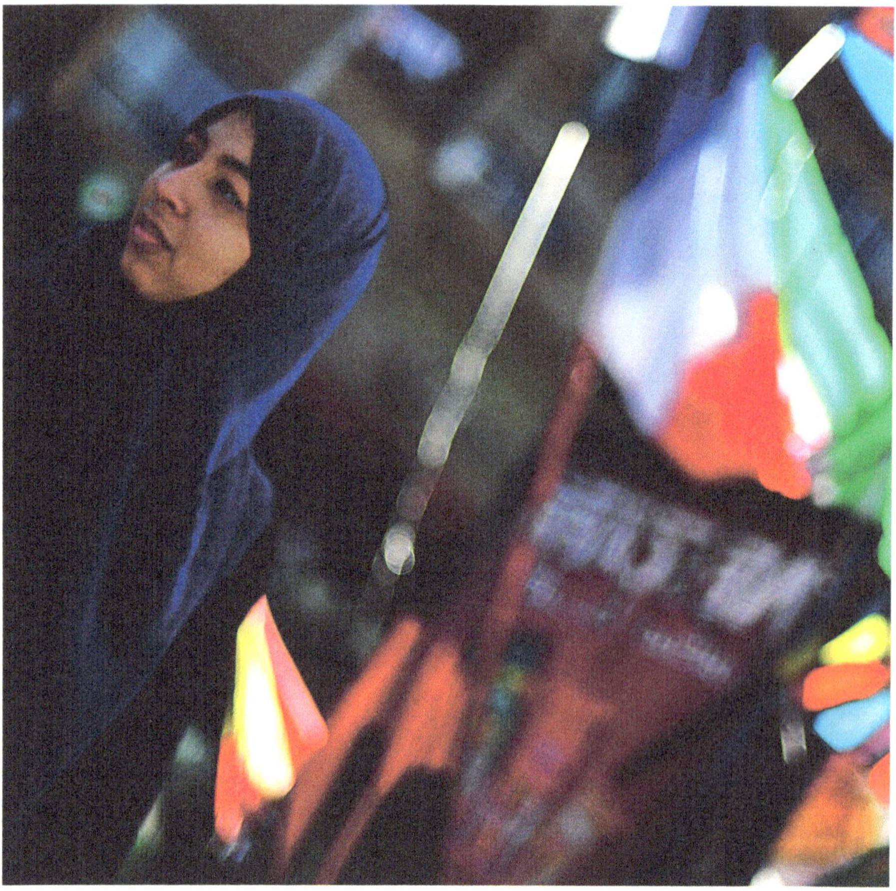

23 FEBRUARY 2013: WE ARE ALL KAHLED SAEED

That includes this beautiful young woman whose face in my shot today is blurry through motion, as I took the photo on the move from the front seat of a taxi. More importantly, her face today is unblemished and innocent, just as Kahled Saeed's was before, at the age of twenty-eight, he was beaten to death by two police officers in Alexandria on 6 June 2010.

He was a quiet, well-adjusted young man with no criminal record who was grabbed by two policemen as he popped in to see friends at an internet café. After an initial blundering in the entrance way of the café, the policemen dragged him to the vestibule of a residential block of flats a few yards away. Before several eyewitnesses, they crushed his skull, dislocated his jaw, broke his nose and inflicted traumas all over his body.

The policemen propped his body up in a sitting position against a wall, as if he was still alive, and left. They later claimed Kahled had choked while swallowing a small bag of hashish in an attempt to prevent its discovery by them.

His brother secretly and bravely took photos of Kahled's face in the mortuary with his mobile phone and published them on the internet. They went viral immediately. Never has such an apparatus proved so pivotal in a country's history.

A Facebook page was set up called 'We are all Kahled Saeed' and it is widely held that it was the circumstances of this young man's death that produced a fundamental surge in the movement that fired the revolution. 'If it could happen to him it could happen to any of us,' everyone said. 'We are all Kahled Saeed.'

Massive vigils were held along the Corniche in Alexandria and along the banks of the Nile in Cairo. Every participant dressed in black and stood five metres from the next in lines that extended for miles.

The two policemen were eventually convicted, after an initial government cover-up, and are serving a sentence of seven paltry years for manslaughter.

I wasn't aware of the details of Kahled's story until today, and hadn't seen the before and after photos. They shocked me to the core and brought home to me more than ever what the Egyptian state had become under President Mubarak. There is a desperate need for reform under President Mursi in the months ahead, beginning with the police force, or else there is a real prospect that many more faces like that of the innocent Khaled will be brutalised beyond recognition. Now's the time for Mursi to grasp the security force nettle.

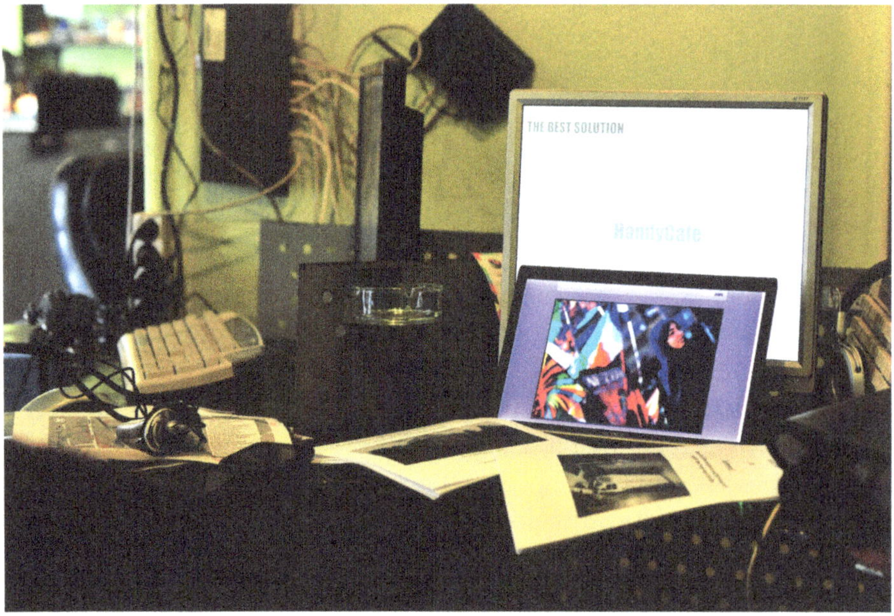
THE BEST SOLUTION

24 FEBRUARY 2014: HANDY CAFÉ

I spend nearly all my waking hours in an internet café. It's very handy, in line with the café's name, as the internet in the hotel is woeful this trip and I need a place to write and make calls. I love how it connects me to real life and gives me energy.

The owners welcome me as a valued customer and I've become a permanent fixture in the corner. I pay money into an account, bring my own laptop to use with their internet cable, passively smoke throughout the entire day and lift my feet first, to let the guy with the broom sweep under my desk and then, later, to allow another guy with a mop to clean the same space. Street kids press their dirty noses against the glass window and make funny faces a foot from my 'enter' key. My power cable trails across the floor and somehow the plug manages to maintain the smallest of purchases in the slack socket half way up the wall. How the charging light stays on, I'll never know.

But this is how it is and how it works – just – in The Best Exotic and Smokey Handy Café!

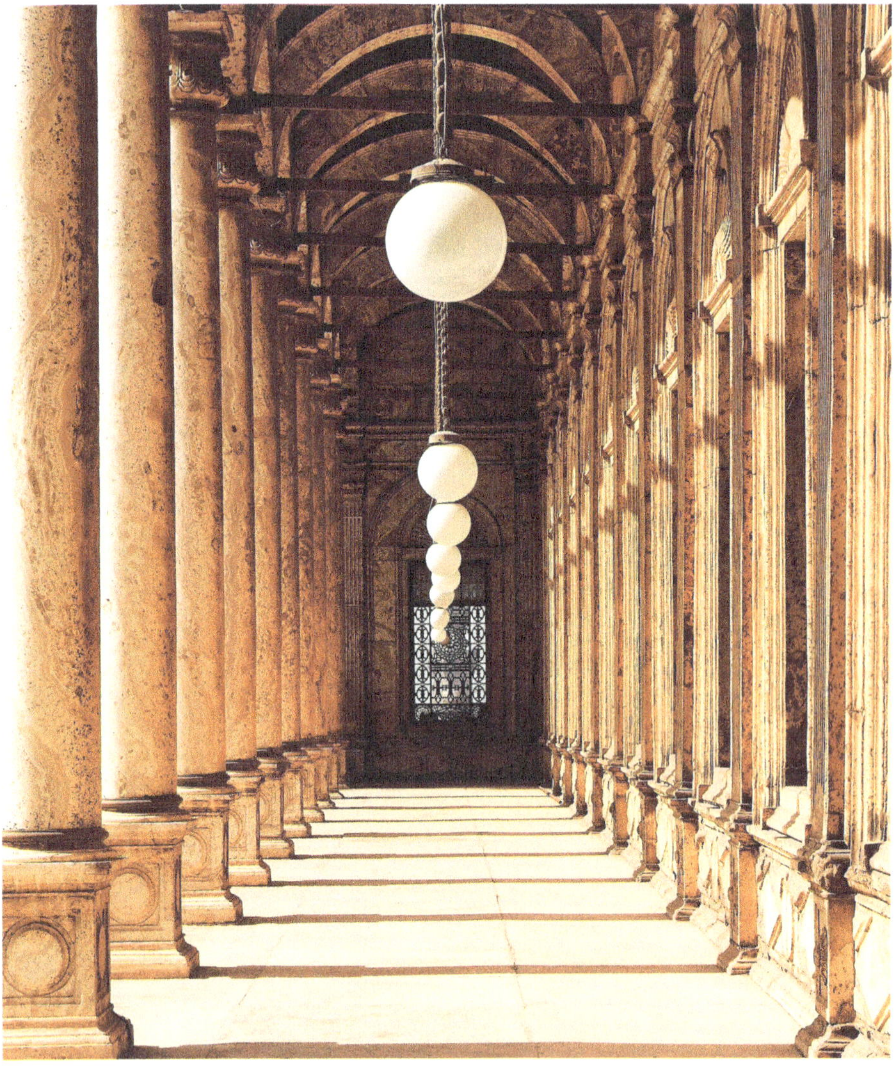

26 FEBRUARY 2012: MUHAMMAD ALI MOSQUE

The taxi ride up to the Citadel today is through the narrow lanes of Old Cairo lined by crumbling abodes and jammed with motorbikes, cars, microbuses, donkeys, carts and black-robed women with large baskets on their heads. Dust and exhaust fumes billow up. It's like watching a television special report through the windscreen.

The Citadel is dominated by the Muhammad Ali Mosque, which was built in the Turkish style during the first half of the nineteenth century by Muhammad Ali Pasha. This native Albanian served as an Ottoman army officer and established his own independent dynasty in Egypt in 1805. He crushed the Mamluks, who had ruled for six hundred years, and is credited with instigating reforms in the military, economic and cultural spheres that set the basis for the modern Egyptian state. His dynasty lasted in form, if not de facto control, until the 1952 Free Officer revolution.

Muhammad Ali is buried in the mosque's courtyard around which four long arcades of high grace extend. It's a surprise to find this order in a city of such disorder. I first visited in September 1981, and my camera lens today is the very same one I used then. It still has a dent where the bus hit it. My photograph of this arcade was the first ever photograph I took that looked great. The sensation was, 'Wow! I can produce something professional,' and for my friends it was, 'Wow! What a fantastic camera!'

I remember feeling aggrieved that no one mentioned the photographer. My camera body then, a professional Nikon F3, played a part but it was really the quality of the Nikkor 50 mm f1.4 prime lens that impressed them.

And it still impresses today as I make this trip to recreate that first shot in honour of the lens's longevity and return to daily use. 'There's something magical going on between that lens and Egypt,' said my friend, the Brazilian photographer Fernando Cohen, recently. I noted he didn't mention the photographer either.

I love the lens's clarity but also the mechanical manipulation required to use it. As I click-click the old-fashioned aperture ring into place, my memories, too, click-click into the sharpest of focus.

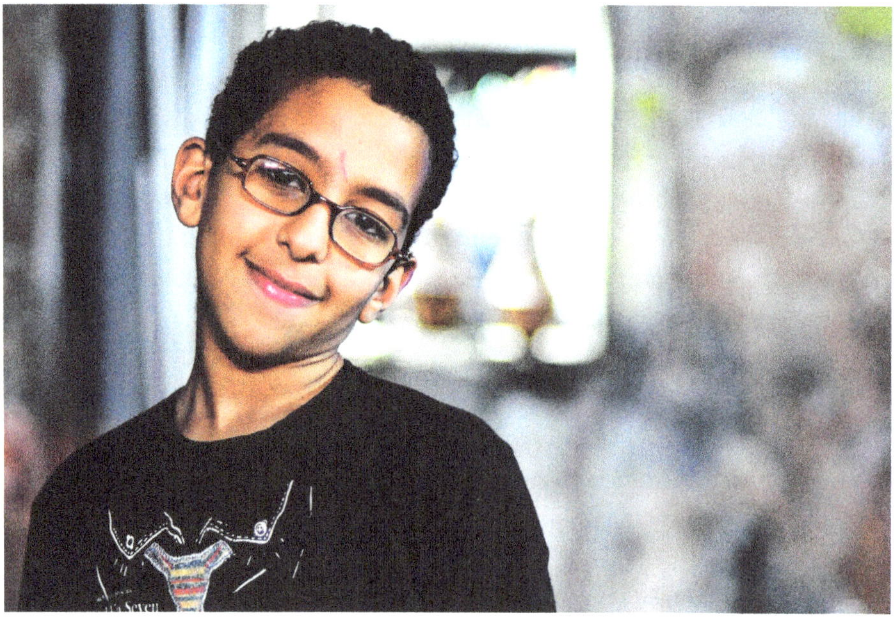

27 FEBRUARY 2013: WHY IT MATTERS . . .

Su'ud makes it matter; progress in Egypt, that is. He must be about eight years old. His elder brother parks cars on a dusty lot and his wizened, gallabeya-ed granddad delivers bottles of Fanta around the block, four at a time. The family live behind the lot in an open basement that has a kitchen cubicle cluttered with jugs and pans and a living area with a baggy old couch, white plastic chairs and a television casting blue, snowy light across the earthen floor.

So, what would I wish for Su'ud at forty? That's in thirty-two years' time, which mirrors the period since I first came here. I'd wish him an end to everyday experiences like tear-gas attacks and unlawful detention with beatings or deadly batterings. A house with a door and glass in the windows. Work that uses every qualification he acquires with enough money not to need to moonlight or go to Saudi Arabia, where he may be radicalised. A police force that helps and protects him in time of need. The confidence and opportunity to cast his vote for someone who represents his interests without fear of intimidation. The survival of that sparkle in his eyes and that he may say, on the day of his fortieth birthday, 'I am a son of Egypt, a land of dignity, development and democracy.'

Su'ud means good luck; I wish him that and more. He'll need it.

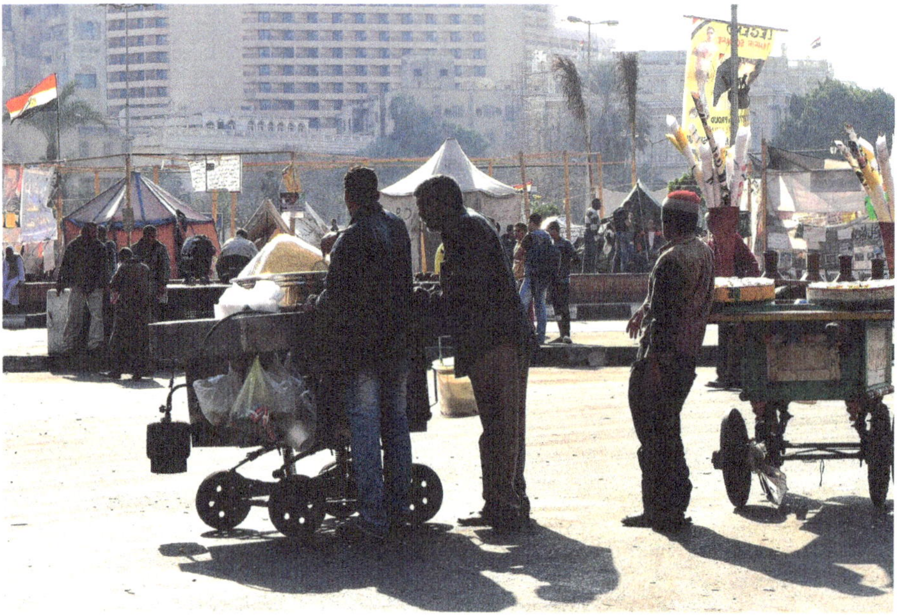

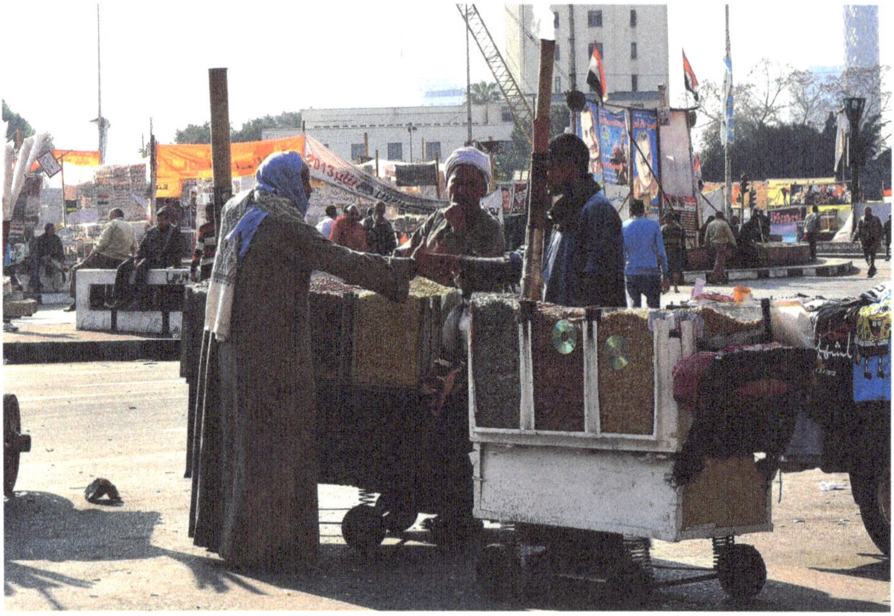

28 FEBRUARY 2013: TAHRIR TODAY

It's very hard to stay away from the magnet of Tahrir Square. There are more tents pitched since my last visit in November and groups of people mill about. I keep my antenna tuned for signs of tension and see several scuffles and fisticuffs over which vehicles can pass through the barbed-wire barriers. Post-revolutionaries control the entrances but there is a large gathering of Muslim Brotherhood members on the raised centre roundabout, a physical stand-off that seems to echo that between the government and opposition. President Mursi has not offered meaningful national dialogue as he continues to press home his Islamist agenda.

I'm not completely at ease and stand with my back against a building to watch developments. It isn't easy for a fair-complexioned, six-foot-three-inch-tall (190 cm) Scotsman, who is also carrying a big camera, to look inconspicuous.

Tahrir Square covers a huge area with eleven entrances, three or four of which have been blocked with large concrete blocks reaching a height of four or five metres. The tops of roughly made wooden ladders poke up from the other side, like the kind a medieval army would have used to scale a castle wall. The sections of road that lead to these barricades are strewn with rubbish and hold large pools of stagnant water from burst drains.

I've just realised that the elevated walkway, which used to circle the whole area in the 1980s like a ring of Saturn, has disappeared. I have vivid memories of it. In strong heat, I used to climb the stairs against descending throngs, circle round and then plunge down through another mass of people to the pavement of the selected radial road. It was a constant battle and you needed to gather your energy to go onto the streets then. You still do.

I move along the pavement to a row of travel agencies. This is the area in Cairo where you can book any trip inside or outside of Egypt or hire any form of transport. I sit on a bench inside one of them, away from the sun's glare, to review the photographs on my camera screen. A woman customer cries, 'No, not Egypt Air!' Who can blame her? I've heard too many stories over the years to climb aboard one of their planes. The agencies are happy just to be open and have some business, no matter if it's only a donkey ride around the block.

This visit coincides with me reading accounts of the pitched, revolutionary battles that took place between 25 January and 11 February 2011 in and around Downtown and on the bridges over the Nile. The flyovers, bridges and slipways formed a hard, concrete battlefield and defined the lines of attack and retreat. It seems all had their moment as the focus of bloody resistance during those days.

It must have been terrifying, as with all battles or wars, to be in the thick of it without knowing when or how it would end. I admire the people who took to the streets with a now-or-never attitude. Many said that if they were to die, then so be it; the alternative of life under the regime wasn't more attractive.

I leave the square by Taalat Harb Street. I'm the only foreigner in view and a man spots me. He's small and wiry, half-drowned by his linen suit. When he stands in front of me I can see his tobacco-stained teeth and the sharp outline of his shoulders through his jacket. I calculate that it's unlikely he's with the security forces and prepare myself for a scam. The museum one is common around here.

'Where you from?' he asks with a smile that slopes down the right side of his mouth.

'Scotland,' I reply in my finest brogue.

'Ah, Auchtermuchty!' He names this small Scottish town to demonstrate his intimate knowledge of my homeland. He's also clever enough to pick a place name whose pronunciation exaggerates the characteristic 'och' sound of the Scottish accent. I wonder if he's attended a geography class at scam-school to learn 'Ja, Feuchtwangen!' to use with Germans or 'Mais oui, Forges-les-Eaux!' with the French.

'Close, but no.'

'Tourist?' he probes further.

'No, working.' Any moment now, I think.

'I'm the Assistant Director of the Egyptian Museum.'

'Really? How marvellous for you!' I don't mention that I've met five of his job-share colleagues in the last month and scan my surroundings for the best getaway route. I decide and start off.

'Where are you going? Wait . . . I can show you . . .'

'I'm meeting a friend – sorry.'

'Mister, I can help you . . . hold on . . .' He's still at my side but struggling with my longer stride.

'Not today, thank you. Give my best to King Tut!' I throw the words over my shoulder as I lose him in my wake. I slip into Café Riche with a sigh of relief.

I'm not sure how he finalises his scam but it will entail going for coffee with a request to pay the bill and contribute to support his family in Upper Egypt, or pressure to accompany him to his friend's stall in the bazaar where the prices are the cheapest in the city. No commitment, of course.

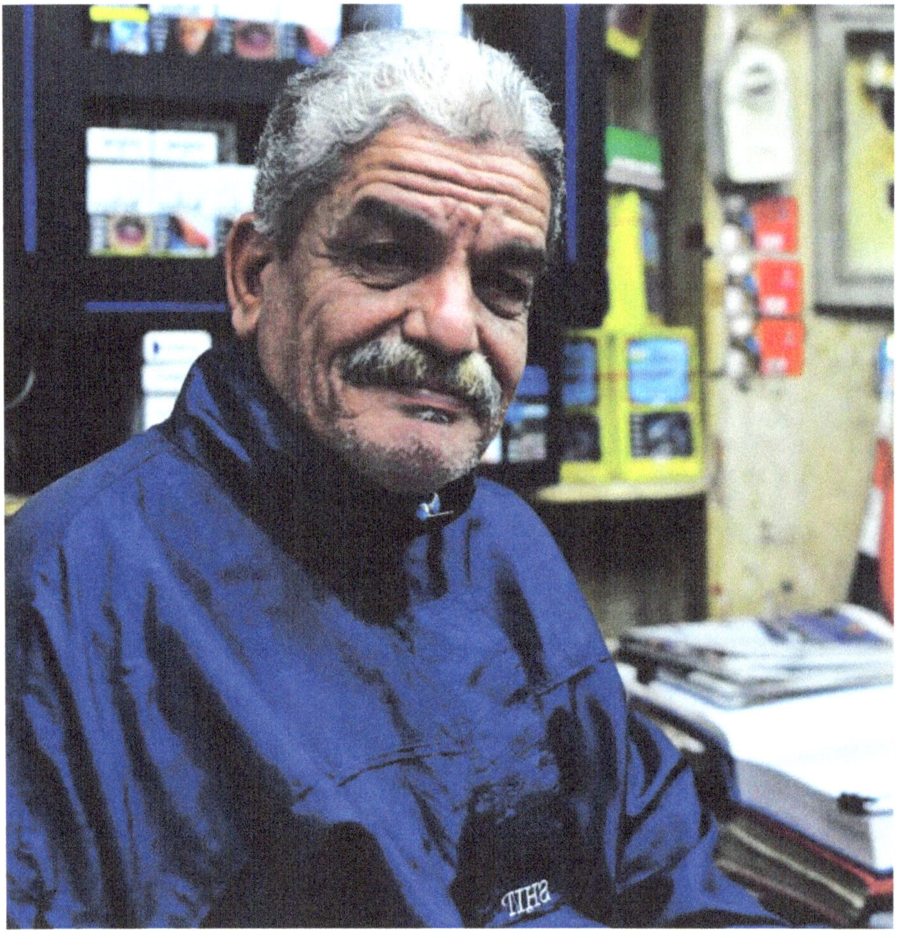

1 MARCH 2013: OMAR SHARIF OR . . .

'May I take your photo?' I ask. I've been into the shop many times.

'Sure! Why not.'

'Thanks.' I kneel in front of the counter, which my subject is sitting behind, and take a few shots, working hard to focus with the manual-focus lens in the low-light conditions.

'Would you like to see? Hey, you look like Omar Sharif!'

He laughs as he looks at the first one. 'Yes, I like it! Pick the best one and let me have a copy, please.'

'Of course . . . and how come you speak such marvellous English?'

He pauses and gives me a look. 'I was a good student at school. I loved English, and after university I finished my language studies at the British Council. My dad had this shop and lots of foreigners came in. I got to practise a lot! Language is not there for studying but communicating.'

'How long have you had the shop?'

'Ooomph! My dad opened it in 1940.'

'1940!'

'Yes, and he passed in 1990.'

'How old was he?'

'Seventy . . .' His look becomes distant.

'And what did you study at university, if I may ask?'

He's not back fully, still distracted as he speaks. 'My daughter's a . . . a . . . what do you call it . . . to do with pharaohs?'

'An Egyptologist.'

'That's it! An Egyptologist.'

'But what did *you* study at university?'

'Economics.'

'And may I ask how old you are?'

'You may *ask*!'

'And? . . . Younger than your dad?'

He gives me a playful look. 'Of course!'

'OK. Thanks again for the photo!'

I leave and he calls me back, smiling.

'Don't forget now.'

'Of course not . . . and what's your name?'

'Mohamed . . . to my friends.'

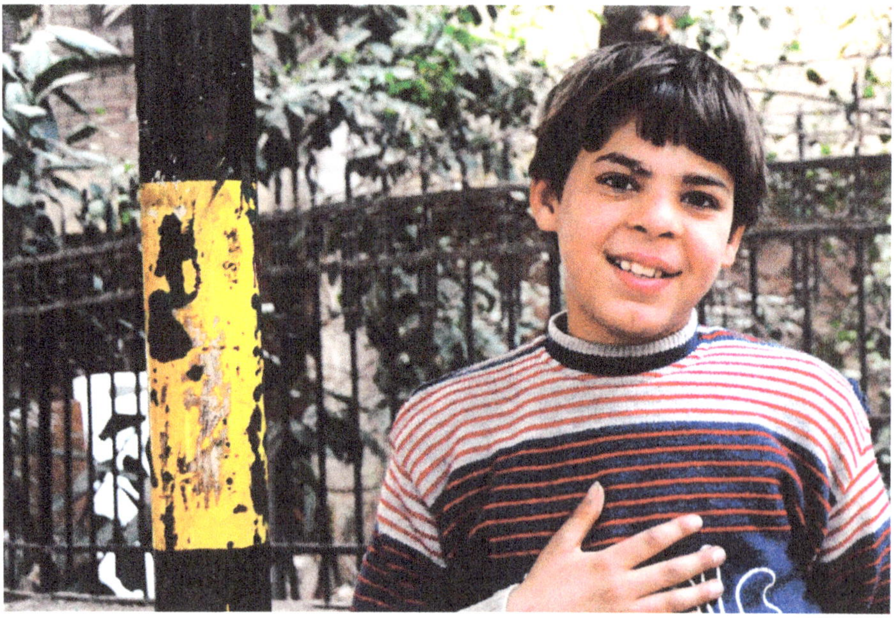

2 MARCH 2013: YASHEEN

Meet my young friend, Yasheen, with whom I coincide various times a day around the Zamalek block. Sometimes he sells me tissues on a street corner, sometimes he spends one of the few pounds he earns and sits at a workstation beside me in The Best Exotic and Smokey Handy Café, playing games at terminal velocity, or presses his nose against the window of whatever establishment I'm in, like today, at the restaurant where we're having lunch. I grab my camera and nip out to see if he'll agree to a photograph, which for the first time he does. He chooses the location and the touching-heart pose himself. He hides his plastic carrier bag of tissue packets behind his back. We make a rendezvous with him at 5 pm tomorrow at another local café to give him a print of the shot.

Now we're out to distribute other prints to a number of people who kindly agreed to give me their portraits over the last few months. Everyone's delighted to receive them and it always creates a stir and requests from their neighbours to take their portraits too. Shona shows the patience of a saint as we endlessly recover our tracks in search of a carpenter whose workshop I happen to have lost. The search will resume tomorrow.

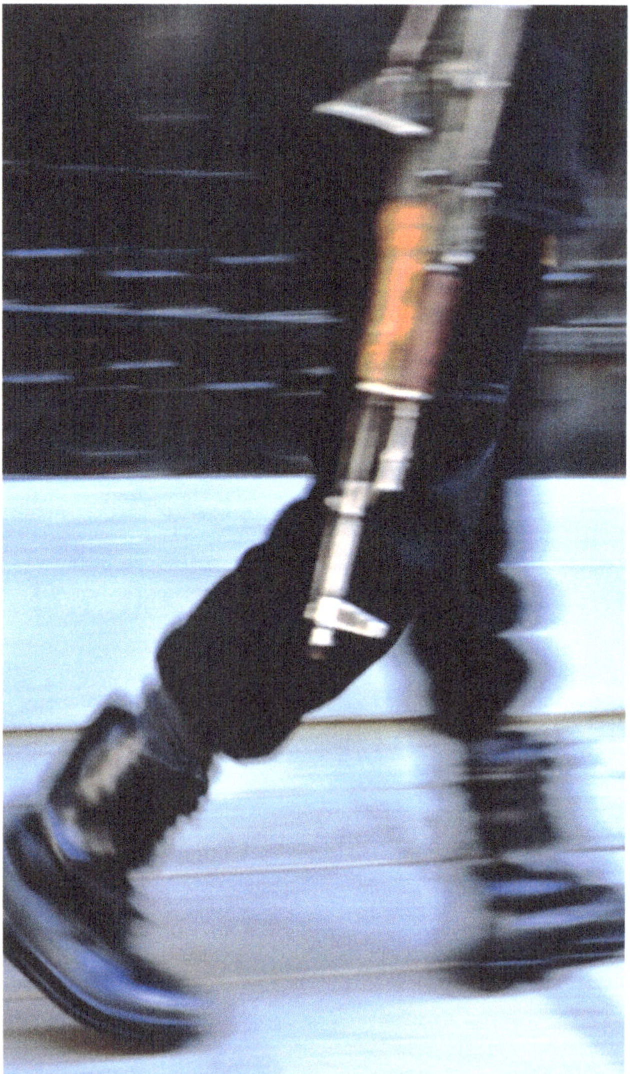

4 MARCH 2013: FARE WELL, EGYPT

This morning, just off Tahrir Square, our taxi screeched to a halt, backed up with its reverse gear whining, executed a fast three-point turn, and raced off down the one-way street we had just come along against the flow of traffic. Our driver had spotted plain-clothes security officers beating up protesters in broad daylight further on and wasn't taking any chances. The Security Forces HQ in Port Said was set on fire during continuing protests against state brutality that has left over four hundred dead in recent months. The worst excesses of the black tunic-ed and rifle-toting General Security Forces continue in Egypt's democracy.

As we leave again, we can only wish the country better times, and hope that all the people, including the secular liberals who played such an important part in bringing down Mubarak's regime after thirty insufferable years, find their voice and the political knowledge and organisation to achieve the goals they desired for the whole country at the time of the revolution.

As I write this at the airport terminal, waiting to board our flight, I see it is already two years ago since I speculated on a return visit to the country thirty years after my first one in 1981 and which did, in fact, come about. How time flies.

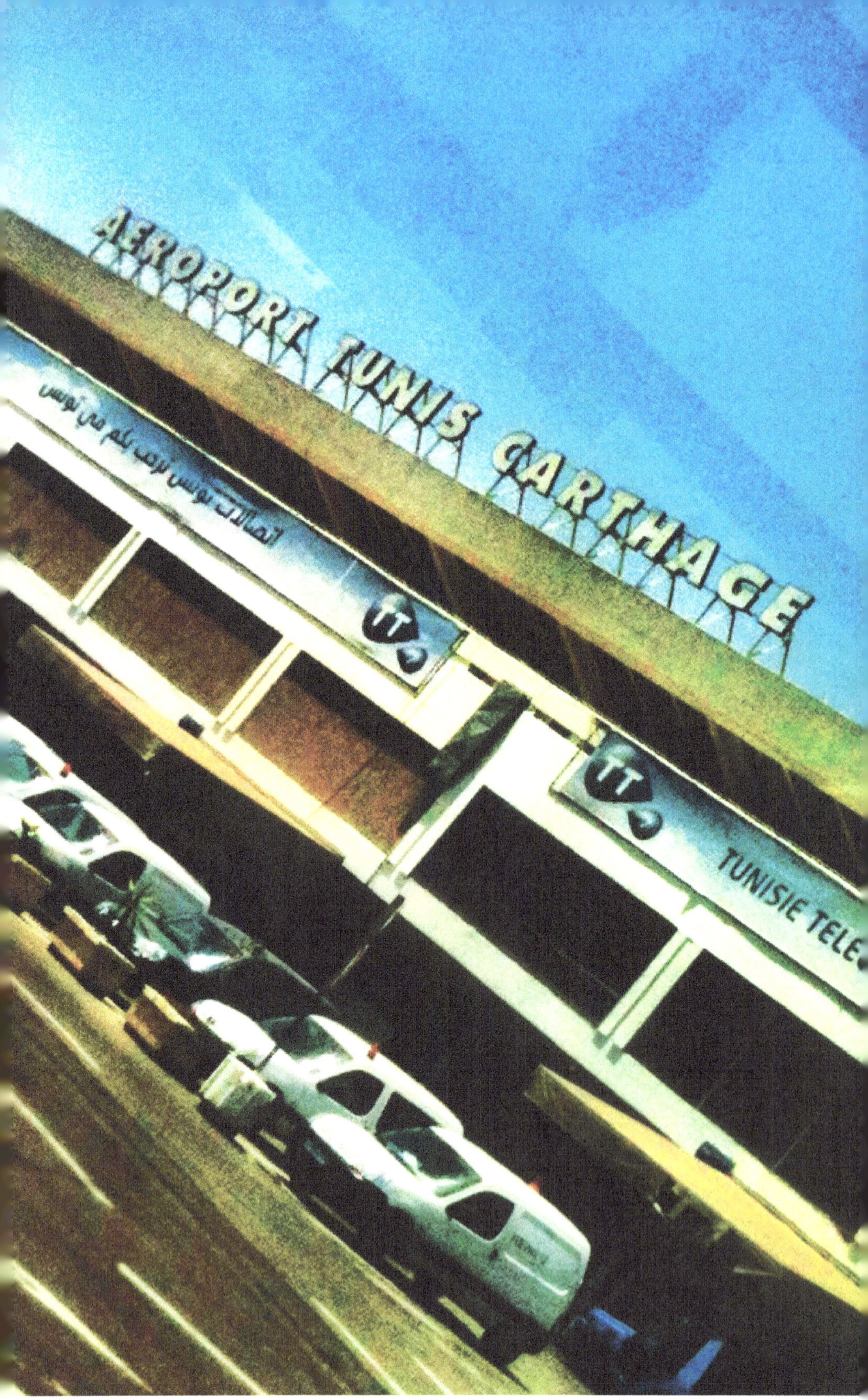
AEROPORT TUNIS CARTHAGE
TUNISIE TELE

Chapter 5

The People Have Spoken

21 JUNE 2013: AT HER MAJESTY'S PLEASURE

The one time I have an invitation to attend The Queen's Ball in Cairo this evening, I get bounced from the first sector of my Swiss flight from Paris to Cairo via Zurich. The next flight with the same airline won't arrive for another twenty-four hours.

I press hard to be re-routed on an earlier flight and make quite a few references to the Queen of England. I'm allocated a seat on an alternative flight via Tunisia. Looks like I will go to the ball, although I'll miss the first dance.

I arrive in Carthage off a Tunis Air flight, which had comfortable armchair-like seats that only planes of a 1970 vintage have. After using all my French to work out the convoluted queueing system for transfers, I now have a boarding card for my onward flight to Cairo.

I'm tempted to stay over and explore the city but I hear the voices of Shona and the Queen, in that order, reminding me of my duty in no uncertain terms. So, I've settled for a cold beer in the terminal building as I wait for my flight to be called. I've also sent this photo to Teleri by email. She spent part of her childhood in Libya next door and probably would have visited Carthage. She'll be delighted to know I'm in one of her old neighbourhoods.

This visit coincides with the first anniversary of President Mursi's election. His approach seems still to avoid politic dialogue and negotiation with the opposition despite his narrow mandate to govern, and he is highly unpopular. The next leg of my journey is with Egypt Air, my first ever flight with them after years of avoidance. I hope it delivers me to my destination more effectively than Mursi seems to be doing on behalf of his country.

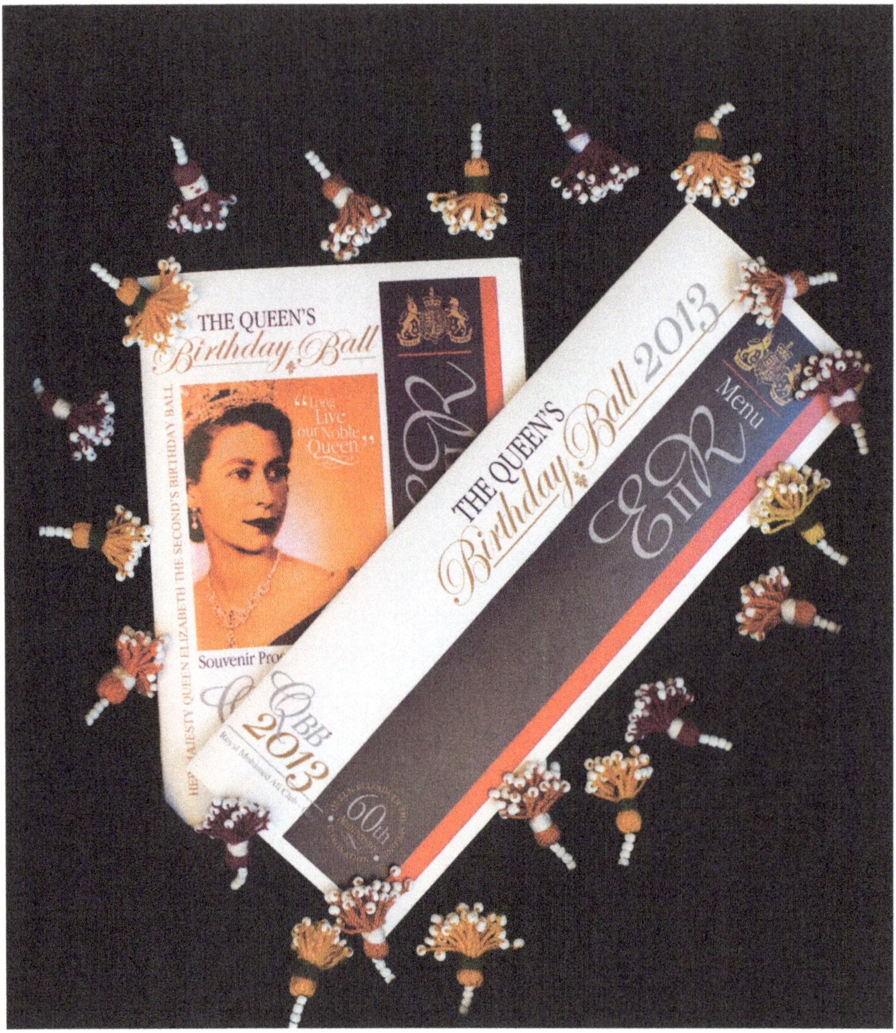
THE QUEEN'S
Birthday Ball
"Long Live our Noble Queen"
HER MAJESTY QUEEN ELIZABETH THE SECOND'S BIRTHDAY BALL
THE QUEEN'S
Birthday Ball 2013
Menu
EIIR
QBB
2013
60th

22 JUNE 2013: TURNING HEADS

After yesterday's 4 am start in Paris, the diversion to Carthage and a very smooth flight with Egypt Air, I did get to the Queen's Sixtieth Anniversary Ball in Cairo, although I was a little late.

Ahmed, who nearly always picks me up from the airport, and Mohammed, the doorman of our building, did a double take after I had dashed up to the apartment in T-shirt and shorts and reappeared five minutes later in a white linen suit with a red silk paisley bow tie and matching cummerbund. It's the first time I've worn a closed-neck shirt in all my time in Egypt and I felt constricted.

I'll long remember the ride along the banks of the Nile to the venue at the Royal Mohamed Ali Club in Giza. We passed fruit stalls, crowded bus stations, coldly lit cafés filled with shisha smokers and backgammon players. Herds of goats sat regally on earthen banks between the cafés and indulged in a spot of people watching.

'Look at that one in the front of the white car. He's got a butterfly strapped round his neck. And in this heat!'

They must have thought I was mad.

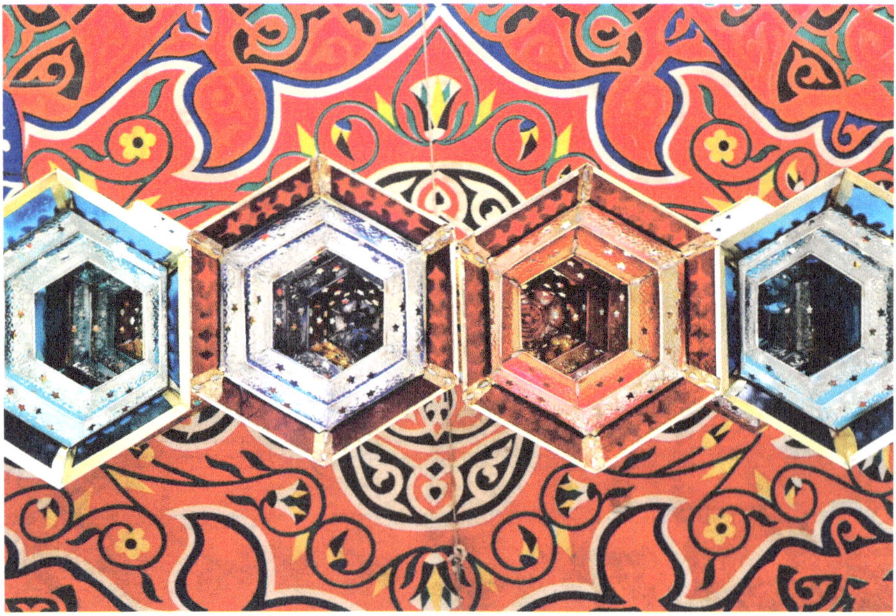

23 JUNE 2013: RAMADAN APPROACHES

Ramadan, the month of fasting, nears and the festive treats spill onto the pavements outside shops: dates, pistachios, dried apricots, *ful medammes*, Persian cheese, pomegranates, okra and all kinds of sweet and sticky pastries. Colourful, boldly patterned awnings provide daytime shade and in the evenings the Ramadan lanterns or *fawanees* are quite magical when they are lit and sway in the breeze. Some say the tradition of the lamps stems from the welcome given to the Caliph Moezz Eddin Allah when he visited Cairo in AD 969. The lamps were hung to brighten the streets and the spirits of the people and have done so ever since. This shot needed a lot of bended knee to allow the 50 mm lens to get any *fawanees* in frame.

Otherwise, it's been a day at my desk, preparing invoices and also setting up sessions with clients in other countries whose working week also starts on Sunday.

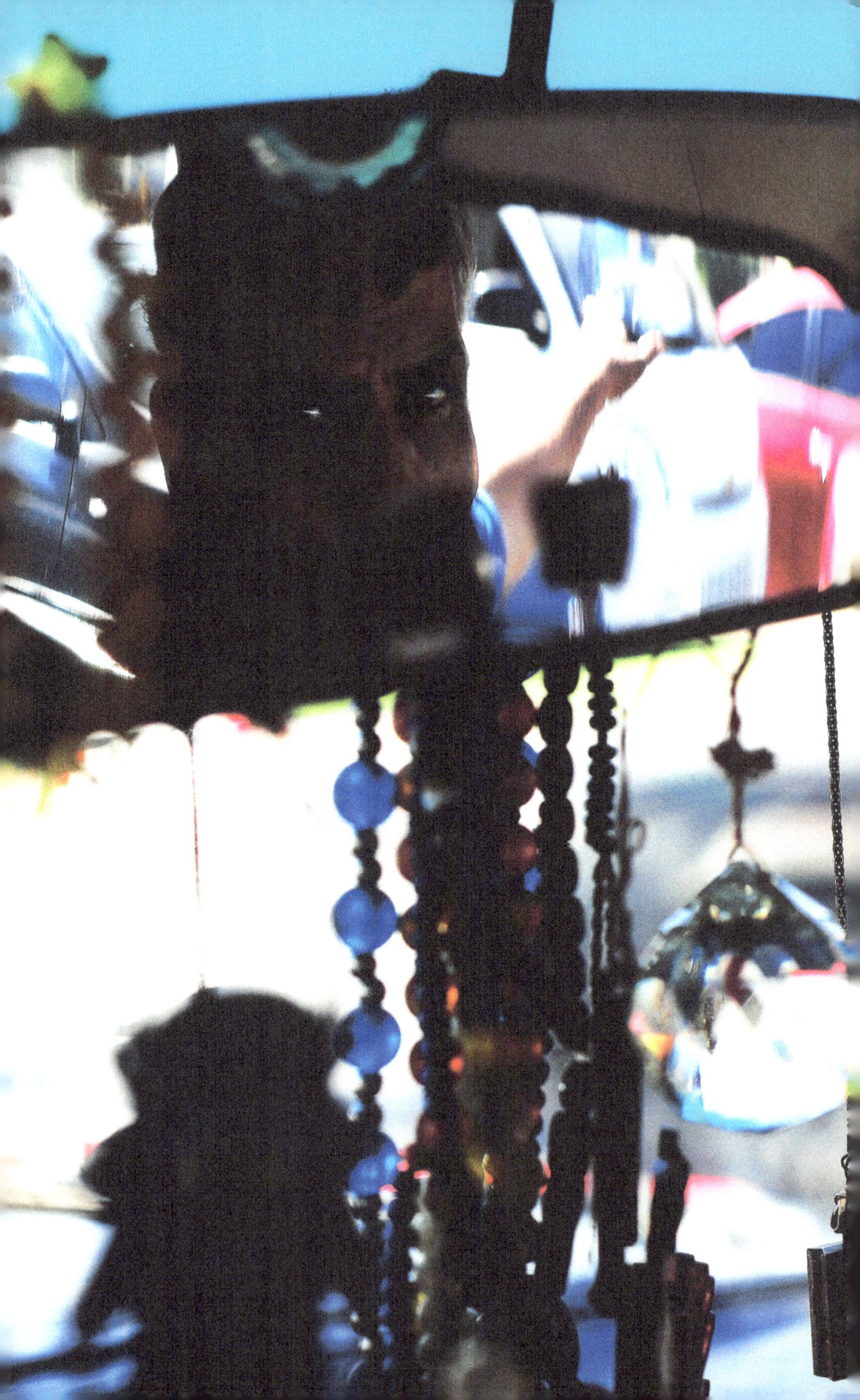

25 JUNE 2013: TAXI DRIVER

It was a mistake to have taken a taxi today. The roads are gridlocked as hundreds of drivers crowd around petrol stations in search of fuel to see them through the weekend and beyond. I cut my journey short and decide to sit it out in a coffee house until the worst of it has passed. Fanciful thinking. Now, on my return leg, the traffic is worse, and tempers fray all round.

My ride is in a forty-year-old Peugeot 504 estate car, which is one of the workhorses of Egypt.

'French,' cries the driver, slapping the dashboard so hard the needles of the dials jump and the engine almost has a coronary. 'You?' He almost accuses me with those piercing eyes.

'Scotland,' I say, braced for a backlash against anything that does not represent Gallic strength.

'Aaaagh,' he spits out the window and, in continuing disgust, sounds his lion-roar horn that has everyone ahead jumping out of their skins if not out of his way, there being nowhere to jump to.

The run on the petrol stations is because of the mass protests that are planned for the first anniversary of President Mursi's election to office, which falls this Sunday. Hardly anyone but his Brotherhood are happy with him as nearly 10,000 street protests over the past year testify; seven times more per annum than in Mubarak's time.

Apart from his supreme-power grab and the intrigues around the creation of the constitution, which was adopted with the support of only 19% of those eligible to vote, he has placed his favourites in key ministries and governorships up and down the land. This has led to outcry and sit-ins. Some of his appointees resigned before the seats of their trousers had touched the chairs in their new offices as crowds barricaded the buildings and prevented their entry.

It happened in Luxor this week after Mursi appointed Adel el-Khayata as governor. He is a member of Gaama Islamiya, whose associates allegedly massacred over sixty tourists with machine guns and machetes at the nearby Mortuary Temple of Hatshepsut in 1997. The fundamentalist terrorists took a leisurely forty-five minutes to stalk and kill their victims, who cowered in the temple precincts. The authorities suppressed all photographs and eye-witness accounts that revealed the full viciousness of the mutilations inflicted, especially those on the female victims. They wanted to minimise both international outrage and damage to the tourist trade. The latter is still to recover. To call el-Khayata's appointment insensitive is an understatement.

Mursi has also nominated relatively junior managers from industry to head up important ministries, again raising questions of suitability and judgement.

The chaos ranges from Giza, where Shia Muslims have been lynched by a Brotherhood-inspired mob, to the Cairo Opera House, which is on strike over government interference with their repertoire.

Sunday is being presented in some quarters of the media as a last-ditch grab for power by a rather unholy alliance of Mubarak heirs, post-revolutionaries and independents in revenge for what they see as Mursi's own power grab since he was elected. There is a possibility that the Muslim Brotherhood will be swept aside with Mursi agreeing to step down in October when fresh elections will be called. The army would caretake in any interim period.

You can tell things are getting serious when Shona's campus announces it will close for three days and we've been told to stay in our apartment, contactable by telephone land line in case the mobile network is cut. We've been instructed to buy in candles, tins of food and stash some cash in drawers for a siege that could last ten days. We've had to provide addresses and phone numbers of next of kin in our home country and the security-alert message system has been tested. These alerts warn of no-go areas due to street disturbances as well as the marshalling points of protesters going to Tahrir Square. They are cascaded by mobile-phone text message through the different levels of the organisation to reach every employee, who must then reply to acknowledge receipt.

I ask the manager of a local hotel if they'll be open over the weekend.

'Yes, we're open and we'll be taking very good care of our guests. Don't worry – you'll be fine too,' he says before continuing, 'We'll get our country back.'

He has a certain glint in his eye.

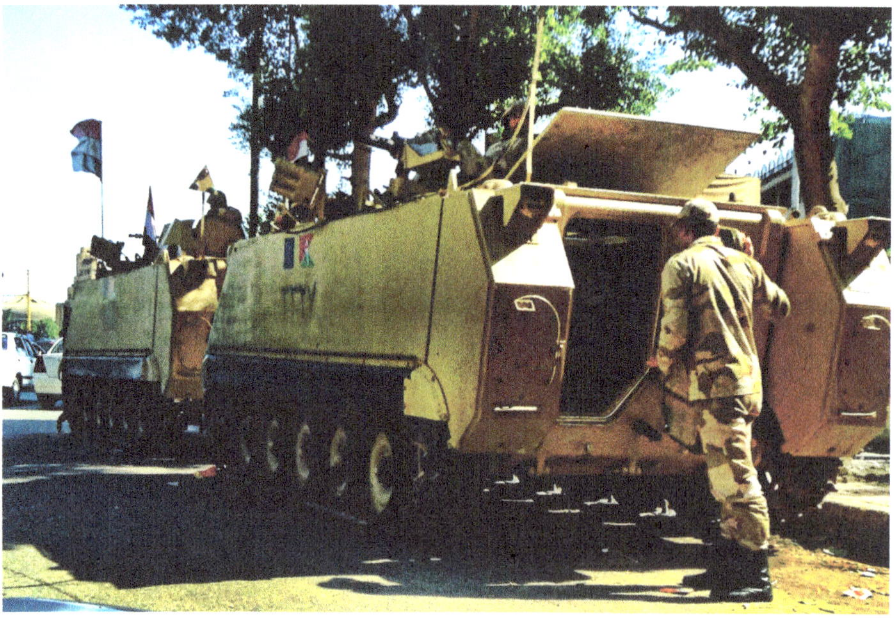

26 JUNE 2013: MILESTONE

Today was a personal milestone for me. My journey with Egypt began thirty-two years ago with a five-week odyssey around its extended block of Mersa Matrouh, Alexandria, Port Said, Aswan, Luxor, El Fayum, Helwan and Asyut. It has included being hit by a bus, and a visit to the pyramids with my head wrapped like a mummy. It's also where I confirmed my ideal state is the world of exploration, discovery and possibility. My visits in the last couple of years have been inextricably linked to Tahrir Square and political developments. It's been a great privilege to observe and experience Egypt at such close quarters, and today I reached another landmark: I did some work in Cairo for the first time in my life.

It wasn't straightforward. My client's driver couldn't get through the traffic to pick me up on time as it was all backed up due to the panic buying of fuel with long queues at the petrol stations. There were reports that tanks had been sighted on the outskirts of the city and rumours that the army intended to pre-empt all the demonstrations by taking power today. Four people worked to get me to a hurriedly reorganised venue away from the business area and my Egyptian and French mobiles rang constantly.

In the end I was taken to my client's home overlooking the Nile and our work focused on future strategy. It seemed appropriate.

When I think back to the young man who arrived one humid night at Cairo airport all those years ago and looked out with a mixture of thrill and trepidation from the madly skewing taxi during the ride into Downtown, all I can say is, 'Who would have thought it!'

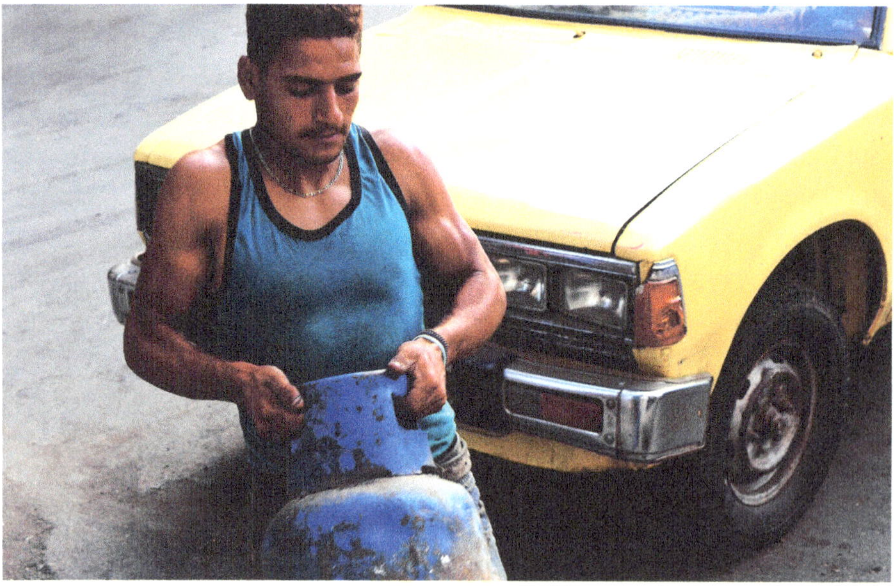

27 JUNE 2013: ESSENTIAL DELIVERIES

Essential deliveries are taking place in Cairo today and the shops are busy with people stocking up not only for the weekend but also the potentially prolonged tug of war, as the leading national newspaper *Al-Ahram* put it, on 30 June, when the nation will both protest against and in favour of the president. The prize is not just the satisfaction of having your voice heard but the presidency itself.

Mursi gave a televised address last night that lasted nearly three hours. He cut a solitary figure as he stood behind the podium in the centre of a low stage some distance from his seated audience in the modern auditorium.

Long national addresses seem to be the way of dictators. I remember watching Sadat speak for hours on TV every night to his people when I was in Asyut, a focal point of unrest in Middle Egypt, a week before he was assassinated. 'His people' in the sense that a jailer has his people behind bars.

Mursi issued self-deprecating mea culpas and called for the opposition to work with him in the national interest. His credibility is open to question: there haven't been any substantive talks with the opposition in the past year and sexual torture remains the staple diet of information gatherers in the prison system; 'Pass me the broom handle,' is the imperative in this day and age of iPhones and Galaxies.

When the broadcast ended, I noticed that the applause from the member-of-parliament audience was strongest among those wearing beards, likely to be his own party members, and merely polite from others. Those wearing uniforms looked nonplussed.

At the end, Mursi moved from behind his podium, taking one or two hesitant steps forward, and raised his arms a few times in salute. He has none of the natural swagger or confidence of a man in charge. This seems to confirm that he apparently acts as the representative of the Muslim Brotherhood's Supreme Guide. Mursi was unknown before being thrust into the presidential election spotlight and tonight he appeared forlorn and adrift.

The camera tracked back to show a wide-angle view of the auditorium from the rear. As the applause petered out those seated in the front row picked up their briefcases and made for the exit pretty smartish. Mursi noticed, abruptly turned to his right and followed suit. The technicians came on stage, unplugged the microphones from the podium and began to coil their cables for storage. I wonder if Mursi will remain unplugged.

I asked a few people today about the impact of his speech:

'It was incredible, he's made everyone more determined to go onto the street on Sunday.'

'Egypt is a powerful and rich country – if only the government would let the wealth flow to all. Mursi has done nothing . . . he doesn't deserve to be president.'

'In the final analysis we are all Egyptians whether Muslim, Christian or whatever . . . we will unite on the street on Sunday to show this.'

'He's hung himself!'

***

I follow Shona's instructions to stock the flat for the possible siege and go off to the local supermarket with a wad of notes.

'Do you have a delivery service?' I ask the store manager.

'Yes, of course. Where do you live?'

'Just three blocks away.'

'No problem, sir.'

He comes round the shop floor with me, recommending local brands over imports, and has a team of men pack everything into carrier bags at the checkout, filling four large trolleys. Some of the staff take photos of the till read-out as a souvenir. Shona did say to prepare for a siege.

'When do I need to be at home to let you in?' I ask.

'Now,' says the manager.

'Now?'

'Yes, now,' he says. 'Lead the way.'

I head off at the front of the four-trolley convoy, each one pushed by a strong Egyptian man. A Pied-Piper-of-Hamlin trail of street kids follow us through the streets, all of them shouting for backsheesh. It isn't credible to plead poverty so I give out some coins and manage to lose them after a couple of blocks.

The men bring everything up to the apartment and into the kitchen.

'Is this the first time you've used our service, sir?'

'It is, indeed.'

'What do you think?'

'Fantastic!'

'See you again, then.'

And they will.

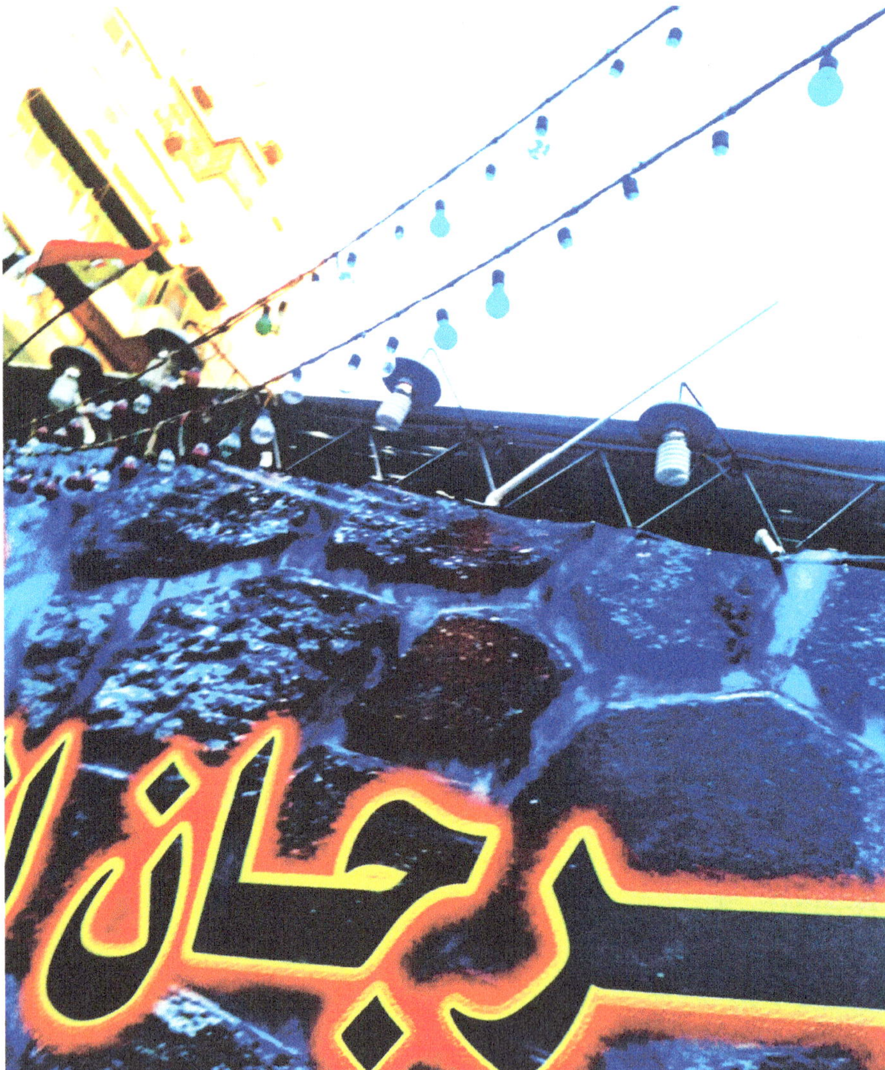

28 JUNE 2013: LIGHTS ON TAHRIR STREET

Ramadan decorations lit up Tahrir Street this evening. Today was Friday prayer day and everything was quiet in our area of Cairo. I was up and out early to do some printing, signing and scanning of a proposal for work and couldn't believe the lack of traffic.

Back in the apartment, Shona and I had great plans to explore the area but somehow the exertions of the week, or the heat drain of it, caught up with us and we fell asleep on the sofas and then decided to use up some of our stock of food for lunch. We were spoiled for choice. It was six o'clock before we headed onto the streets. We decided against carrying the big cameras in case it was misinterpreted by some people.

Several cascade messages came through, warning of protesters moving in one direction or another, but we didn't see anything of note except for the long queues at the petrol stations and A3-sized posters for sale at roundabouts saying, 'Mursi – Go out.'

We worked our way through the back streets of Dokki to Mohandessin for a steak dinner. Afterwards, we came across some dazzlingly illuminated late-opening ladies clothes shops with windows two stories high. Shona decided to try a few things on and I was brought a chair to sit on and then a cup of very sweet coffee as the trying-on session took on a time dimension of its own. She bought four items and a 30% discount was very welcome.

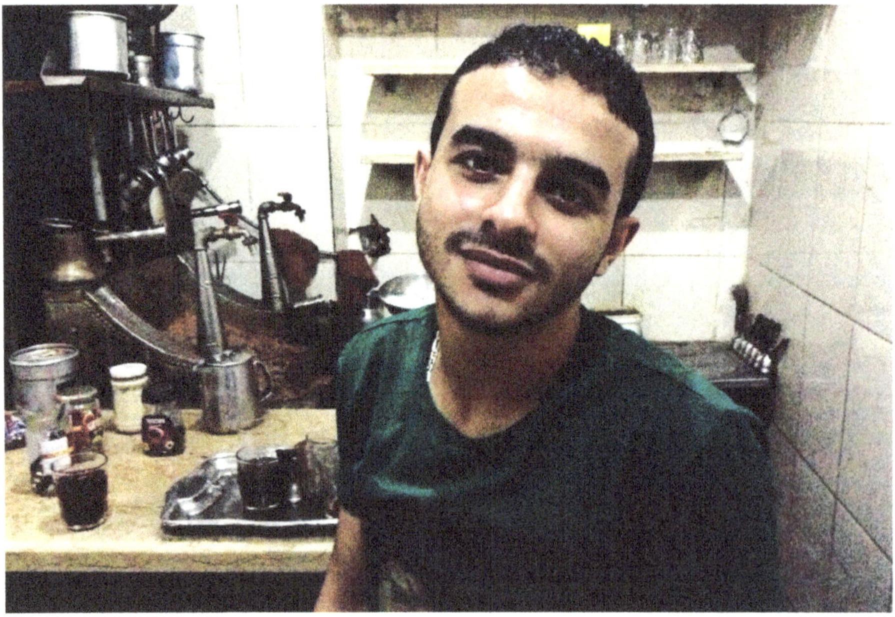

29 JUNE 2013: THE CALM BEFORE THE STORM

It's another quiet Saturday. We gauge the 'safety' temperature through the news channels and the university's cascaded text message alerts. We don't know what tomorrow will bring in Cairo but there are violent demonstrations today in Alexandria. A young American student has been killed there while taking photos with his smart phone during a confrontation between opposing factions.

Here, things are calm enough for us to go out to stretch our otherwise house-bound legs, do a little birthday-present shopping and have a beer before sundown.

Tahrir Square is a half hour walk from where we stay and one of the main thoroughfares used by protesters to reach the square, passes five minutes from our front door. It feels safer to be within easy walking distance of our flat in the evenings.

Walid, here, works at a tiny coffee shop nearby – think of a large cupboard – and delivers to many local shops and businesses. I have portraits of at least one of his brothers and I think his father also. His name means 'just born' and, in the pharaonic scheme of things, that's more or less true in his case.

As the darkness gathers and the drum beat for tomorrow and whatever it will bring deepens, I hope passionately that he can grow up in true freedom; freedom of a kind that this country has not known in 5,000 years and certainly not since the revolution of 25 January 2011.

There are so many 'just borns' in this country, all our Walids.

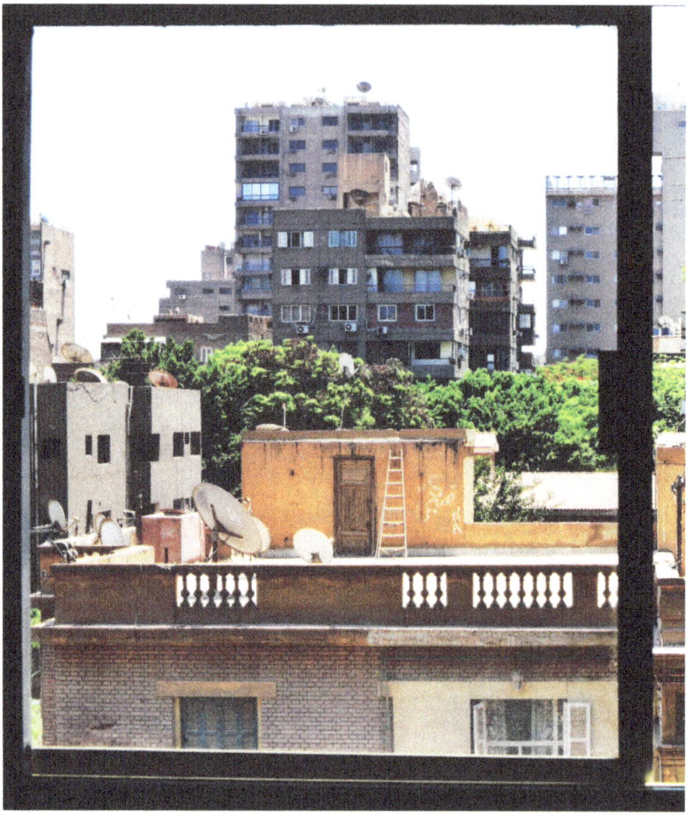

30 JUNE 2013: INSIDE LOOKING OUT

We obediently stay in our flat in Cairo until we receive a cascade message with the advice that we can go out, but need to be back by 4 pm. We leave the apartment in heat so great that you feel sweat beads pop out of your skin. We're amazed that the square adjoining our street is traffic free on this first, normally busy, working day of the Egyptian week.

We decide on a quick dip in the local hotel's open-air pool to cool us down. From the terrace we hear whistles, cheers and the banging of metal in the street below. We look over the wall and see groups of local youths band together before making their way to the main concentrations in Tahrir Square and around the Presidential Palace. There are also groups of well-off silver-haired couples waving their flags as they pose for photos for their family albums, before they too head to Tahrir. The mood is good humoured, as it seems to be in the square at the

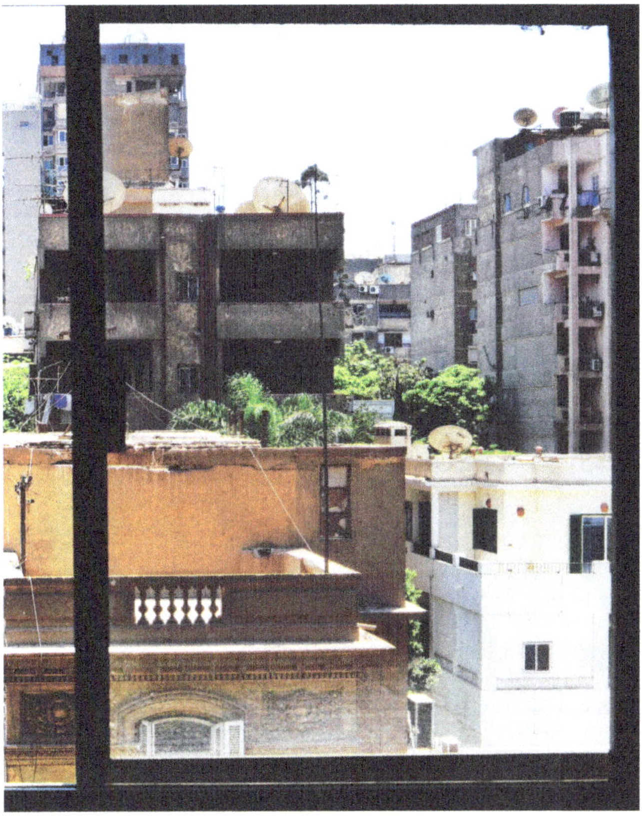

moment from the pictures transmitted by the local TV channels and shown on big screens around the pool.

The commentators say that the turnout is greater than during the protests against Mubarak and the crowds do seem dense and extensive in the wide-angle shots of Tahrir. It'll be interesting to see how the night pans out and the noise levels in the street below develop in the hours ahead. Many people say they won't go home until Mursi resigns.

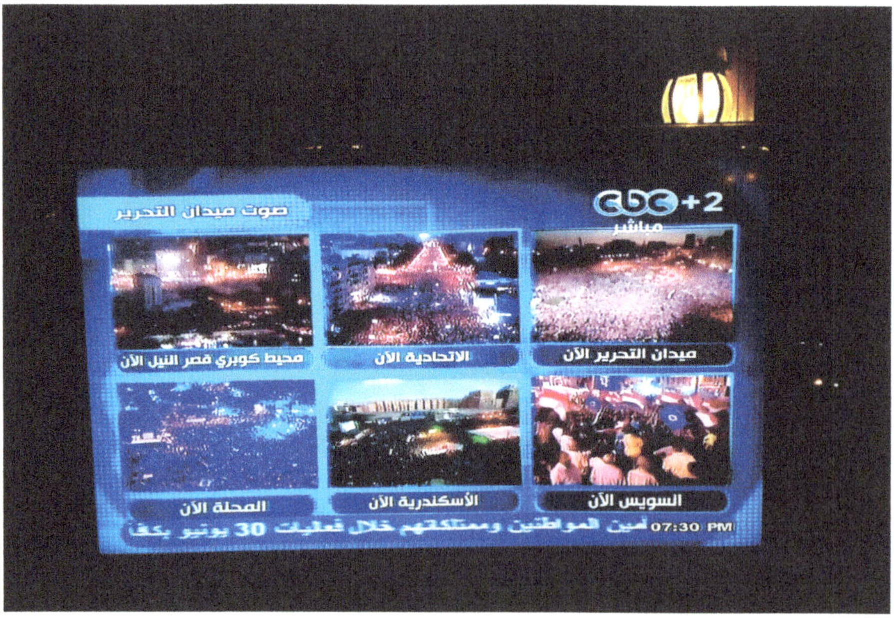
صوت ميدان التحرير
CBC +2
مباشر
محيط كوبري قصر النيل الآن
الاتحادية الآن
ميدان التحرير الآن
المحلة الآن
الأسكندرية الآن
السويس الآن
07:30 PM

1 JULY 2013: CAIRO SPREAD

Cairo was spread out across the TV screens beside the hotel pool tonight. You can see a crowded Tahrir Square here, top right insert, and the avenue leading to the Presidential Palace, centre top. It's the second night in a row the people have taken to the street.

'So, how was yesterday?' I ask an Egyptian who had been to Tahrir.

'Can you believe it! Thirty-three million people on the street.' He seems to weigh them all in his outstretched hands.

'That's incredible,' I say.

'Mursi only got fifteen million when he was elected, and he hasn't kept the contract since.'

'So what's going to happen?'

'We'll be on the street till Tuesday and if he doesn't resign then . . .' He says something I can't make out.

'Sorry, what did you say?'

'Then, there'll be a BIG surprise!' He shouts as if I'm deaf.

The surprise may be less of a surprise now that the army has said it will step in if there's not a consensus in forty-eight hours. As the prize of the presidency is tantalisingly within reach, there's no incentive for the opposition to agree anything. Let's prepare to be unsurprised.

Mursi was elected by a small minority of the voting population with a limited mandate to oversee the country through its first phase of democratic transition and, more importantly, deliver some degree of economic improvement for the vast population. Those opposed to him claim that he usurped all power including that of the judiciary, forced through a new constitution without due process or consultation and appointed loyal supporters, mostly unqualified, to lead the principal regional authorities up and down the country. They also claim that he maintained a regime of oppression in his jails and watched the leading economic indicators plummet while he prioritised the Islamisation of the social mores against the popular will. It seems hard for him to defend himself against the vox populi, which tonight is again being aired vociferously around Cairo and beyond.

On TV, we watch army helicopters drop national flags on the still-cheering crowds in Tahrir Square before we fall asleep to the thudding of the same rotor-blades audible in the sky above our flat.

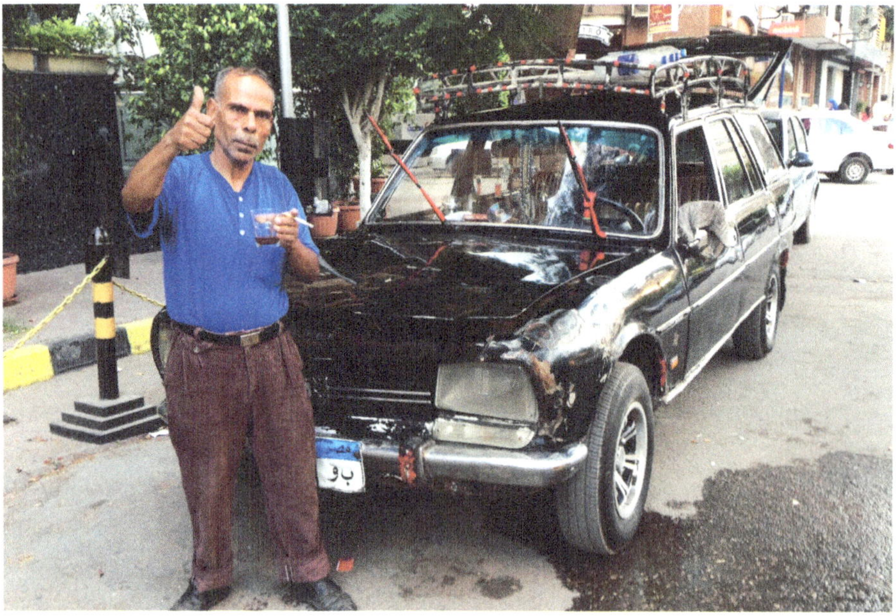

2 JULY 2013: PLAN B

My demon taxi driver from the other day has become my best friend around the block. Jemil, or Jimmy to foreigners, has fitted a new engine to his ancient Peugeot 504 station wagon. The bonnet is open and he's busy with an oily rag as I approach.

'Hello, Jimmy,' I call out.

He turns to me. 'Look. New,' he shouts. He points to the engine block and hits the front wing so hard the solders are nearly put asunder. 'Horse! Aswan! Anywhere!'

Aswan is a twelve-hour drive to the south and I've no doubt the car would make it. I've also no doubt that when Jimmy shouts, 'Anywhere,' that would include Paris. So there it is, our Plan B for our escape home. What a journey it would be: north to Alexandria, then along the El Alamein road through Mersa Matrouh and the Western Desert into Libya, across Tunisia with a stop in Carthage, before crossing Algeria to reach Tangier in Morocco, where we would catch the ferry to Algeciras in the south of Spain, turn right along the Costa de Sol to Malaga, sweep up past Valencia and Alicante to Barcelona, before passing through Perpignan and Lyon en route to Paris.

I can't wait to tell Shona tonight. The Peugeot would make it, Jimmy too and we wouldn't have to worry about the luggage allowance. We could also offer a lift to President Mursi if he needs a ride out of town, as looks likely.

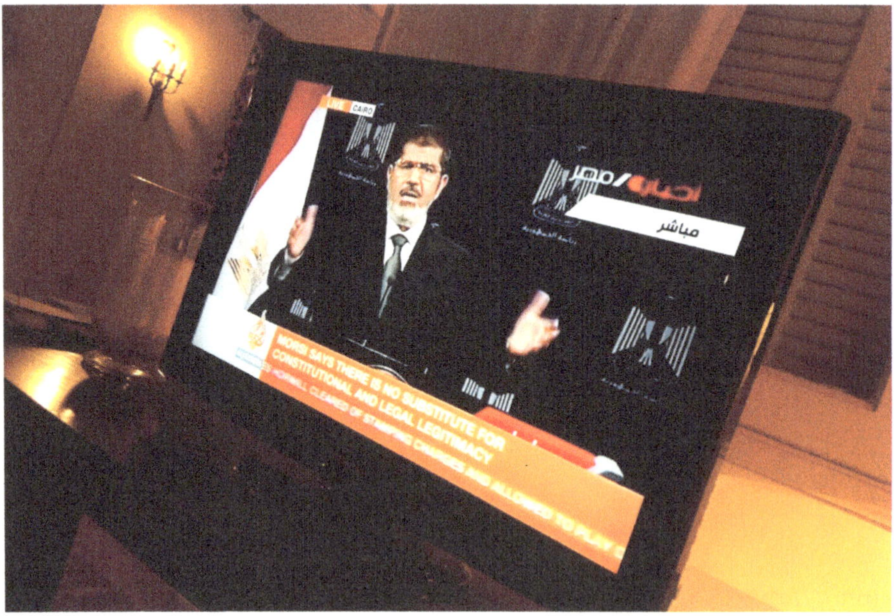
LIVE
CAIRO
مباشر
MORSI SAYS THERE IS NO SUBSTITUTE FOR
CONSTITUTIONAL AND LEGAL LEGITIMACY

3 JULY 2013: MURSI'S LAST STAND

President Mursi made what could well be his last stand tonight. He spoke for forty-five minutes to the nation in a live televised speech that was translated simultaneously into English on the Al Jazeera Middle East channel. He's neither telegenic nor a practised orator. His stiff gestures and rigid expression sapped conviction from his claims that he will defend his legitimacy with his blood and that he has God's blessing. Nor did his numbers seem to be accurate; his constitution was approved by only 19% of the voting population, not the 64% he claimed.

He placed the blame for the current protests on the 'runt of the former regime'. Given thirty-three million people protested against him on the streets all over Egypt on Sunday, that claim too seems a misrepresentation or self-delusion.

There was no acknowledgement that any of the protesters' demands were legitimate, nor an indication that any might be addressed. His calls for national dialogue after a year with no such dialogue lacked credibility.

The army deadline to reach a consensual solution to the issues expires today at 4.30 pm local time. With sixteen people shot dead overnight ten minutes' walk from where we live, one can only think that that is most unlikely. Meanwhile, we begin the process of looking for an earlier-than-planned flight out of the country as instructed by the British consular service.

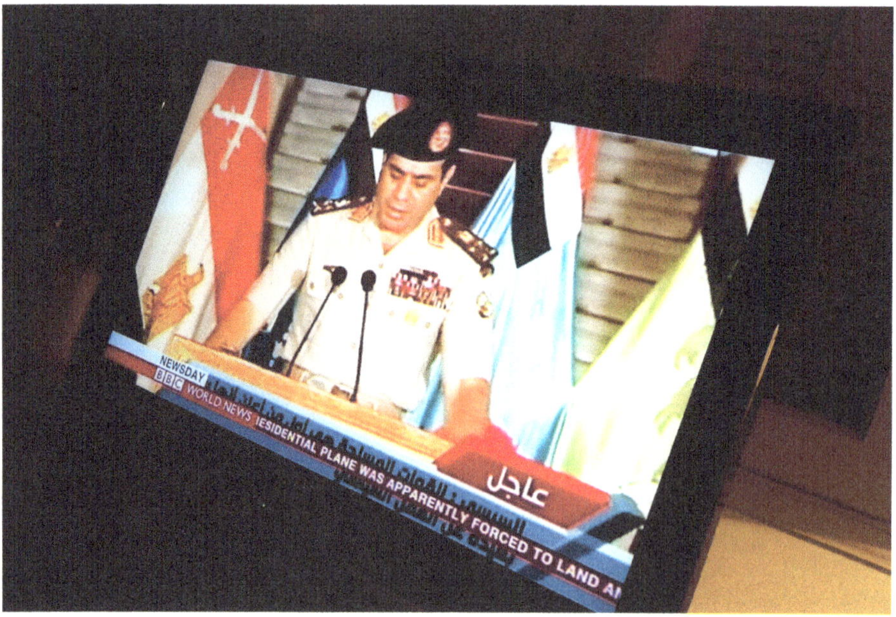
NEWSDAY
BBC WORLD NEWS
PLANE WAS APPARENTLY FORCED TO LAND
عاجل

4 JULY 2013: ANOTHER FREE OFFICER

General Sisi has taken power in Egypt today. He's the fifth in the line of Free Officers to rule the country since the revolution of 1952. Sisi's stated rationale and methods are the same as then: a response to the voice of the people backed by the use of the State's armed forces. The people are euphoric.

Through our open windows I can hear fireworks and crackers whizz and explode, car horns blare and unending cheers rise to the stars. It's deafening. The hope of the people is palpable after a year of frustration in which a government elected on a very narrow mandate sought to follow a path of Islamisation supported by only a small minority of the population. For the first time in thirty-two years I feel optimistic for Egypt. Perhaps now the aims of the 25 January 2011 revolution, which include increased salaries, lower food prices, better education, respect for human rights and democracy, have a genuine prospect of realisation.

Some write that this military coup is better termed the frustration of a fundamentalist coup, the latter being a long process patiently executed over years rather than the incisive blow of a military coup. Fundamentalists carry out good works and provide improved social services among the illiterate peasant classes who grow cotton and rice in the Nile Delta or cultivate sugar cane, corn, wheat and bananas along the Nile Valley. The villagers become accustomed to set-piece meetings where food is distributed and during which the organisers impart the tenets of fundamentalist values.

In parallel, over half a century of dictatorial oppression by Egypt's ruling regime concentrates the country's wealth in the hands of an elite who use it to finance their lifestyle of detached villas, private schools, sports clubs and premium brand cars. The middle class are frustrated by the lack of opportunities to use what qualifications they have, their salaries falling below their needs and their inability to influence the running of the country. The poor search through stinking urban rubbish tips for handfuls of rice to eat or bones to boil, and remnants of old clothes to wrap round bare feet. All but those closest to power rise up in revolt and, against all expectation, the regime is overthrown.

The fundamentalists are also surprised by developments. They respond with agility and use their greater political organisation and astuteness to out-manoeuvre the revolutionaries, who lack aligned leadership or political experience. The fundamentalists mobilise their grass-root supporters, who recall the benefits they received over the years and vote for the fundamentalists obediently at the polling stations.

A Muslim Brotherhood member becomes the first ever elected president of Egypt with the backing of 19% of the eligible voters fulfilling a long-cherished dream of the movement. He projects the image of a human-rights-respecting democrat to the outside world but follows the values and instructions of the supreme council of his own party, which seeks to Islamicise the country based on the strictest tenets of Sharia law. The fundamentalist coup is accomplished and the next phase of the movement's ambitions starts.

There is a problem, though. The narrow Islamist agenda and unimproved living conditions are unpopular with the majority of the Egyptian population. Its sense of identity, developed over the last hundred and fifty years with Western influences, is offended. The people rise up again, in even greater numbers, and the army withdraws its support from the president. It goes further – it arrests and imprisons him.

It remains to be seen what the next chapter in Egypt will bring.

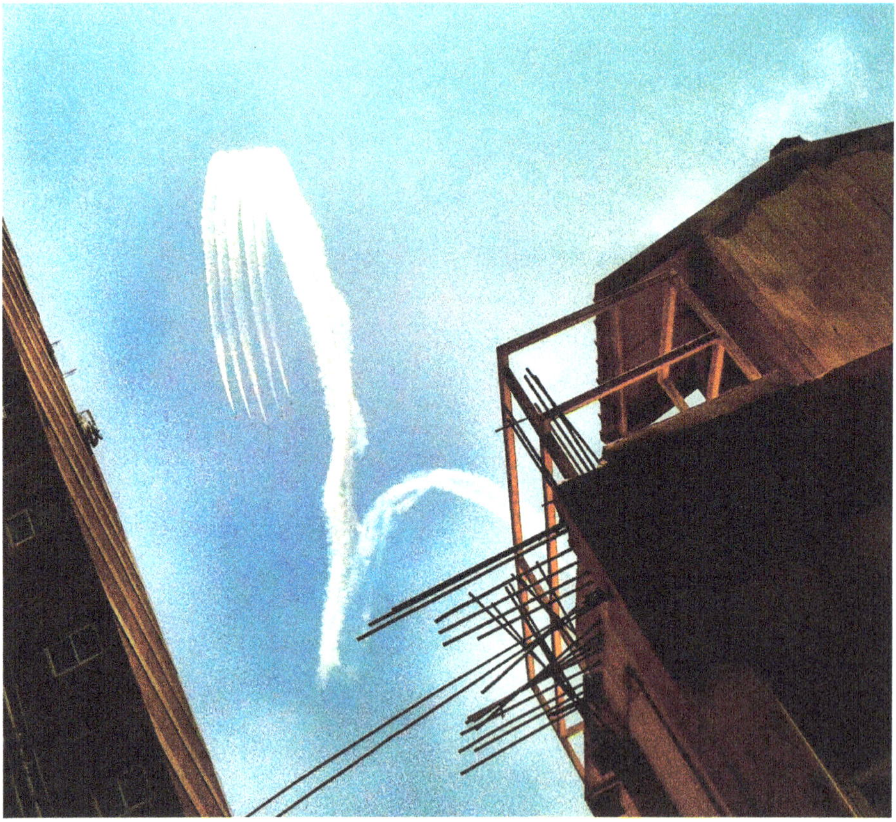

5 JULY 2013: THE NEXT LIFE

'So what do you think of the changes?' has been my standard question today around the block where I live in Cairo. Here are some of the responses:

'Beautiful!'

'Fantastic, fantastic!'

'We are finally achieving the revolution!'

'I voted for Mursi, but never again!'

'Religion is between God and your own heart; it's not for politics.'

'It's wonderful . . . like the next life!'

It was a fair cross-section of society, from taxi drivers and café owners to students, shop owners, lawyers and businessmen.

Air-force jets looped-the-loop, tracing giant white hearts and the red, white and black of the national flag in the sky all day long. Helicopters flew low with giant flags fluttering from inverted flag poles pointing down from their bellies.

As dark fell, our taxi drove past the garden night spots along the banks of the Nile where party crowds of young people gathered. They clapped, whistled, cheered and banged the roof of our car before we headed for a more open section of road.

The eternal sensations of Egypt floated through our open windows; the heat, the dust, the scent of jasmine, the twinkle of stars and lanterns, accompanied by local music from the radio with its unnerving runs, swoops and wails of violins. Below the radio, the taxi meter ticked away with its ubiquitous green LCD animated running pony beside the price, showing that all was well and we were truly on our way.

No one knows exactly where Egypt is going. The route map appears to be that the Head of the Constitutional Court, Mr Mansour, becomes interim president. He will lead a body composed of representatives of the original revolutionary opposition, the latest rebel movement leader and representatives of the mainstream mosques and Christian churches. Its stated aim is to complete the objectives of the 25 January revolution in a genuinely pluralistic way, to establish a secular constitution and design and implement an economic recovery plan. The aim is to improve educational, health and living standards for the nation's ninety million people, 45% of whom live in poverty with less than two dollars a day income. It's a big job for a short period.

Back in the flat, we watch Interim President Mansour speak on television.

'We must always stand in Tahrir Square, not literally, but in our hearts,' he declares. The programme editor cuts to scenes of streets in Downtown where the atmosphere has changed for the worse as supporters of the deposed President Mursi react. Stones, lumps of concrete and blazing cars litter the asphalt and gangs of youths charge down slip roads with sticks and metal bars. They've covered their noses and mouths with scarves, no doubt soaked in vinegar to protect them from the effects of tear gas. I fear what this 'next life' will look like, as I put out the light beside my bed.

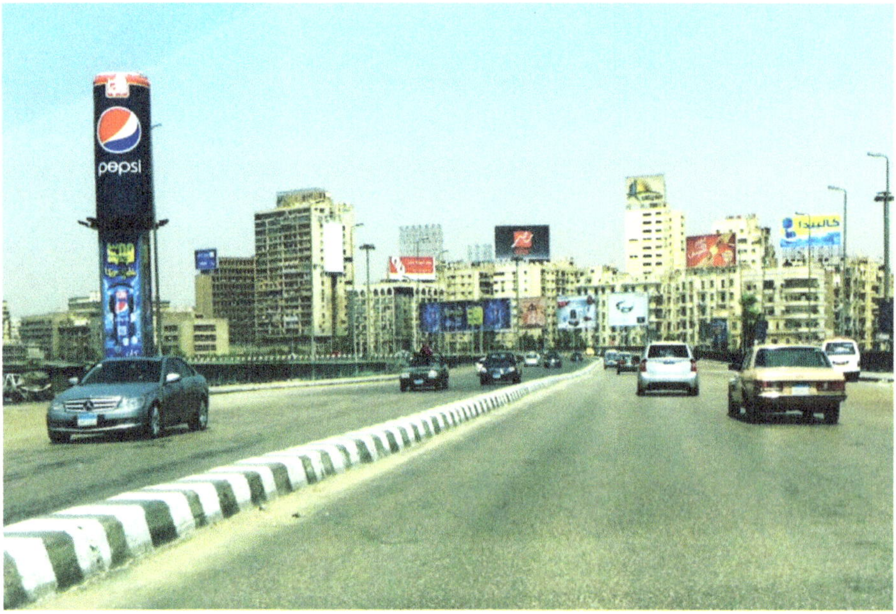
pepsi

6 JULY 2013: 6 OCTOBER BRIDGE

I awake this morning to the sound of gunfire. At first it's the determined stuttering of machine guns in bursts of a few seconds. Then the isolated cracks of rifle shots. I wonder if I should wake Shona, and screw up my eyes to read my watch face. It's 6.30 am. Maybe better if we move to the interior of the apartment away from the windows, I think, but have no idea how we're going to get to the airport later. There's no option; we'll just have to get into the car and hope for the best.

A few minutes later, I realise the rifle shots are nearer, more regular and focused just outside the apartment. I hear shouts and resolve to wake Shona right away. We don't have a moment to lose, I think, as I roll over . . . and then it all falls into place; the raging battles we'd seen on TV before coming to bed, and which had dominated my dreams, have been replaced by the hammers and drills of the building site across the street.

I've heard the same sounds every morning for the last two weeks but only now after the pitched battles that have scoured the streets of central Cairo have they taken on such a sinister tone. I feel relieved and kiss Shona's forehead. 'We'd better get up and packed,' I whisper.

The worst of the fighting last night took place on the 6 October Bridge that you see here. It's been cleared of stones and burned-out car wrecks and the traffic flows normally as we cross at 1.45 pm. People died all over Egypt as Muslim Brotherhood supporters, allegedly incited by their deputy leader's incendiary speech, took to the streets. In Cairo, people attempted to storm the police headquarters where the deposed president is held and others attacked the anti-Mursi crowd in full celebration in Tahrir Square. Worse scenes took place in the hotbed of Alexandria.

We manage to negotiate several roadblocks and diversions and arrive at the airport an hour behind schedule but still in time to catch our flight. Rising above the Western Desert of Egypt on departure is always a bittersweet experience for me, full of a deep longing to be down there still, mixed with the relief and guilt of escaping the daily toil of it all. It certainly was when I took off the day after Sadat was assassinated and it's the same now in this latest swirl of uncertainty. In a country that lacks embedded protections against abuses of government power – votes of confidence, judicial review and so on – the checks and balances to Mursi's actions had to come from somewhere. It's not surprising that that somewhere was the army.

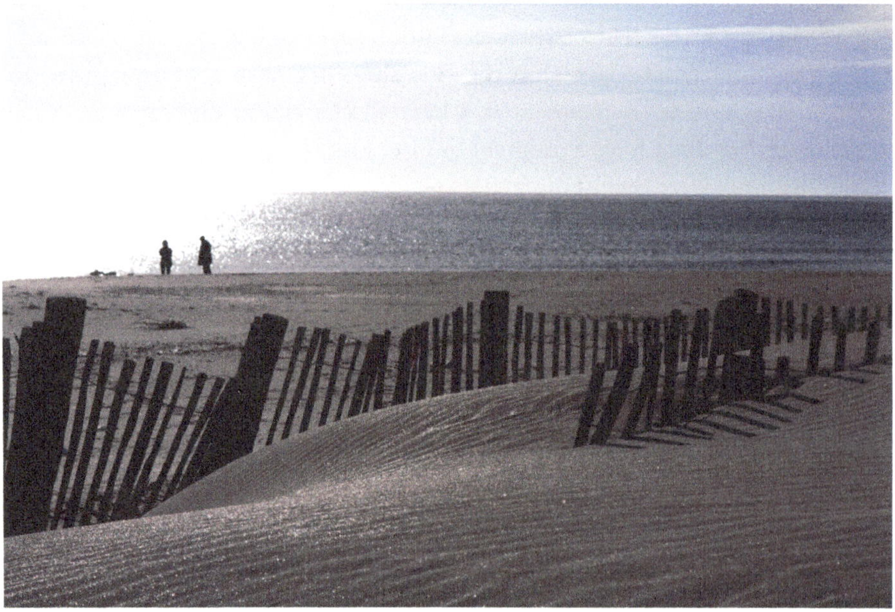

The Mediterranean by Teleri Williams

7 JULY 2013: THE SPARKLING SEA

I left Cairo in tumult yesterday as it was when Teleri Williams's parents were forced to flee Nasser's coup in 1952, two months before her birth. She was very much in my thoughts as the plane gathered height and I looked down on the sparkling sea, like diamonds cast on pale blue silk. I recalled Teleri's reply to my email from Tunis just the other day, in which she shared details about her car trip with her family when she was only eight years old from Tunis to Benghazi. 'Some day I must show you the photo of our car beneath the Italians' triumphal archway at the border . . . with nothing but desert either side of it!' she wrote.

I didn't know that Teleri had unexpectedly passed away as we were leaving Cairo. She was a marvellous writer and poet and it is a tragedy that the world will be denied the further fruits of her voice. When I say she was with me in the sky yesterday showing me 'her' Mediterranean and the necklace of communities where she lived around it, I know I'm not mistaken. She is at one with it as never before.

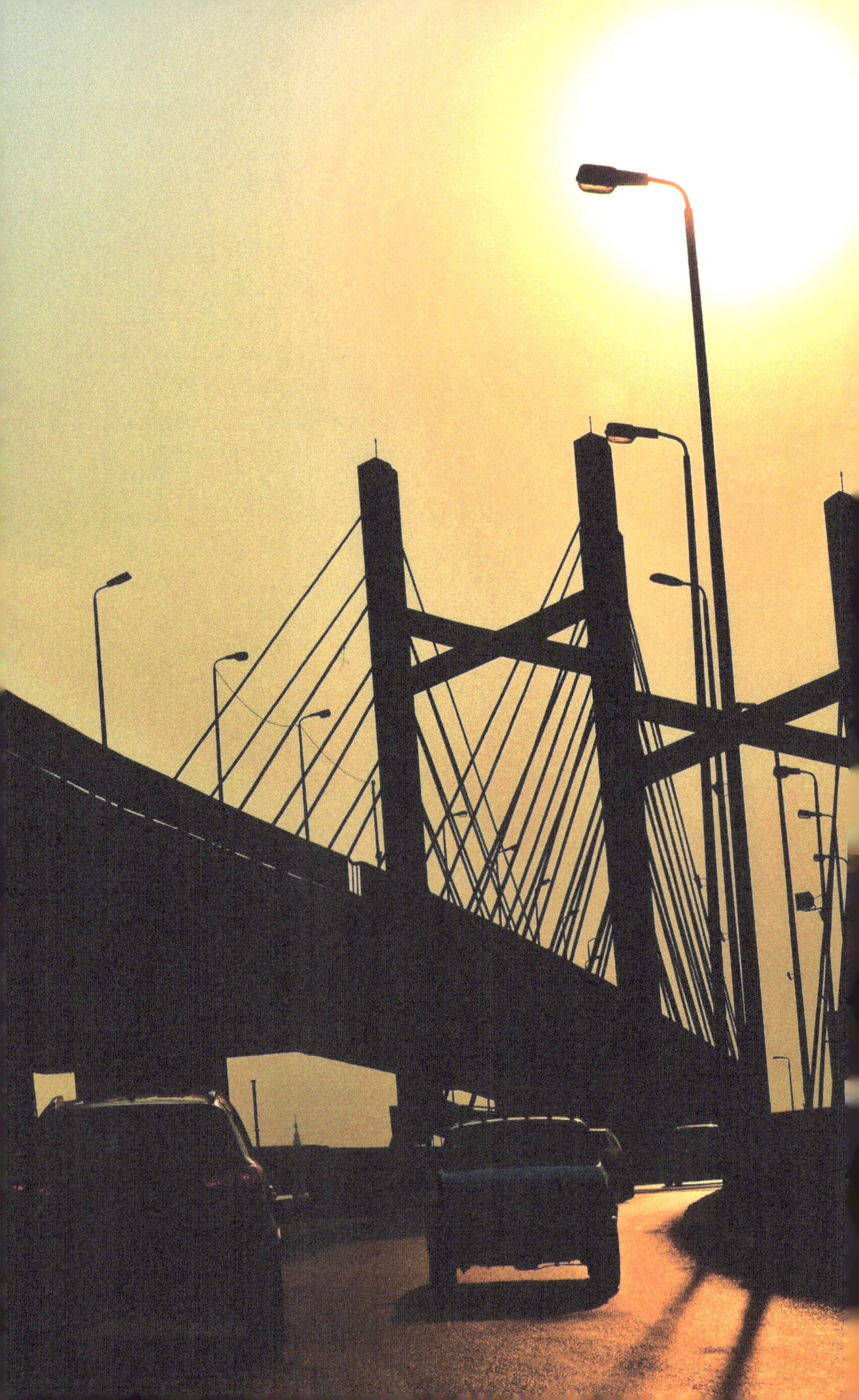

Chapter 6

All Quiet, Really?

16 OCTOBER 2013: OF KILLINGS AND CURFEWS

It seemed half the Western Desert was in the air above Cairo today as we came in to land. Peering through the sand, the vast dun-coloured city with its broken-down hovels and rubbish-strewn wasteland looked like the coat of a scabby dog. On final approach, we swept low over the Nile at Tahrir Square. It's been three bloody and tumultuous months in the history of Egypt since we were last here but it all looked exactly the same from above. Hopefully this visit will tell us something of what is happening on the ground.

In August, six weeks after we last left the country at the time of Mursi's ousting, Interim President Mansour's government showed its ruthless side. It ordered the clearance of various encampments in Cairo, including at Rabaa al-Adawiya Square where Islamist supporters of the former president had continued their protest. The security forces attacked with bulldozers, armoured personnel carriers, tear gas and rifles loaded with live ammunition. The assault lasted twelve hours and over eight hundred Islamists were killed, many unarmed and shot in the head and chest. A virtual state of emergency is in place with a midnight curfew every day except Fridays when it is 7 pm.

I'd been led to expect army tanks stationed every hundred metres, but we saw none on the way into Downtown. The traffic seemed normal, albeit lighter than usual due to this being Eid al-Adha, four days of religious celebrations also called the Feast of the Sacrifice. It honours the willingness of Abraham to sacrifice his son Ishmael. Lambs are sacrificed and divided into three parts, the first for the family, the second for relatives and friends, and the third for the poor. Special prayers are said in halls or open fields; there are family visits on the first day and then on other days visits to parks or resorts or cinemas. Children traditionally receive new clothes, and everyone tucks into *kahk*, small sweets filled with nuts and dusted with sugar.

We drove past several barbeques at the road's edge. Their aromas drifted through our open windows and will linger in the night air long after the midnight curfew hour.

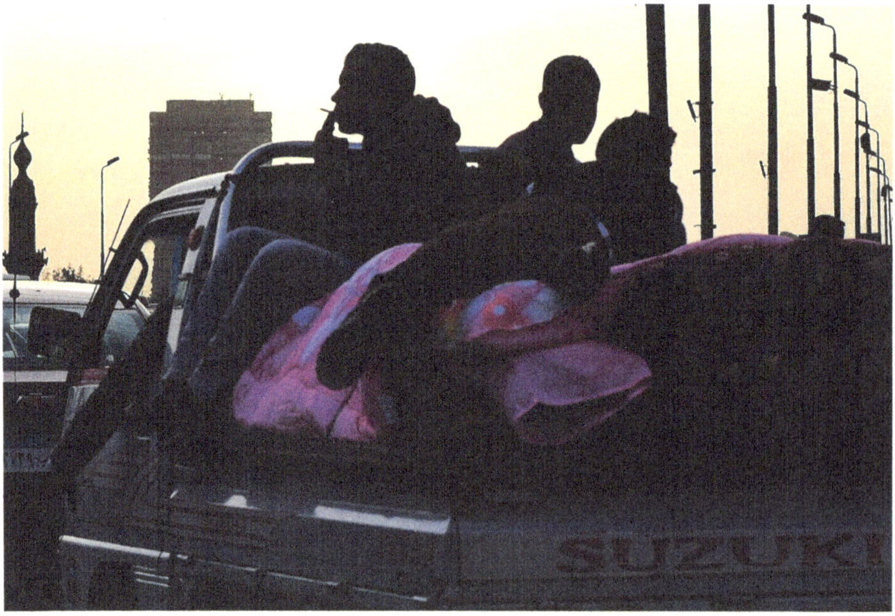
SUZUKI

17 OCTOBER 2013: ALL QUIET

All is quiet in Cairo today and Shona is in full nest preparation mode. She needs to make any apartment we stay in feel like home before she can focus on work and brings many of her favourite items with her like small bowls and scarves to decorate each place. She also buys flowers, cushions, posters and baskets locally to complete the look and feel. I clean the flat with multi-use cleaning fluid and rolls of kitchen paper to wipe or prise out sand and dust from every groove of the window frames, the wardrobe interiors and along the top of the skirting board. It's a good team effort and I know Shona's pleased to have me here to help.

We go out in the late afternoon and hail a taxi, crossing from Dokki onto the island of Gezira before heading north to Zamalek, of all the areas of Cairo the one we call home. As tomorrow is the first day of the weekend, there's the usual Thursday-night congestion at roundabouts and bridge crossings. These young men on the truck are also engaged in nest making. One of them will be getting married and the tradition is for the groom's friends to help set up the happy couple's first home with essentials like a mattress and chairs. A festive mood prevails and we see many couples stroll across bridges over the Nile while brightly lit riverboats host parties on the river below.

We dine in a Italian restaurant, which we've been told is owned by the son of Omar Sharif; one day maybe we'll meet the star of *Doctor Zhivago* and *Lawrence of Arabia* here. We ask if they're open tomorrow.

'Yes, but only from 1 to 5 pm. Then we close to let everyone home before curfew,' they said. Tomorrow is prayer day and has an earlier curfew of 7 pm as no one knows what trouble might flare up after afternoon prayers. We all have to get home leaving sufficient time for our taxi drivers to get back to their own homes too.

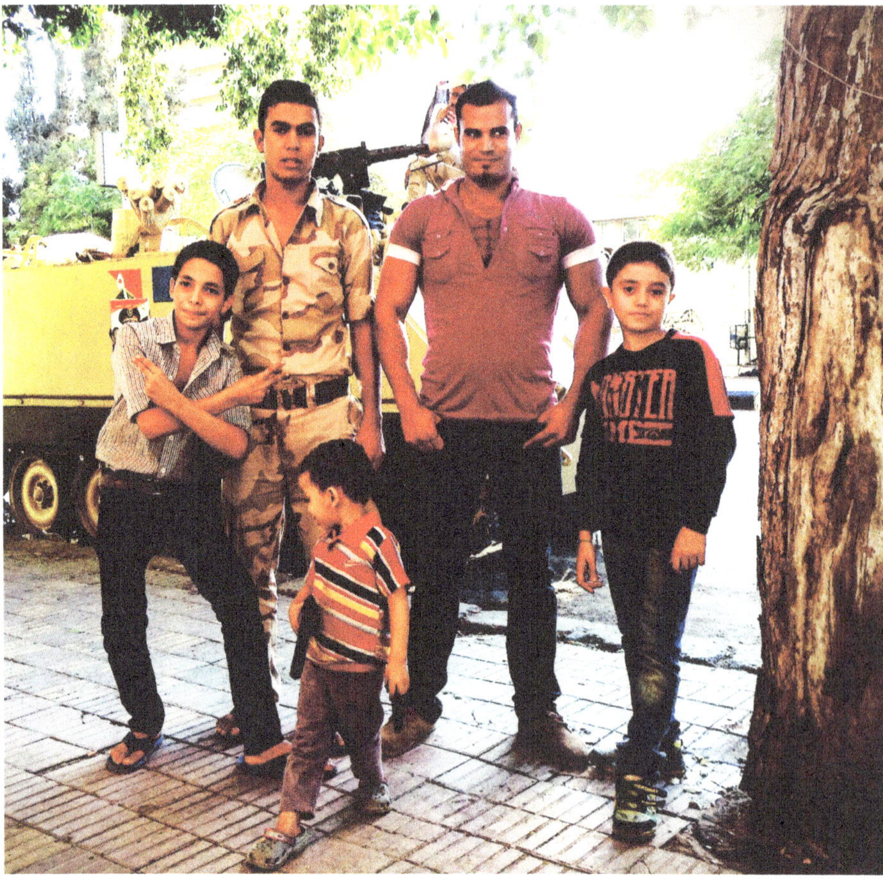

18 OCTOBER 2013: GUN SHOT

In the late afternoon of this Friday prayer day, keeping an eye on the curfew clock, we walk along a busy road towards the university area, just south of Dokki, which has been a hot bed of Muslim Brotherhood resistance. There have been numerous fatal shootings here since our last visit. The army monitor the area more closely than others so we're not surprised to find an armoured vehicle parked up beside the kerb with its crew engaged in various activities. One soldier mans the machine gun on top of the vehicle, another prays on a mat in the shade of a nearby tree, and a third asks to take our photo.

We happily pose before requesting a reciprocal shot. The uniformed boy-soldier you see is delighted to collaborate and calls others to join the group. One soldier hurriedly slips on his boots and, at the last minute, the small boy with the gun joins the line-up. I'm honestly not sure if it's a real one borrowed from the soldiers or a toy. I don't waste time in arranging them nor do I insist they all look directly at the lens, just in case it is the real thing and the gun-toting kid suddenly takes aim.

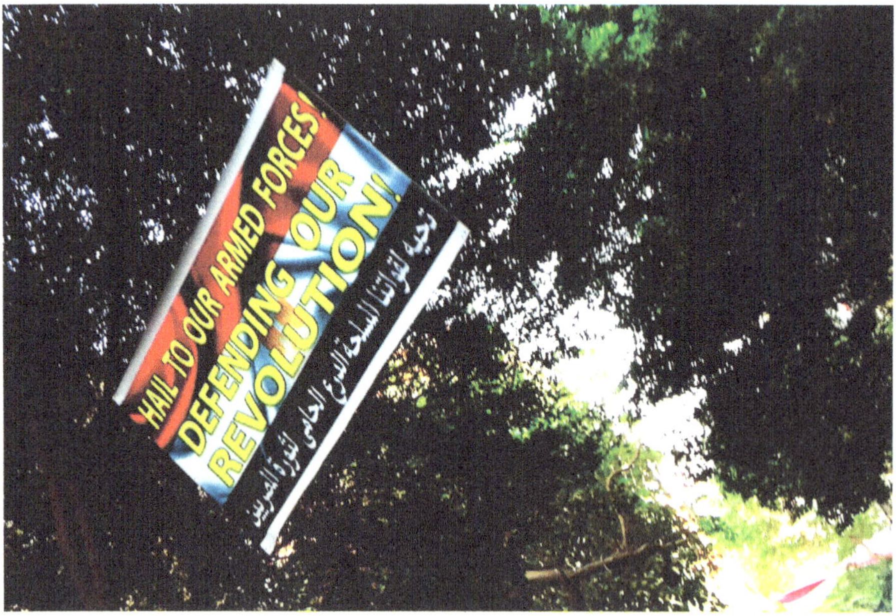
HAIL TO OUR ARMED FORCES!
DEFENDING OUR REVOLUTION!

19 OCTOBER 2013: HOW ARE THINGS?

Since I arrived back in Cairo three days ago, I've been asking people how things are. Here are some of the replies:

The Driver: *Better. A lot better. Getting back to normal. Inshallah.*

The Tour Operator: *Recovering. Tourists are coming back. Don't think Sisi is here for ever. We'll be able to put in our own man soon. And that's good.*

The Financier: *Everyone's happy! People are investing again . . . everything's moving. Thank God!*

The Boutique Owner: *Before it was the army that ruled. Then the police. Now it's both. And they're still beating us up. There'll be no major change if this continues . . . but the people are very happy.*

On a rough poll I make it nine to one in favour of the latest developments among the section of the population I come into contact with, which includes shopkeepers and cleaners. I haven't spoken to any Muslim Brotherhood supporters who will have a different view, especially in the light of the protest camp killings. None of the people I spoke to mentioned these deadly events.

The Islamist coup is clearly over and I viewed the high-energy dance routine on Egyptian TV last night, with naked-chested young men twirling scantily clad ladies in acrobatic manoeuvres, with a sense of schadenfreude. Only three months ago the Brotherhood minister of culture, with no electoral mandate whatsoever, played what turned out to be his last hand. He ordered the national ballet to lengthen its tutus.

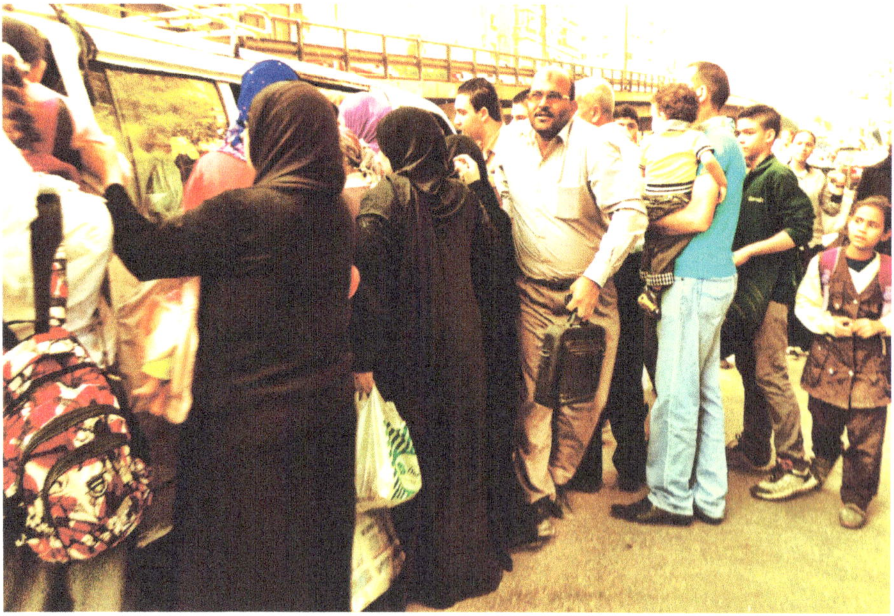

20 OCTOBER 2013: CAIRO CRUSH HOUR

Cairo's traffic was gridlocked today as the city came back to life after the religious festival of Eid al-Adha. The quadrant of streets around our apartment was noisily backed up all day long, making it all but impossible to venture to other parts of the city. For those who had no choice there was the usual squeeze to board one of the city's microbuses.

I didn't go out until three o'clock when the schools closed. It brought home, once again, the need for the unblocking of every system and process in Egypt to provide basic services and a future for the multitude of smiling playful kids who rush out the school gates every afternoon after class.

They keep coming and coming; the population has risen from forty-odd million in 1981 when Mubarak came to power to nearly ninety million today and there's no stopping it. If the current birth rate continues the population will reach one hundred and sixty million by 2050.

Government policy has been to encourage birth control and a maximum of two children per family as the country cannot educate, create jobs for or provide welfare support for more. The rural poor ignore these top-down policies. They see additional income produced by having more children as an essential insurance policy for their old age. Muslim clerics are split on the issue – those closest to centres of education advocate birth-control measures as long as they are reversible, while the rural less-educated clerics continue to preach that children are a gift from God and that procreation should not be interfered with.

Egypt's education on birth control is not working and the education system is regarded as one of the worst in the world. Successive regimes have failed to positively impact either. It seems time for someone to enrol the rural poor in a greater support for and practice of effective birth-control methods. 'Out of Egypt I called my Son,' said the prophets in biblical times. I wonder who will emerge now to lead the people.

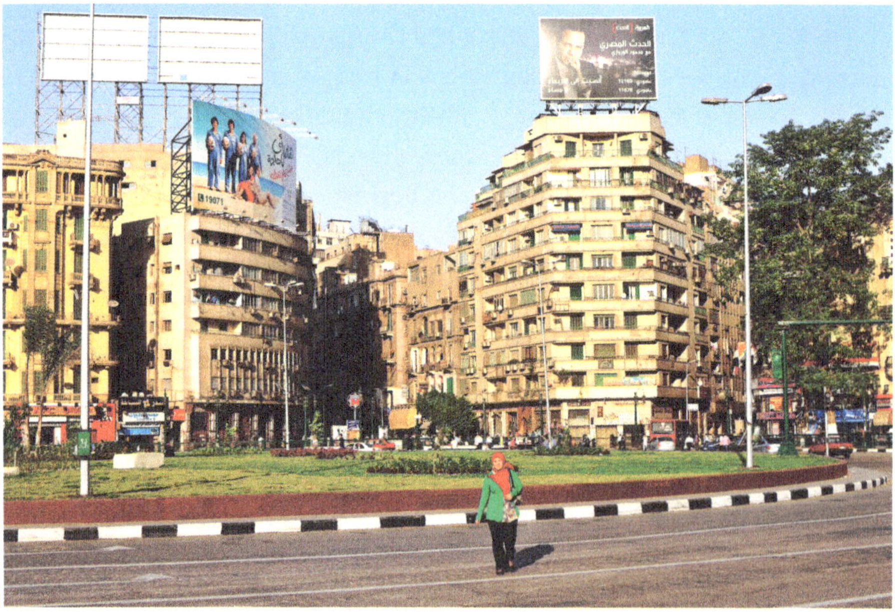
الحدث المصري
19071

21 OCTOBER 2013: BACK TO TAHRIR

I've just walked round Tahrir Square. It's the first time I've seen traffic circulate there since 1981, although there was a thirty-year gap between my first two visits. The kerbstones of the central roundabout are now painted black and white and the greenest of new grass, saplings and shrubs grow where the revolutionaries' encampments once stood on scuffed dirt. It could seduce you into thinking that things are back to normal but for the fact that a wedding party was gunned down yesterday at a Coptic Christian Church in Giza in broad daylight, about fifteen minutes from where we stay. The assassins arrived on motorbikes and opened fire from their saddles as the wedding party posed for photographs outside the church after the ceremony.

Now in Café Riche in Talaat Harb Street the tables are occupied by groups of men from different generations, their discussions quite heated. There's a haughty walk-out right now by a young man declaiming in English, 'What we need is a leader with guts!' Our collective look follows him through the swing door onto the street. The door settles back to its closed position, the older men at his table shrug, and we turn back to our dishes of baba ganoush, pickles and roast pigeon.

Things are far from settled and I wouldn't bet on the fresh grass of Tahrir Square remaining untrodden by protesters for long.

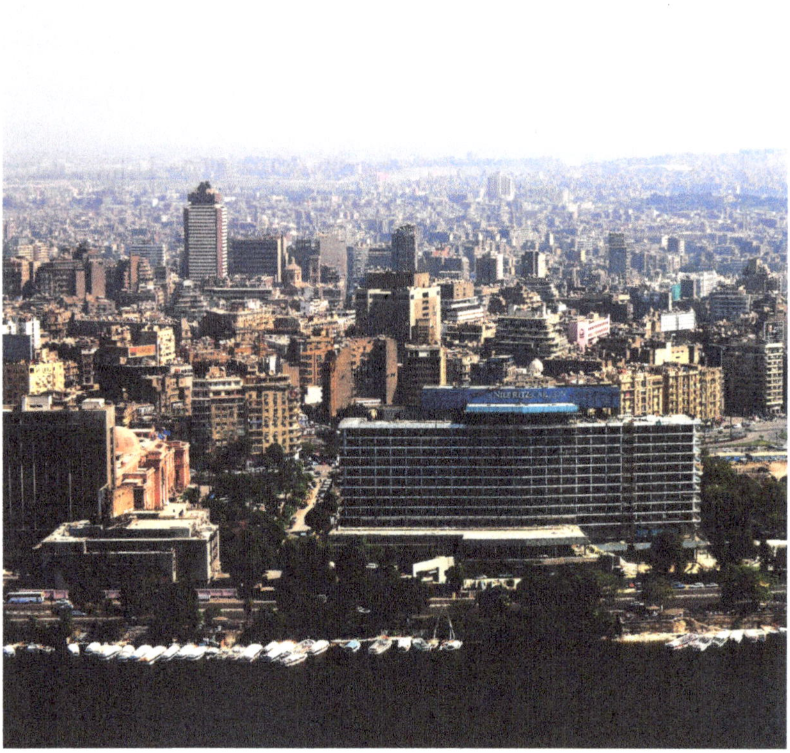

22 OCTOBER 2013: THE LIE OF THE LAND

Here's the lie of the land as seen from the top of the Cairo Tower, for many years the tallest building in Africa at one hundred and eighty-seven metres although there's now one taller in Johannesburg.

You can see Tahrir Square, with its grassy roundabout, to the right of the former Nile Hilton, which is centre foreground with blue signage on top. The pink building, slightly obscured to its left, is the Egyptian Museum. Half of its dome is behind the tall burned-out building, formerly the HQ of Mubarak's National Democratic Party, torched during the revolution on 28 January 2011. Just out of frame to the left is the 6 October Bridge, which is often the scene of fighting, and the one to the right of frame is Qasr El-Nil Bridge, opened in 1931. It carries El Tahrir Street from Dokki and was built by Dorman Long Ltd of England, which was also responsible for the Tyne Bridge, Newcastle, and the Sydney Harbour Bridge, Australia.

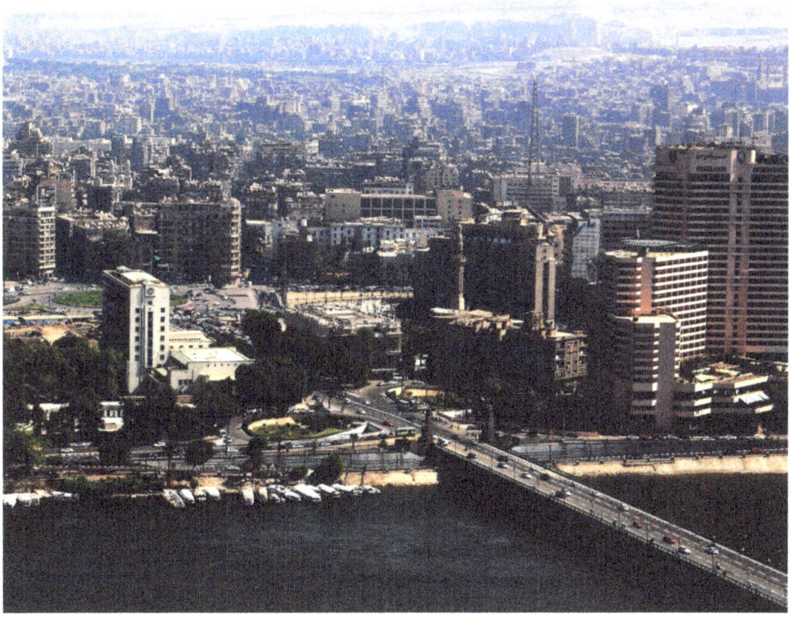

I can see where I stood in the square to take yesterday's shot, but it's a little complicated to explain. If you look closely you'll see the yellow buildings that form the background to it – they are almost in the exact centre of the frame, just above and to the left of the green grass of Tahrir Square.

My second objective today is to find Yasheen, our street-kid friend. I head to the block where he usually hangs out.

'You Mister Flowers?' shouts another older boy loaded with red and yellow carnations as he dodges through the traffic to cross the street. There's no punctuation indicated by his intonation and I almost reply, 'No, I'm not Mr Flowers,' but stick to my task instead.

'Yasheen?' I point directly at him and then hold my hand at his chest level to indicate a smaller boy. 'Where is Yasheen?'

This taller flower seller shrugs his shoulders. 'You no flowers?'

'No, I'm not. I mean yes, no flowers. Not today, anyway...Yasheen?' I try again.

'Yasheen?' He mimics my pronunciation and his brow furrows.

'Yes, Yasheen.' More waiting.

'Excuse me, may I help?'

I turn and look at an elegant Egyptian lady with a silk headscarf and dark glasses who's stopped beside us on the pavement and who has just addressed me in English.

'Thank you. I'm looking for Yasheen.'

'Yasheen?'

'Yes, Yasheen. A boy. He sells flowers here.'

'Yasheen?' She and the flower seller exchange looks. He gets there first.

'*Has*im?' He tries.

'*Has*im?' I echo.

'Ah, *Haaas*im!' says the lady. She turns to the young man and there's an exchange in Arabic.

'He's not here,' she says.

'Yes, I know he's not here, but does he know where he is or when he's coming?'

She translates.

'He wants to know why you want to know.'

'Because . . . because, I'm his friend.'

She absorbs this before translating. They both turn and look at me. Closely. Intently.

'And I want to measure his feet,' I add.

An unconvinced 'Ah-haaa!' nod comes from the lady.

I pull my key-ring measuring tape from my pocket and extend it to what looks like a Hasim foot length.

'See?'

They still don't seem convinced.

'Look, I've known him since he was a little boy and I want to bring him some nice training shoes from Europe like these.' I point down to my brown leather moccasins. 'Well, he saw my trainers the other day – they're in my suitcase now. And he loved them.'

She passes all this on to the flower seller. I look at my watch as I have a plane to catch.

'He says Hasim's size thirty-seven. He wants a pair too, size forty-three.'

It's time for me to go.

'Thank you both very much. Sincerely. I'll see what I can do.'

I get onto the road to the airport. Youssef, the driver, is in a less than talkative mood, partly because he's munching a large bagel he's bought from a roadside stand. Crumbs tumble down his shirtfront as I ask him about the political situation.

'What do you think of Mursi now?'

'Stupid,' he replies instantly and looks at me, clearly wondering if I am too.

'And what will happen at his trial?'

He takes his right hand off the wheel and draws his index finger slowly across his neck.

Better leave it there, I think.

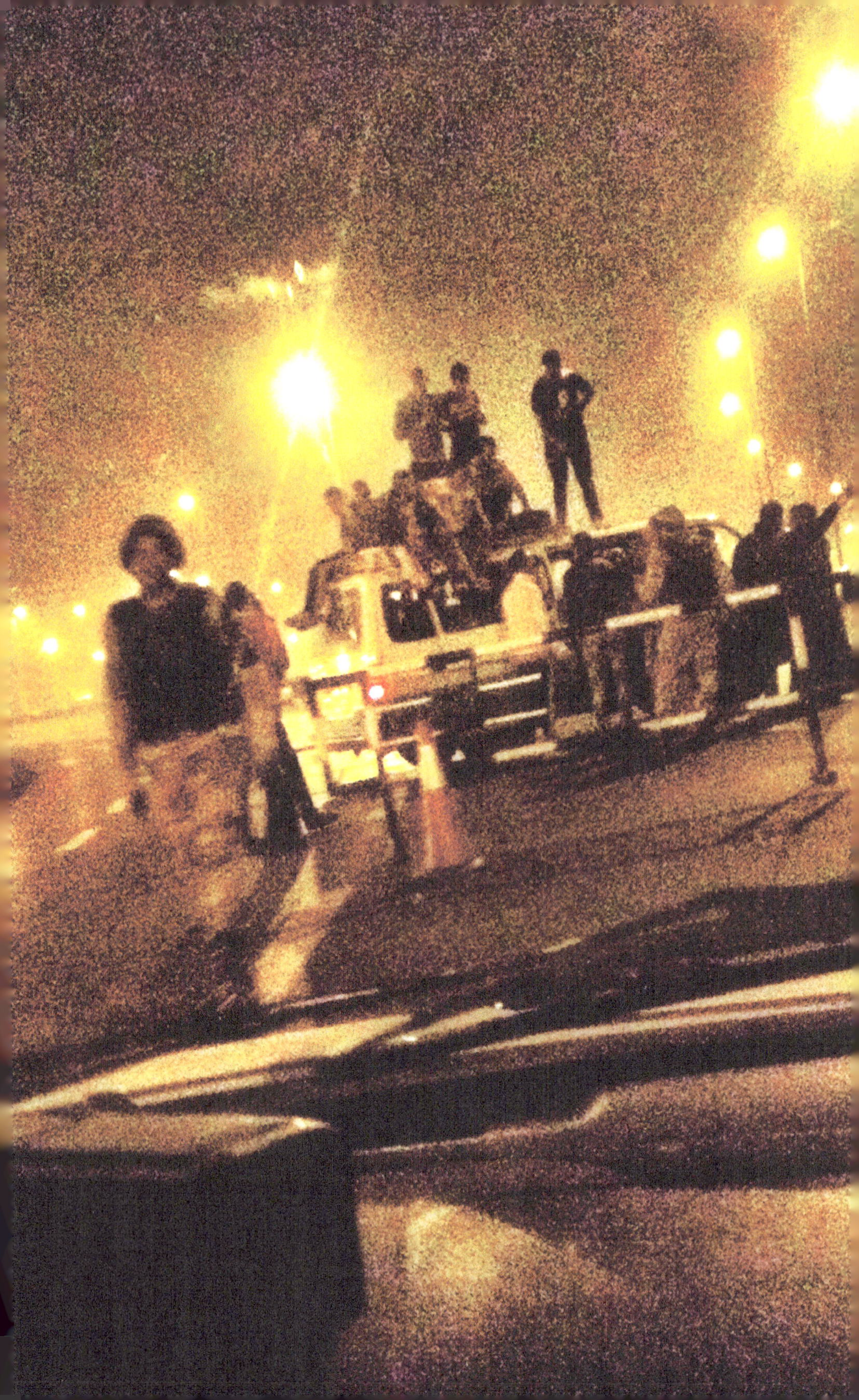

Chapter 7

In Search of a Decent Man

9 NOVEMBER 2013: CAIRO CURFEW

He picks up on what seems like the twentieth ring, but says nothing.

'I'm Alex . . . Is that my driver? . . . Where are you?'

'Duh . . .' a voice replies.

I hand my phone to the man behind a car-hire desk in the airport arrival hall, signalling for him to speak. A flurry of Arabic leaves his lips and he hands me the phone back. 'Asleep,' he says. It's two-thirty in the morning, but it's no excuse.

A wizened, elf-like man leans into me immediately. 'Where you go?' he asks.

'What about this man?' I ask the car-hire rep. 'Is he reliable?'

'This one . . .' the rep says, leaning across his counter to pinch the old man's short white frizzled hair and tugging on it as hard as he can, '. . . this one's got experience.' He laughs and I laugh too, but he doesn't help me negotiate the price.

'Idiot!' My new elf driver shouts as he pulls away in the dark from the first army checkpoint with a petulant squeal of his tyres. 'Won't let go straight . . . need small roads.'

They are small roads. I lose count of the three-point turns we do in a warren of deserted back streets. My driver bounces the car up high kerbs to cross pedestrian walkways. Its plastic farings scrunch and sound as if they'll fall off.

The floorpan scrapes on concrete. We drive up one-way roads the wrong way, flashing our lights at the occasional on-coming car. We pick up speed down a clear empty carriageway only to round a bend and see barbed wire stretched across the road. Soldiers sit on top of armoured cars on the other side of the barriers and swivel their large machine guns towards us.

'Don't worry,' my driver says as he brakes to a halt. 'I know other way.' He turns the car round, all the time holding my passport open at the photo page in his gear-changing hand.

We stop at five more checkpoints. At some, the soldiers just look in; at others, they ask my nationality.

'Scotland,' I say.

'SCOTLAND!' my driver shouts as if playing a trump card. Several soldiers crowd round my window and signal for me to lower it. I do. They're no more than boys and jostle for a look at me. They spot my iPad mini on my knee and beam broad smiles from under their helmets as they point it out to their colleagues. I think, puppies, but remember Shona's last text saying, 'don't dare ask for photos if you get stopped,' so I don't . . . but I'm sorely tempted.

We speed towards the next checkpoint and, for a second, I wonder if elf-man intends to run it in a final show of bravado for his Scottish passenger. His approach is fast enough to cause the soldiers to take a step back and I see the ends of their rifles rise by a few degrees. My driver applies the brakes and changes down through the gears, revving the engine high each time.

He's got my passport wedged in his mouth this time and a captain whisks it away through the open window. He turns to examine my photo under the spotlights and thumbs through the pages, scrutinising the Egyptian visas.

'Purpose of trip?' he asks in clear English.

'Tourist . . . visiting my wife.'

'Egyptian wife?'

'No, British. She's working here.'

In a well-practised movement, he closes the passport and tosses it through the window as if dealing a playing card. A tiny movement of his index finger signals us to go on our way and my driver releases the clutch. He doesn't leave any rubber on the road this time.

'Last time tonight. Don't worry. Welcome to Egypt,' he laughs, as we speed towards the Nile.

Half an hour later, I text Shona so as not to wake the household by ringing the doorbell, 'Outside door on landing.' The door opens and it's even bigger smiles. Nice to be home.

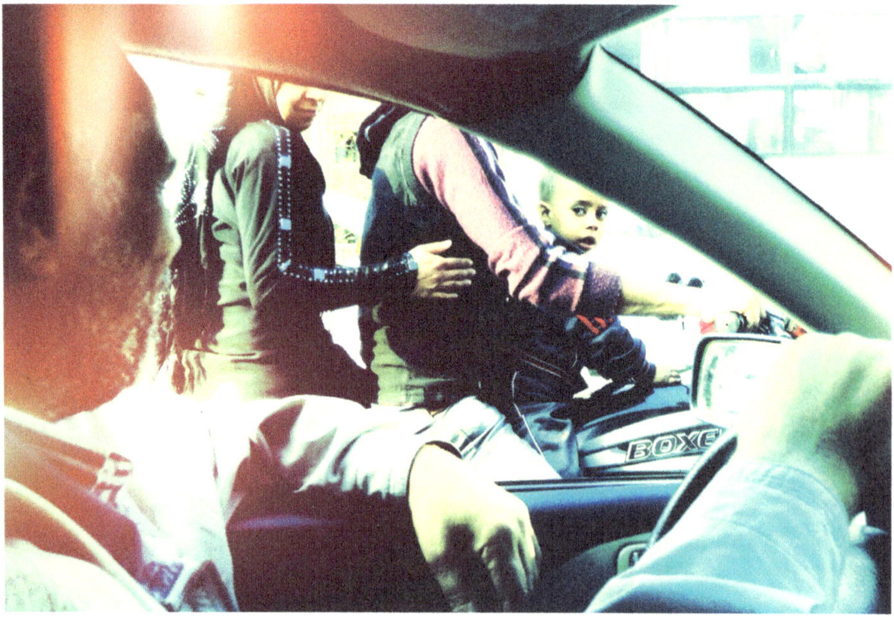

10 NOVEMBER 2013: THE CLOCK'S RUNNING

The sixty-day time limit set by Interim President Mansour to present a new draft constitution ran out two days ago, with nothing to show for it. 'Not to worry,' they say. 'If you define it as sixty working days, we've still got until 3 December.' Very Egyptian, but time is still short to reach this important milestone of the political roadmap set out when Mursi was ousted.

The drafting committee are drawing fine distinctions in it to maintain the Islamic identity of the country while establishing more independence from the Al-Azhar religious institution. Sharia law has always underpinned the country's legal system and this venerable and independent body has had a high degree of influence during centuries on the way the law has been applied in the governance of the country. When Mursi was in power there was a move to apply the principles of Sharia law more strictly.

Other non-constitutional matters press. Butane gas canisters are in short supply now that the cold weather is setting in and men in the street begin to wear baggy jackets over their galabeyas. It looks like there will be a repeat of last winter's gas shortage, which was allegedly caused by the Mursi government's mismanagement. The poultry farmers are upset as they need heat to incubate their chicks as the temperatures fall.

Rabid dogs are another headache for the city fathers at the moment. There's no rabies vaccine to be had and they do not have enough vets with fire-arms licences to cull the dogs humanely – as humanely as you can from fifty yards with a rifle. Popular discontent on these matters, rather than the delay in drafting the constitution, highlights what's important to the man on the back of the city's motorbikes.

Still, everyone continues to be content with political developments, including an Egyptian Christian woman I spoke to, one of 10% of the population who has this faith. 'Thank God, we don't have Mursi to deal with anymore,' she said. Aly, my driver today, had an exchange through his open car window with the father of this family on their motorbike. 'Good people,' he said, turning back to me. 'They're very happy now.'

I waited but nothing more was forthcoming. We can only hope and pray that this marginal momentum is maintained up to and beyond 3 December when the draft constitution is published, but I can't help worry about what further resistance to Mansour and Sisi is planned.

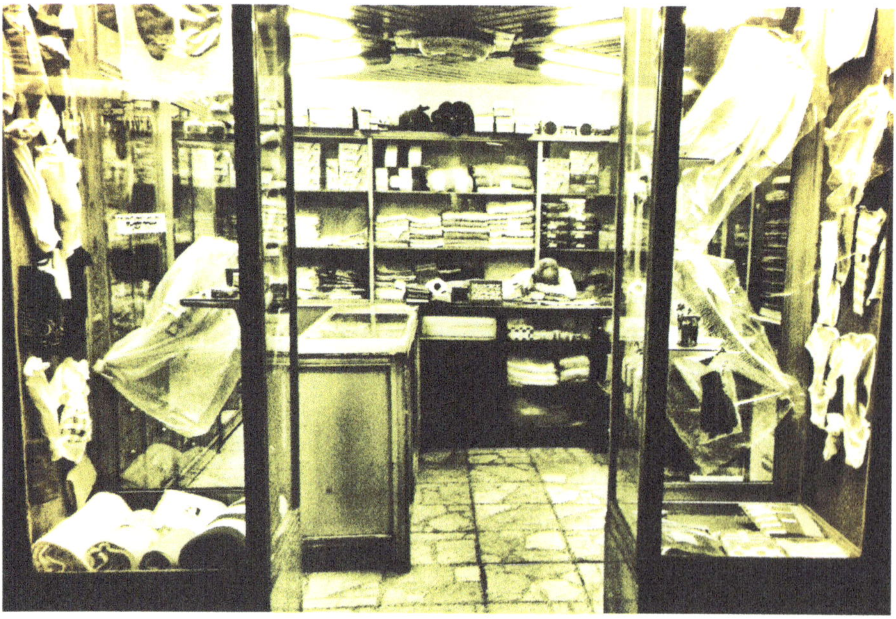

11 NOVEMBER 2013: SLOW TODAY

There are many brightly illuminated window displays in Downtown Cairo and other areas like Mohandessin and Maadi. Rows of them dazzle shoppers with a high-voltage glare. It's as if the shops are plugged directly into the power supply of the Aswan Dam. But not in the stretch just off 26 July Street in Zamalek where this one is located. Many here are unchanged in decades and cater for the vast array of local daily needs from lingerie and aspirins to dustpans and sofas with a traditional style of personalised service.

Trade is slow and many of the predominantly male shop attendants stare into the distance or fall asleep at their counters as they wait for a customer. Others sit on low chairs and run prayer beads through their fingers. Tinny transistor radios or snowy-screened portable TVs, squeezed between bags of beans or bolts of cloth, provide some distraction. Boys from the local coffee shops, often the size of cupboards, deliver small glasses of sweet tea or Turkish coffee and provide a little social interaction.

Several shop owners are pavement proud, as much as you can be in the dusty conditions, and have done up their small stretch with smooth concrete slabs or marble. The more energetic spill buckets of soapy water on them and push or pull the black slops to the road side with hard rubber strips attached to the end of poles.

The problem is that the proprietors don't discuss their pavement plans with their neighbours or consider what has already been laid next door. No two adjoining sections ever share the same appearance or level, requiring the shopper to be as focused as a jump jockey or they will sprain an ankle.

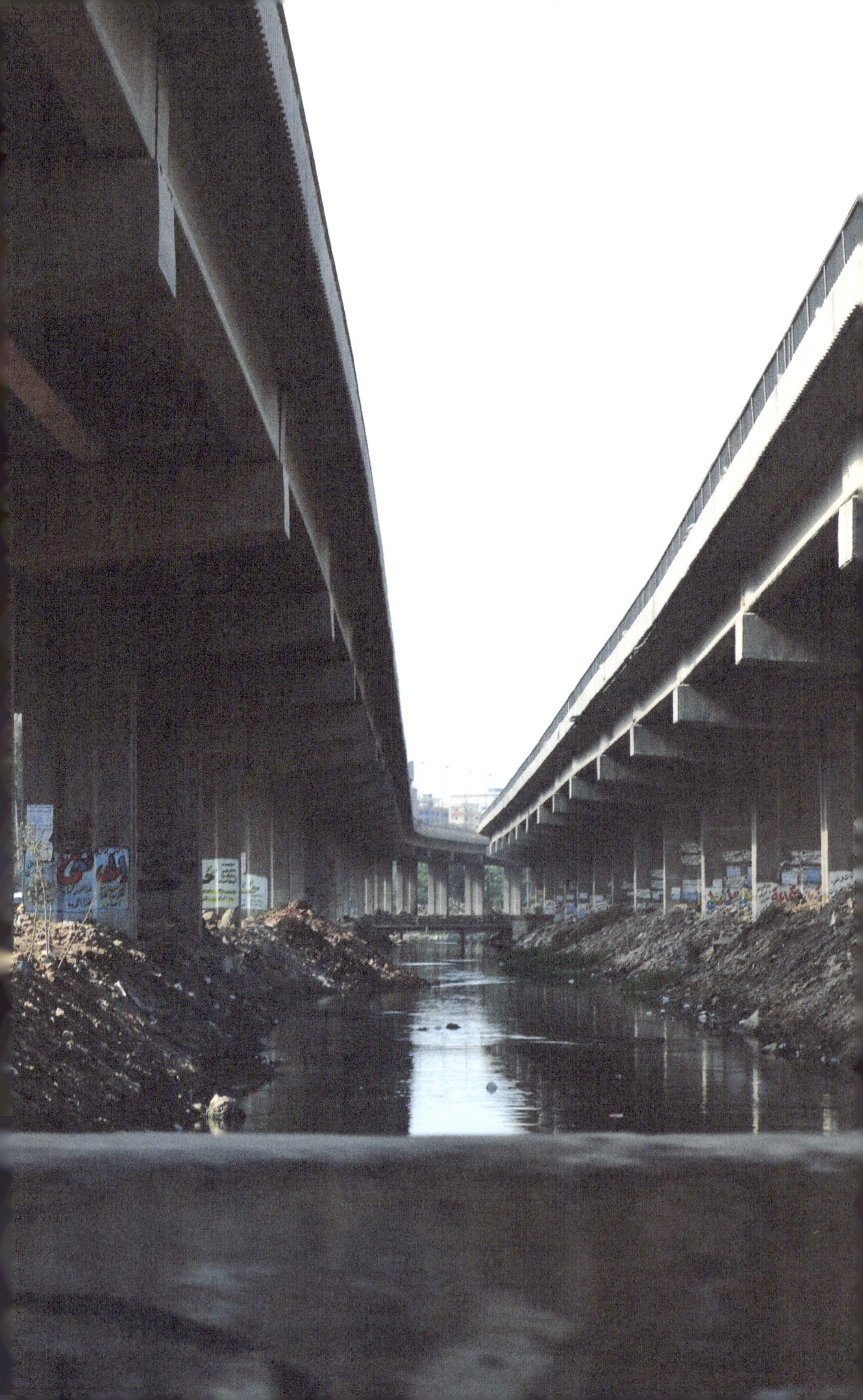

12 NOVEMBER 2013: INFRASTRUCTURE CHANGES

I had lunch with an Alexandria-born investment fund manager in an upmarket Cairo restaurant today, two tables away from the Egyptian finance minister. The table in between was occupied by four security officers recognisable by the white curly communication cables running down their necks into their black jackets. Oh, and they weren't eating.

The conversation at my table turned to the economy. I asked if the recently announced inward investments in technology and food manufacturing, along with the Saudi bail-out and the increase in national reserves from thirteen billion to nineteen billion Egyptian pounds, signified the emergence of a papyrus shoot or two of economic improvement.

'Not a bit of it,' my companion answered in his direct manner, born of his years of study in the US. 'Look, there will always be exports and imports, and foreign countries lining up to invest, especially those with the petrodollar, but unless there are deep infrastructural changes, no hope.'

'Like what?'

'Like cutting the subsidies across the board, and that means food and fuel prices going up for the whole population. And putting up taxes. You know, don't you, that no one pays taxes here? Why would they? No one comes and knocks on your door if you don't pay. There's no developed sense of responsibility as in the West.'

'And what about democracy?'

'Democracy! No chance.'

'Why not?'

'Because no one can read. How are you going to get people to understand anything if they're not educated?'

'So, there's a lot riding on the choice of the next president and his government . . .'

'Yes, but what politician is going to cut subsidies and put up taxes? No one. That's why you need a strong man like General Sisi in charge.'

This last remark was loud enough for the finance minister to hear. The intercoms crackled.

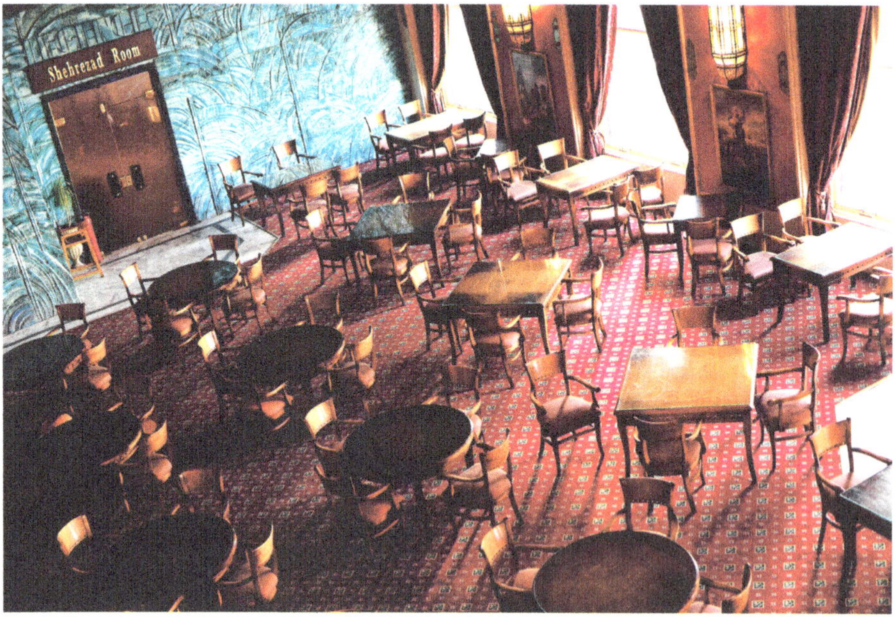
Shehrezad Room

13 NOVEMBER 2013: IS THERE ANYBODY THERE?

I've given myself the day completely off, no work whatsoever, not even a peek at the emails, but there are still essentials to deal with before I leave the apartment. I fix Shona's suddenly cancelled access to her email account, put her jewellery into a locked cupboard out of sight of the cleaning lady and sort out clothes for the laundry. I'm on the local square by 9.45 am in search of a driver and feel that surge of excitement of being about to explore a still-foreign city.

'Was Shepheard's Hotel burned down during the 1952 revolution?' I ask the bagel-eating Youssef, who's behind the wheel again today.

'Yes, yes, but it's back . . . the outside's the same, the inside's modern.'

'Really?'

'Do you want to go?'

'Sure, let's do it!'

The stimulus around visiting Shepheard's Hotel is the British Remembrance Day two days ago. I had recalled how Cairo was the centre of operations for the Allied campaigns of the Western Desert in the Second World War and thought it must be marked somewhere. On 11 November itself, I went to the Anglican All Saints Cathedral. The compound and refugee centre were open but the church building was closed. I tried without success to find someone with a key to the sanctuary to check if there was a war memorial inside.

I researched the headquarter locations for the British Army. There were two, one in the old Semiramis Hotel and the other in an apartment block in The Garden City. The former certainly doesn't exist; it's now the multi-storey Intercontinental Hotel. The latter would be too hard to find without a specific address. The bars of the Continental Hotel and Shepheard's Hotel were reported to be great meeting places, but the first is derelict and the second burned down . . . or so I thought before I spoke to Youssef.

Shepheard's was the first of the world's fabled luxury hotels. It established the template for the Savoy in London, the Waldorf Astoria in New York and the Ritz in Paris. If you remember the scene from the film *Lawrence of Arabia*, when the title character played by Peter O'Toole sweeps into a hotel bar in Cairo in search of an ice-cold beer, it was Shepheard's he entered.

Everybody who was anybody came here . . . Lawrence Durrell, Evelyn Waugh, Mark Twain, the explorer Richard Burton, Noel Coward, Douglas Fairbanks, Mary Pickford and so on, before the war brought Generals Wavell, Auchinleck and Montgomery, plus Winston Churchill and my personal hero Major David Stirling of the Special Air Service. My research also unearthed a photo of the legendary terrace of Shepheard's during the war.

I stand above its modern re-incarnation, which is in an ugly new building, built on the very same spot a stone's throw from the Nile in one direction and two stone's throws from Tahrir Square in the other. Before the original Shepheard's, it was the site of Napoleon's Egyptian HQ.

The bar's empty apart from the sound of a vacuum cleaner. I take a few shots from different angles and heights and then throw out a plaintive enquiry, 'Is there anybody there?' It's met with silence; even the cleaner has moved on. 'Tell them I came, and no one answered. That I kept my word,' I said. It's a small way to remember the efforts and sacrifices of those who fought in all theatres of war to preserve the freedoms we enjoy today, including North Africa where the battles of Tobruk and El Alamein took place.

Later I visit Old Cairo, entering a church, synagogue and mosque located within the same square kilometre. All have the same primary building materials of bricks, stone and mortar, and all are inhabited by mammal bipeds – Homo sapiens is the species, I believe – with an average height of five feet seven inches, brown-olive skin and producing the same language. There must be something in the air, then, that makes each group here and around the world want to beat the hell out of the others as they have done for centuries and centuries. But even the air smells the same.

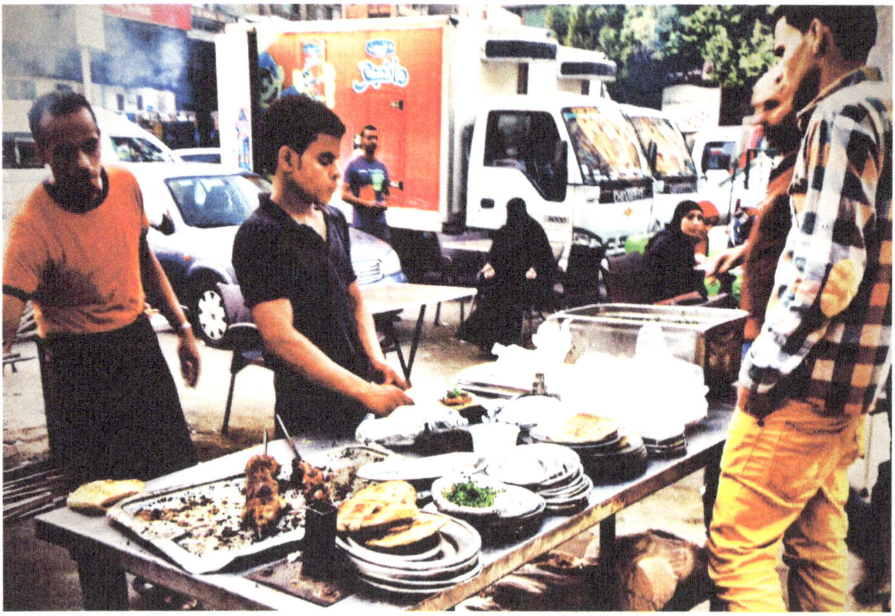

14 NOVEMBER 2013: GET INTO THE KITCHEN

Sheref, an unemployed Arabic teacher, is behind the wheel beside me today. He's in full flow. 'Egypt doesn't need a special man. It's not that hard. We just need a decent man, different from the bad gentleman who was Mubarak and the bad ignoramus who is Mursi. Both of them thieved it all away. Egypt's a rich country. I'm not in the kitchen but the ingredients are all there . . . you just need to mix them up in the right way. We've got oil, we've got the Suez Canal, we've got monuments sitting all over the place. Some of the costs are very low . . . I mean, you put a statue in a glass case with a light bulb on it and that's it. People come along and pay to see it. The trick is to redistribute the money better and educate people. Until they're educated, I wouldn't even let them vote; the peasants in the countryside are too easily bought by the bribes of the Brotherhood.'

Sheref's theme of education and re-mixing ingredients was taken up by Iris Boutros, strategist and economist, writing in a column in the *Daily News Egypt*. She challenges her prosperous and educated countrymen to design a better education system. She asserts that the present system is well funded but performs very poorly because the spend is focused on the wrong areas; 'There are more administrators than teachers,' she says.

She invites them to design a system from 'behind the veil' so that they are blind to the point where their own children or grandchildren will enter the system in the future. They may enter a school in a Nile Delta village or a school in an upmarket suburb of Cairo. The key is to ensure that all have the same prospects of gaining a great education. Only in this way, she argues, will an equitable distribution of resources and opportunity be achieved and social justice realised.

It was quite a challenge to get a photo to illustrate today's narrative but you'll see a veil in this street kitchen if you look closely.

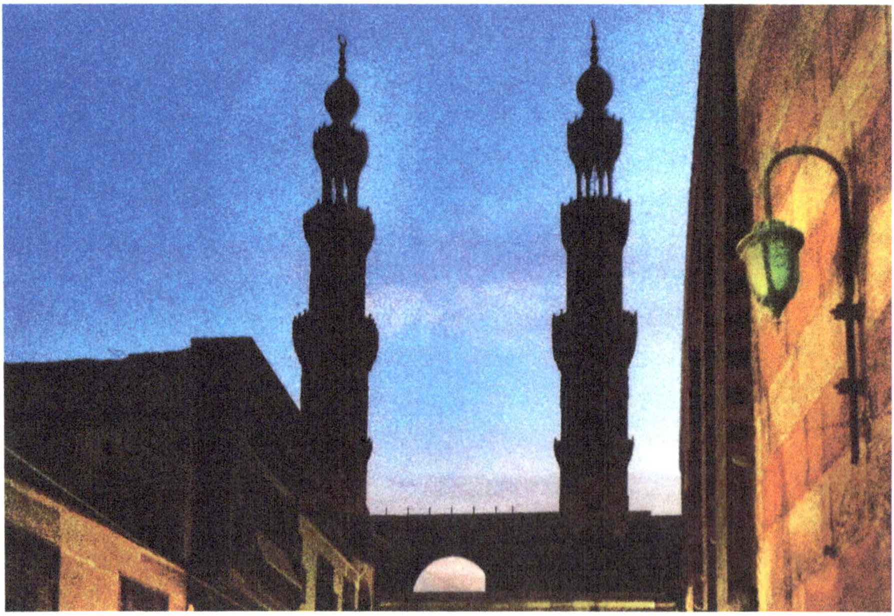

16 NOVEMBER 2013: A WALK IN CAIRO AT DUSK

It's one of those walks that you know you'll remember for a long time. Your path serpentines through a world that's not yours and every step brings impacts that assail all of your senses at once . . . flashes of fuchsia, the wail of the call to prayer, the pungency of rabbit cages, the cool brush of cotton galabeyas against your leg, and the piquancy of spicy chicken liver.

Although the way is narrow and winding and crowded, there are a number of highways that operate simultaneously, each with express deliveries in progress. There's the ground-level highway where porters rush cotton bales to their destination and threaten to skin your ankles with their trollies' sharp edges. At chest height, another highway is reserved for silver trays full of glasses of hot sweet tea or cool sugar-cane juice that pitch dangerously as their bearers strive to keep their cargos on board. The head-level highway is for trellises, piled with rondals of bread or marrow-shaped sponges, which career along and threaten to poke your eye out.

You walk past the colourful stalls of bra vendors, tahini sellers, juice pressers, cheese makers, fishmongers, bakers and butchers. The tent-makers pull reams of patterned cloth through their sewing machines, which chatter like old women. Fez-makers form their trademark red-felt hats on the brass moulds of their heavy presses positioned over blazing fires in the cast-iron furnaces below.

You're greeted with 'Welcome to Egypt!', 'Hi! Come in!' and 'Where're you from?' An old man, blind in one eye, won't take no for an answer as he leads you by the hand into an ancient mosque. He indicates for you to slip your shoes off at the threshold and wraps your wife in a prayer shawl to cover her head. His hands point out all the things he wants you to look at from the carpets to the carvings in the ceiling overhead and then cup, conveniently, for a five-pound note to be dropped into them.

Rising above the hubbub of shouting and shooing and tooting and clucking, magnificent minaret after minaret stand sentinel in silence, somehow giving you reassurance and confidence for the way ahead, as they have done for so many for so long.

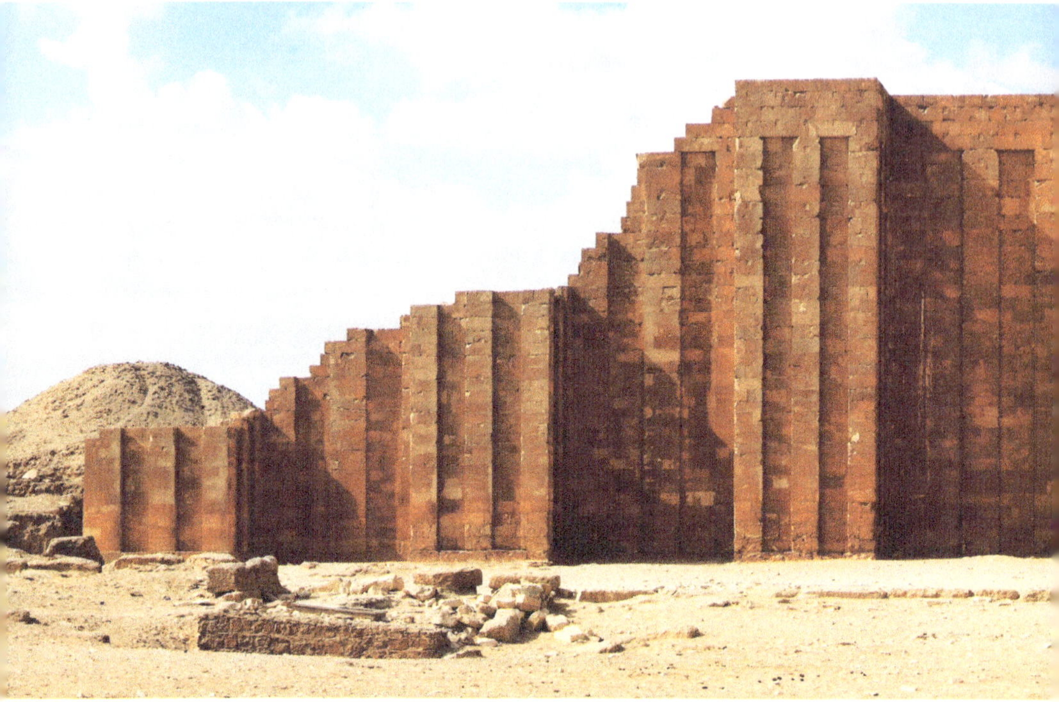

17 NOVEMBER 2013: SAQQARA

Today we visited the stepped pyramid of Saqqara, pronounced Sa'ara, given its glottal stop, about forty minutes' drive through open fields to the south of Cairo. It felt like a visit to a ghost town, open and sparse with very pale fine sand underfoot. The pyramid is made of equally pale sandstone.

There were no other tourists whatsoever, and ten stray dogs came running to our driver, who knew them from before and had brought bread to feed them. There was the usual attempt to sell us souvenirs by a few men holding their goods in their hands.

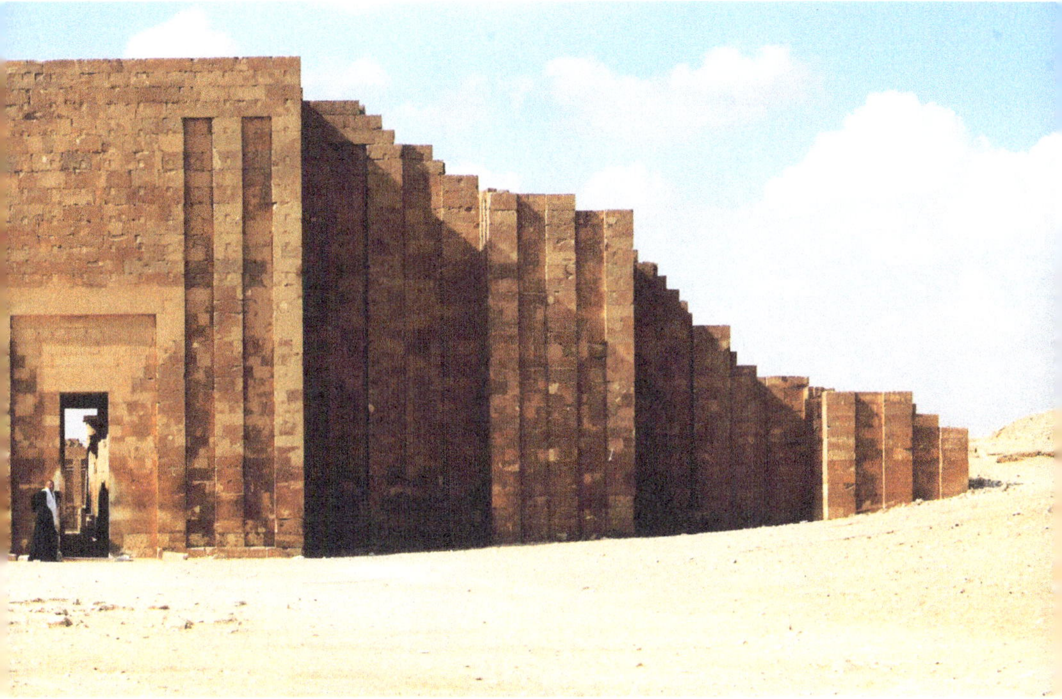

The photo above shows the funerary complex of Djoser. The nearby Saqqara pyramid itself was half covered by a wooden scaffolding that made it look like a giant prospector's mine from the Wild West, but there was no sign of activity. The sun hid behind clouds turning everything an ash colour, but then would burst through to highlight at least twelve other pyramids on the horizon. It seemed like the land of the dead and that's no surprise given that its original function was to serve as a burial ground for the ancient Egyptian capital of Memphis.

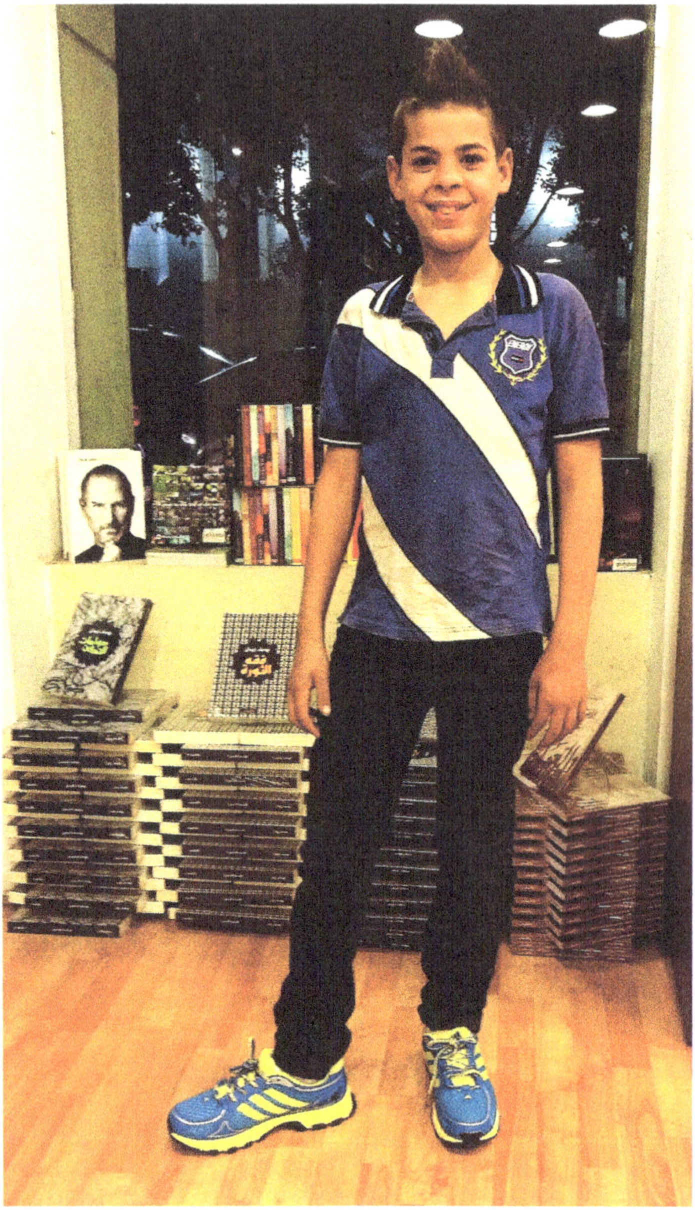

18 NOVEMBER 2013: HAPPY YASHEEN

Here's Yasheen / Hasim our Cairo street-kid friend resplendent in the new Adidas training shoes that we've just presented to him. As soon as he saw us, he quickly put down his bunches of flowers and darted across the street. I`m sure he knew we had something for him, especially after Shona managed to pin him down the other week to measure his feet.

His face lit up as he opened the box and pulled out this flashy pair, which are as near to mine in appearance as we could find. Christmas had certainly come early to the streets of Cairo today.

It seems silly, but we were relieved that Hasim knew how to put on socks, as his feet don't look as if they have often been covered, and he made a decent hand of tying his shoelaces. I helped pull the shoe-tongues up and pressed down on his big toes to gauge how much room there was; couldn't have been better. We had brought insteps in case the shoes were too big but Shona's prudence in insisting on a physical measuring paid off handsomely. He was up and literally running on the spot.

He and I dodged into the nearby bookshop to borrow their light and grab a few photos before we were both thrown out as undesirables. A few handshakes and hair ruffles later, he was off, running back to his pals but not before he had checked if we would top up the account we run for him at the internet café where we first met. A smart kid.

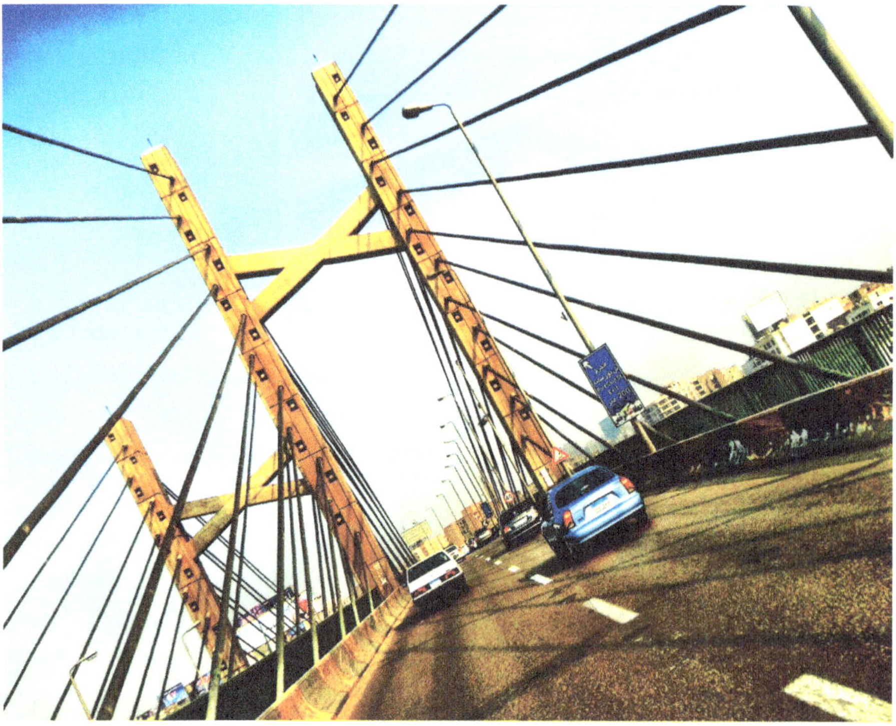

19 NOVEMBER 2013: BOOKEND BRIDGE

I photographed this same bridge when we arrived five weeks ago so these bridge shots act as bookends to this visit. As I type seated in the front seat of the car, I reflect that we arrived in a time of great uncertainty. There had been a new bout of killings in the immediate lead-up to our arrival and a strictly enforced curfew was in place, with the city full of checkpoints and armoured vehicles at every strategic corner. Ex-President Mursi, who was 'elected democratically but ruled autocratically', as one commentator pithily put it, was due for trial and no one knew what the reaction of the Muslim Brotherhood would be. We weren't sure how foreigners, with or without cameras, would be received in the street, especially near the university area bordering Giza where we live and which was the scene of the deaths of many Brotherhood supporters as we slept in our beds down the road at the end of June. Then, we had witnessed Mursi's last hurrah on television one night and General Sisi's bienvenue the next, helicopters drowning out the noise of the streets as their rotors battered the air above our heads.

Now, I can report a relative calm. There's no obvious hostility or resentment as we walk the streets and our big cameras have been on show from time to time, too. The curfew has been withdrawn and relieved service providers from café owners to taxi drivers can work all the hours they need to pay their bills. The turf of the Tahrir Square roundabout is still green but tanks continue to move into position around it every night at dusk, with barbed-wire barriers ready to be pulled quickly across every access road. The young soldiers on top keep their fingers tightly on their triggers.

There's still not a tourist to be seen in the bazaars or the mosques or out in the valleys and plains of the dead where the pyramids stand. The microbuses continue to overflow with commuters, daily income for the average citizen remains pitiful, and throngs of people scavenge on the great rubbish tips of Mother Cairo, headscarves pulled tight over nostrils to keep out the stench of Cairo's detritus.

The people in general are very happy with political developments, a draft constitution will be presented before the end of the year and much clamouring will take place. Some will vote and many will still not have learned how to. Mursi will come back to the courthouse and be tried and found guilty of something, probably murder. It looks like mass protests will be banned and people who support the Muslim Brotherhood or similar groups will be pushed underground. Radical fundamentalist elements will turn to violence to pursue their aims. Bombs will go off in the metro system and policemen will be shot dead on guard duty.

Life in Cairo will continue as it has and always will. Must close now – we've arrived at the terminal.

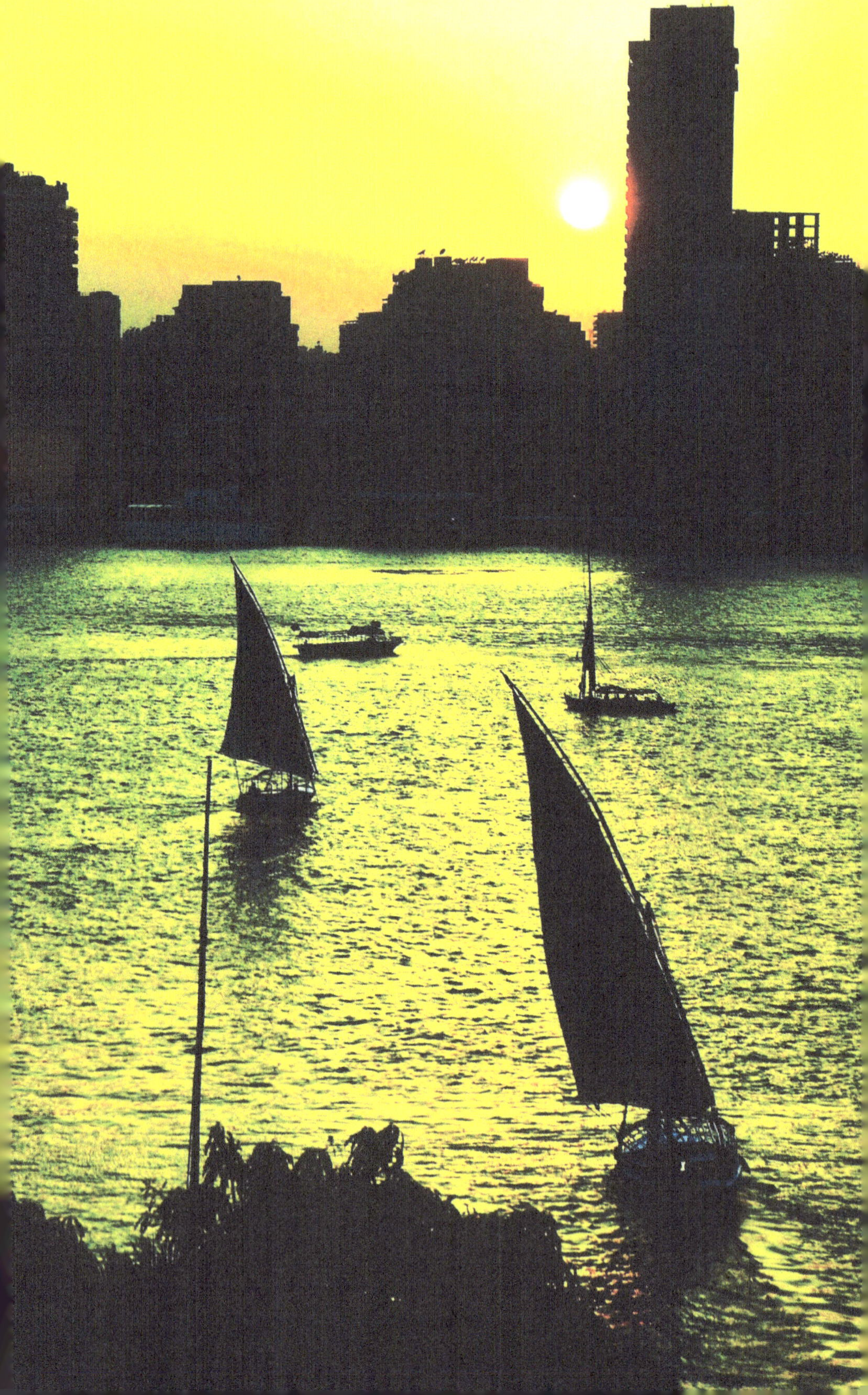

Chapter 8

The Strong Man

25 APRIL 2014: THE NILE AT DUSK

I've never seen Cairo looking as good as it did today when our plane banked over Gezira Island in the golden hour before sunset. The buildings around Tahrir Square stood out like ingots and appeared to form a guard of honour, while the Egyptian Museum housing the treasures of Tutankhamen bordered the scene with its cherub-pink walls.

During the drive through dusk to Downtown with the windows lowered, the warm air fluttered under my linen shirt and around my torso as I sat with my elbow out of the window. From the radio came the swooping wails of a string section accompanying an Egyptian singer that conjured all the passions of this place into our cabin.

There is nothing finer than the Nile at dusk. Egypt's very existence amid a vast desert is the result of its life-giving qualities. It hasn't all happened naturally without the hard toil of the country's people through the millennia. They worked under a strong sun to dig the irrigation channels and man the water wheels that lift and carry the Nile's lifeblood to the corner of every field. Egypt came into being and is sustained through the cumulative efforts and constant tending of its people.

It's now over nine months since Mursi was ousted. Interim President Mansour oversaw the clearance of the Islamist protest camps at a huge cost in human life last August, imposed a three-month state of emergency, complete with curfew, which expired in October, replaced it with a new Protest Law banning all demonstrations and assemblies without prior permission in November, designated the Muslim Brotherhood, which provided the country's last president, a terrorist group in December and brought in a revised constitution in January, which attracted controversy in its drafting process but, on the face of it, was well supported in the vote.

The constitution confirmed previously established civil rights including the equality of women, maintained Sharia law as the source of legislation but added that its interpretation be based in the relevant texts and collected rulings of the Supreme Constitutional Court rather than Sunni doctrines and the larger community. Military influence was extended by requiring the approval of the Supreme Council of the Armed Forces for the appointment of the defence minister.

The next milestone is the presidential election due next month. The favourite to win is former General Sisi, whose reputation as a strong man appeals to a significant section of the population. Let's hope he remembers that Egypt's existence depends on the individual contribution of every citizen, whose dignity needs to be honoured and rewarded.

It will be interesting to see how he prepares to take his place in the unending parade of presidents next month.

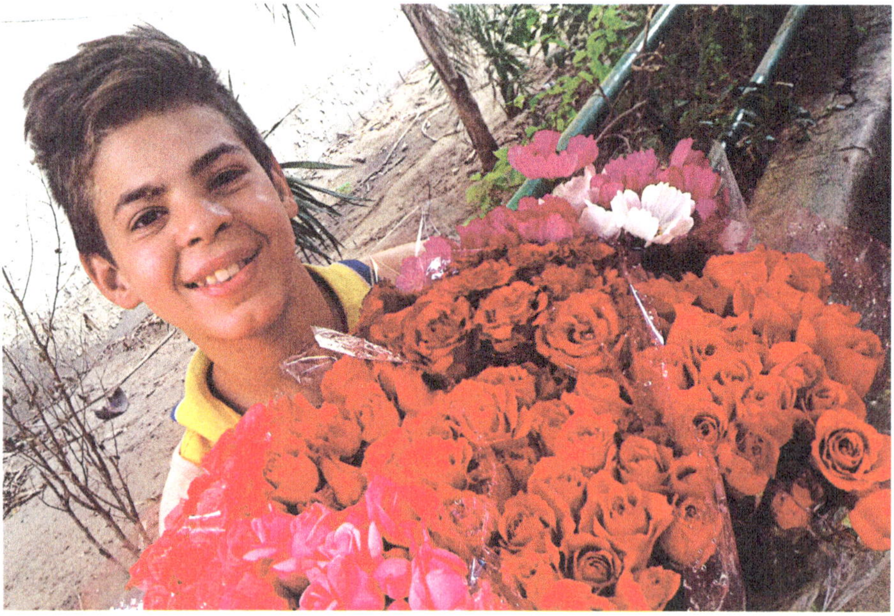

27 APRIL 2014: YASHEEN AGAIN

Yasheen/Hasim spots me first. He picks up his bunches of flowers and runs across the road towards me.

'Hello, Mister!'

'Hello, Hasim. Where are your shoes?' I point to his bare feet, my question clear. Gone, kaput, scuffed, ripped up, he conveys with a whole body's worth of language.

'What a shame!' I say, half wondering if they were sold the minute we turned our backs four months ago. We'll never know, but he isn't asking for another pair. He says something beyond my understanding, but points to my ring finger, which means he's talking about Shona.

'She's in Cairo but not in this area just now,' I say, motioning too.

'Tomorrow?' he asks in English.

'No, she can't make it tomorrow. Are you here every day?' I show him the calendar on my iPad mini.

He pulls my arm to take me across to the kiosk girl, who speaks English 'fifty-fifty' as she puts it. 'Most days,' she says.

Hasim's keen to know, and practise, saying our names. The girl tells us his father disappeared or died long ago. He lives with his mother and an older sister and a younger brother in a suburb somewhere. Yasheen screws his face up and twists his body away when I ask him why he doesn't go to school, but my mention of English seems to catch his attention. Shona and I have some ideas about this, but it'll take some more research.

He doesn't ask me to, but I buy two bunches of flowers, white lilies and large purple daisies, as Shona is keen to brighten up our flat. I manage to get across that Shona will be here for a while and we'll both see him soon.

He looks thinner, probably just losing some of his baby fat, but much more dirtily dressed than before, more like a kid living on the streets. There really isn't anything to him as I squeeze his shoulder as we say our goodbyes.

My Egyptian mobile bleeps. It's a text from Shona: 'Explosions in metro. So you know. Traffic will be worse maybe. Take care. Xx'

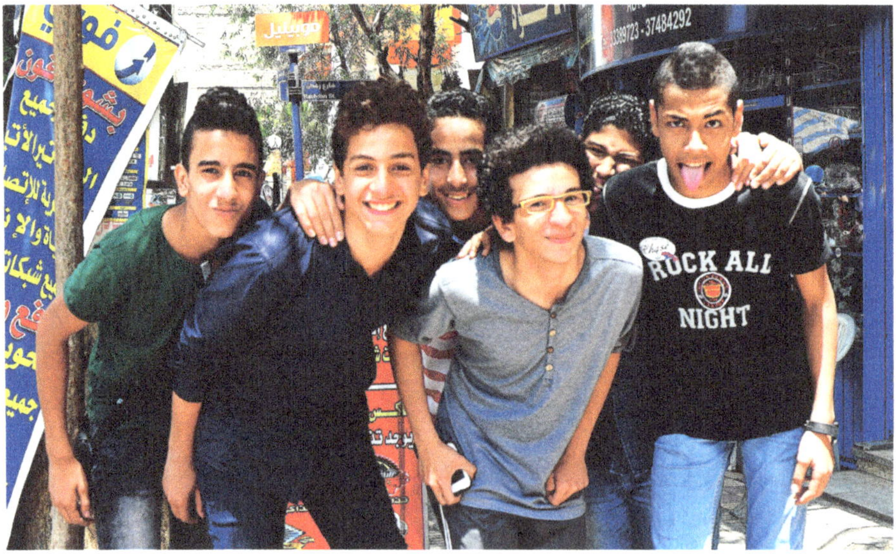
ROCK ALL
NIGHT

28 APRIL 2014: THE NEXT GENERATION

Here you see some of the next generation of Egyptians. These young men were fizzing with energy today on this busy thoroughfare near the University of Cairo when they insisted I take their photograph. I wonder what lies in store for them and if they will escape the oppression and persecution that every generation has suffered stretching back to pharaonic times. They belong to well-off families and are private-school educated, which may protect them, but not everyone is so lucky.

This morning a judge sentenced six hundred Muslim Brotherhood members to death after cursory and derisory trials. Four homosexuals are doing hard labour for their 'debauchery'. Many journalists face trial simply for exercising their profession. All this under the rule of Interim President Mansour, who presents a placid face in public. One can only speculate on what role General Sisi plays behind the scenes.

A primary duty of national leaders is to grow their country's prosperity and ensure it's shared equitably among the population. It's not to permit corrupt practices that concentrate the wealth of the nation in the hands of an elite to the detriment of the wider population. That way lies revolution.

Egypt is entering the third cycle of this kind in as many years. The people overthrew Mubarak for this behaviour, and Mursi too. It is an open question whether the Mansour–Sisi period will break the pattern. I wonder if any of these next-generation young men will in the future.

The one on the right with his tongue hanging out was the instigator of this photograph. Afterwards, he took time to ask me where I'm from, shake my hand, and thank me very sincerely. My money's on him.

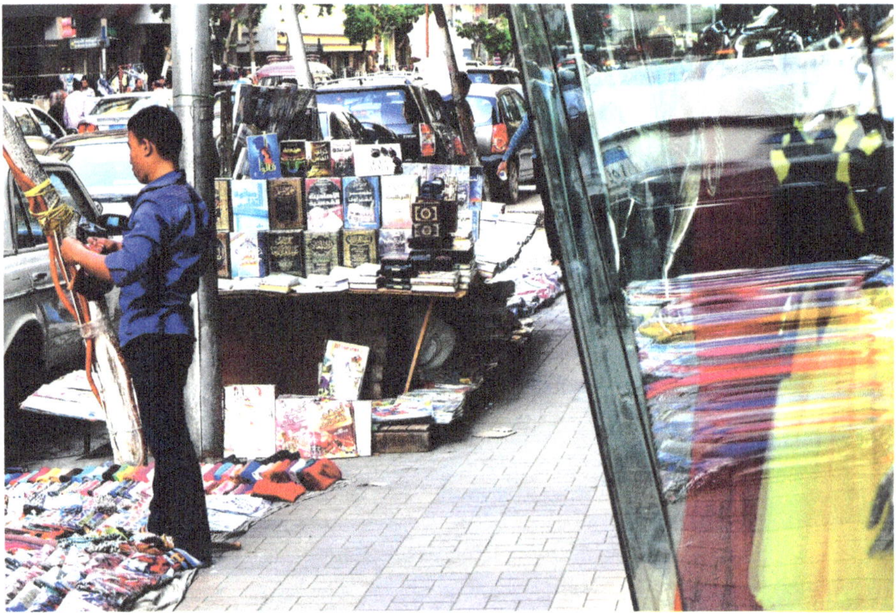

29 APRIL 2014: DOWNTOWN

There's still something grand about Downtown, Cairo. The European inheritance is evident in a mix of architecture that merges Regent Street, London, with Boulevard Haussmann in Paris. Now, thrown into the mix, we have the brash commerce of Argyll Street, Glasgow, seen in the gaudy window displays and cheap colourful goods hawked on the pavements. The Americanism Downtown appears on all the road signs and equates to the original Arabic for middle city. The name emerged when the Hollywood greats visited what was then the most glamorous destination this side of the Atlantic. They would be shocked to see it today, although there are signs of improvement.

At the end of Talaat Harb Street, Tahrir Square continues its rehabilitation as a giant roundabout with new bushes and painted kerbstones. The shell of the 1960s Hilton Hotel that backs onto Tahrir is finally, after years, showing progress in its refurbishment with glass in its upper-floor windows. The pedestrianised streets around the Stock Exchange, free of tanks at last, are decked colourfully with the red and yellow plastic chairs of the shisha cafés attracting the early-evening crowd. If you want a beer go to the secluded Kings Bar in the Cosmopolitan Hotel or the high roof terrace of the Odeon Hotel, although you will be accompanied by the ghosts of previous patrons rather than living people.

Dirt and decay still predominate. Outhouses in which servants slept on the rooftops of the elegant apartment buildings are crumbled and vacant. Faded portraits of performers of yesteryear curl in dusty glass cases in the hallway of the Bela Studios of Photography. Cats poke their heads into piles of garbage strewn in every alleyway off the main boulevards.

The mood is positive, though. Sisi, the next president for sure, gets an overwhelming thumbs-up from everyone I speak to: 'a good man', 'a strong man', 'a great man', 'just what we need'.

'Why?' I ask. Only one reason is given, and it's heartfelt . . .

'He got rid of Mursi.'

Let's see how long his honeymoon lasts or, put another way, how long Tahrir Square remains a roundabout before it's called into use again as the focal point of national salvation. Your guess is as good as mine.

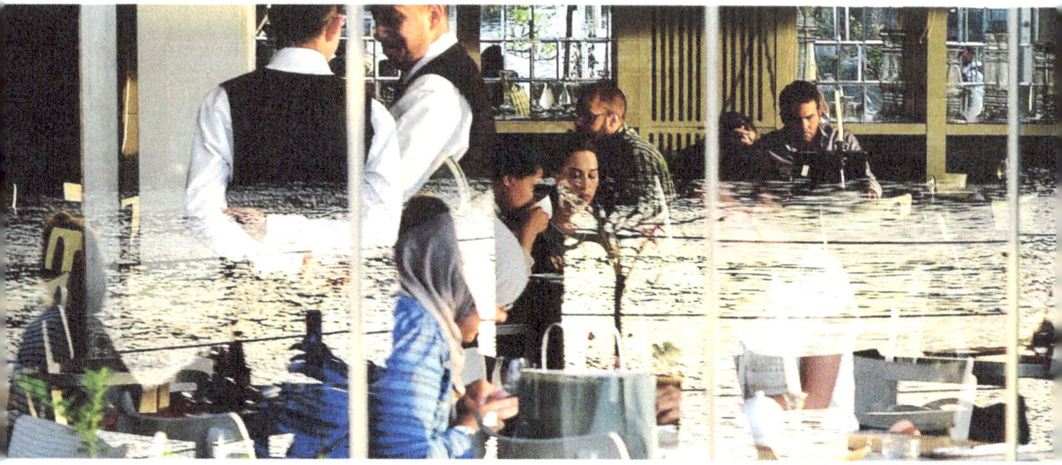

30 APRIL 2014: THE RIVER OF LIFE

The river, here, is the Nile at Cairo and the lifestyle is that enjoyed by the most affluent levels of Cairene society, including those who live in affluent areas like Maadi, where I went this evening to dine with Samir, a young lawyer. He arrives late, plumps his ample frame down on a cushioned dining chair and dabs his moist forehead with his handkerchief. He's grateful that Sisi saved the country from the overtly ideological and inept Muslim Brotherhood and delighted that the former general will take power next month. Samir puts a lot of faith in the people coming back onto the streets to overthrow Sisi were he to set off on an undemocratic frolic of his own like Mubarak or Mursi.

'In any case,' he says, putting down his glass of water, 'Sisi can only hold power for eight years and then has to give way under the constitution. We'll see what his economic programme is in a couple of days. The indications are that it will have a strong emphasis on grass-roots education and rebalancing wealth through higher taxation, which has already started. It's what we need, and I think the affluent are beginning to accept the sacrifice they have to make.'

Such faith in constitutions and the altruism of the rich, I think to myself.

Samir also shares some insights into the workings of the judicial system, which look very strange from outside of the country and which have brought strong international condemnation in recent days and weeks. He claims that there's method in the madness. He said that death sentences are passed en masse

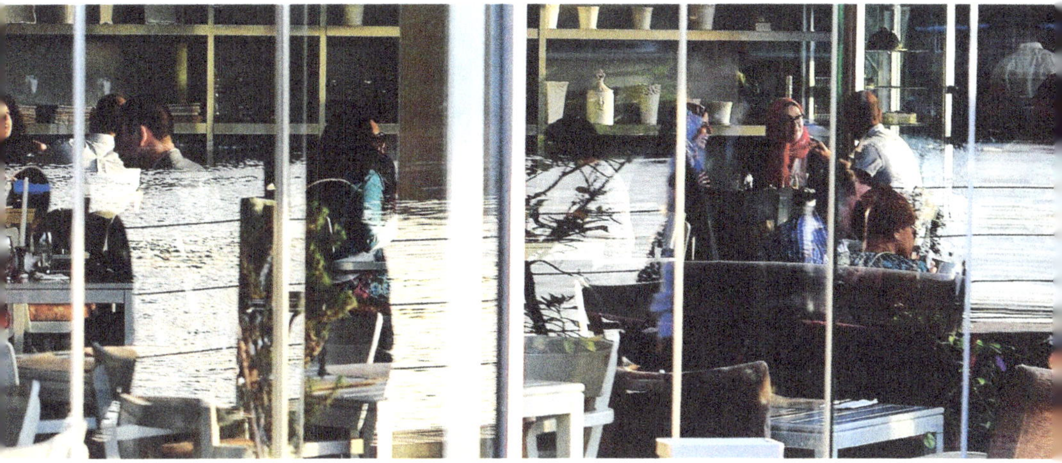

and in absentia when defendants fail to appear in court to defend themselves against the charges. The aim is to incentivise the accused to come forward and test their case fully. If their alleged involvement in the crime merits something less than capital punishment then their sentence will be reduced. The alternative is to live their life on the run under constant threat of arrest and hanging. I have a strong sense that even if the person does come forward their individual case is not fully examined and that a batch-processing approach is applied to multiple defendants with less than fair results.

Later, at home, I come across photographs equal in their barbarity to those of the injuries inflicted on the late Kahled Saeed, the young Alexandrian man who was murdered by police in the lead-up to the 25 January revolution. These latest photos show the lynching of a police chief allegedly by several of the accused in one of the recent high-profile murder cases. The sight of his near-naked and brutalised body being trailed round a town square on the end of a rope tied to the back of a motorbike with hundreds cheering was medieval in its horror.

There are clearly many twists and turns for this country to navigate in the coming months.

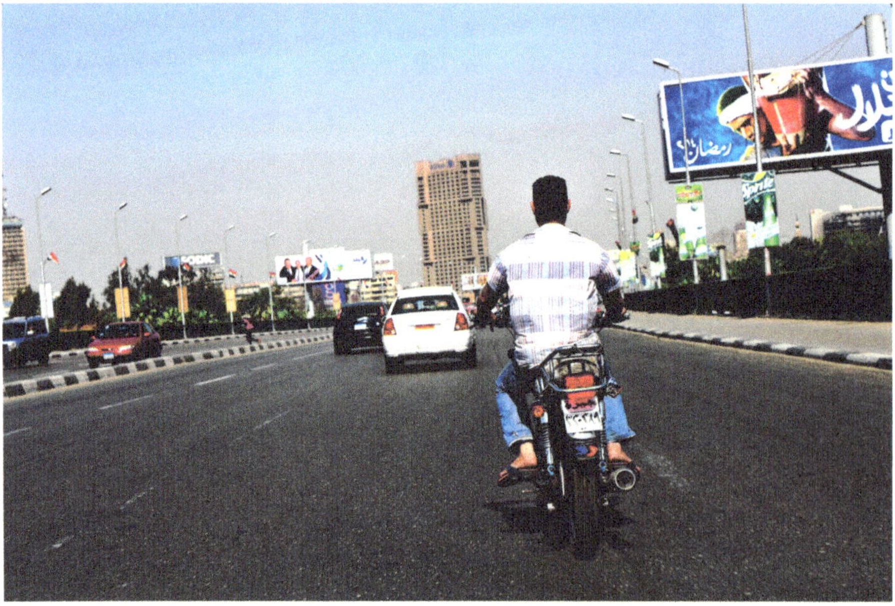
رمضان
Sprite

1 MAY 2014: ALL ROADS LEAD TO TAHRIR SQUARE

'So, why will a Sisi presidency be good for the country?' I ask my favourite question of the trip, this time to the retired father of one of my friends. He has handsome aquiline features and I can almost detect a genetic line that runs from pharaonic times to the present. He's invited me to his private club beside the Nile and dabs his Egyptian-cotton napkin against his trim, silver-grey moustache after taking a sip of mango juice. The humidity is high and large fans stir the air at our table in an attempt to alleviate the worst effects of the conditions.

'Because he's a Mubarak.' He sees my surprise. 'Not the Mubarak of the last twenty years, but the Mubarak of the first ten years.'

'And what did that one do?'

'It's not only *what* he did, like upgrading the telecommunication infrastructure. . . you may remember when you first visited in the early eighties that when you picked up a telephone nothing happened, no sound, no clicking, nothing . . . not even when you hit it.

'No, the thing is *who* he was. He came as a military man with great discipline and follow-through. He was on top of all his ministers, making sure the projects were executed. As Head of Army Intelligence he knew exactly what was going on, who was doing what, and what the security risks were, both external and internal.'

'Then what happened?'

'He got sucked in. He became corrupt and created an inner sanctum of men who controlled everything. It all stank. He was untouchable and wanted to make sure his son followed him into power.'

'What's to stop the same thing happening again?'

'The people.' He waved his hand, indicating those seated at the tables on the terrace. 'No one will put up with it again. Just as no one could put up with Mursi, although I'm surprised he went so early. You know, I voted for Mursi. I wanted away from the old regime and I'm glad I did. It gave the Muslim Brotherhood a chance to show what they could do after complaining for so long.'

'And what did they do?'

'They failed. They didn't know how to pick their fights. They went for everything and missed the big wins that would have united the people.'

'Like what?'

'Like the police. Everyone hated them. They ran amok under Mubarak; abusive and intimidating. If Mursi had reformed them everyone would have been delighted. Instead, he pampered them.'

'How many people are like you?'

'A lot. At lunch here last Saturday, we went round the table and shared who voted for Mursi last time and who'll do so for the Brotherhood again. Most people did vote for him last time, and now seven out of ten won't.'

'You are all very open about how you vote . . .'

'Yes, we're all interested in politics now – there was no point before – and happy to share our experiences. We're all learning . . . and one of the learnings is that we need a strong man like Sisi just now, disciplined and knowledgeable with a sense of the bigger picture. He's the head of our MI6, after all. His victory is foretold.'

'And after Sisi?'

'We'll organise proper political parties, and a new generation of young people, educated, interested and connected, will vote sensibly in a way that is not driven by ideology. We are ahead of our neighbours in the Middle East. The real Egyptian, whether Muslim or Christian, is not an extremist imposing medieval ways on others.'

'Are you optimistic, then?'

'Very.'

My shot today shows a motorcyclist on 6 October Bridge heading in the direction of Tahrir Square, which lies about six minutes further on, as many millions have done on key occasions over the last three years to ensure not only that their voice was heard but, crucially, that their will was followed. He, in all probability, would have been among those throngs of people who came out to topple firstly Mubarak and then Mursi.

Today our man on the back of the Cairo motorbike looks as if he is going on a simple errand, but the message also seems to be that the people know this road well, and are prepared to travel it again en masse, if necessary.

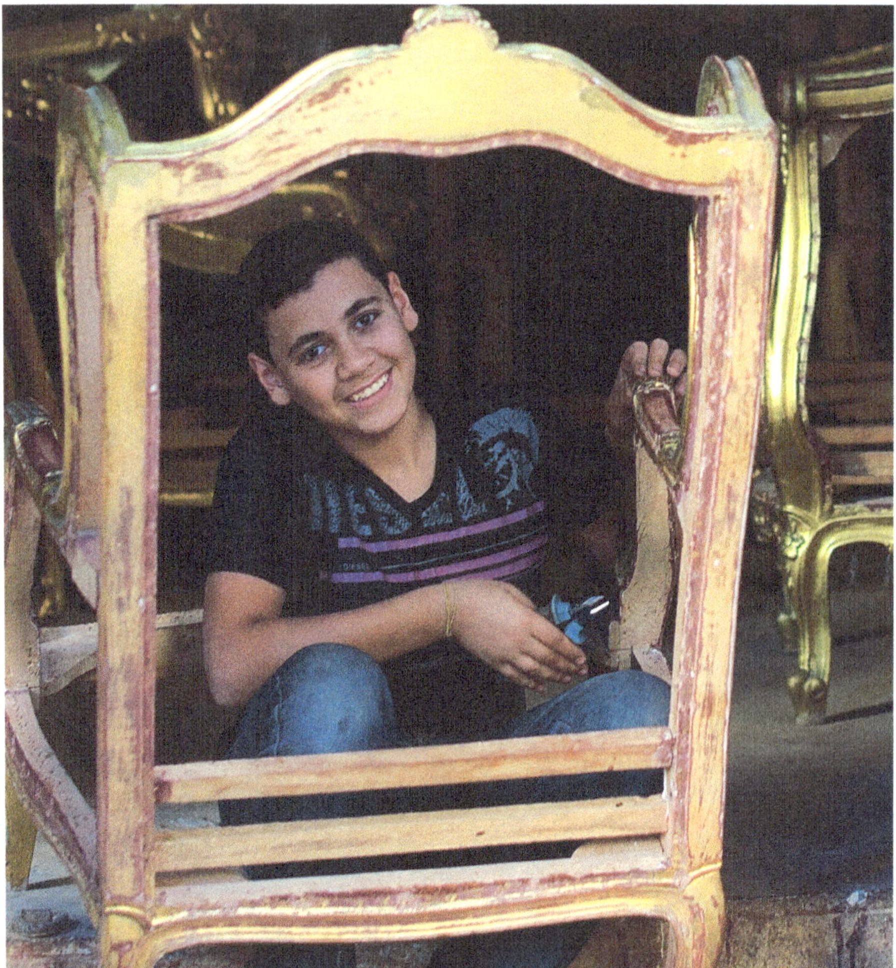

2 MAY 2014: FRIDAY, FRIDAY

It's been a quiet day around the Cairo block. Prayer day again, the first day of the weekend, and the streets are nearly empty of people and cars in our area. Shona spent all day in bed feeling unwell and I went out to get her some throat lozenges, passing a furniture workshop where this young lad was helping his grandfather.

Later, in the evening, I crossed the square by myself to get a bite to eat. It struck me how very quiet and calm it was. I can remember, in very recent times, the square full of big police vans. Black-uniformed men milled around on the street corners or lay across their vehicles' high roofs like panthers on branches. The sight always tightened our chests. Also, at the height of the Mursi troubles, how we timed our return to beat the curfew. There was no traffic but we would look left and right before walking briskly across the open square. Nearby Cairo University was the scene of many shootings and there was a risk that a fleeing gunman would coincide with us as we made the hundred-metre dash home.

Tonight nothing, just a few teenagers chatting on the street corners as they do everywhere, keen to be out of their homes and in each other's company.

It would be wrong to think that there's no risk though. There is an attempt against a policeman somewhere in the wider city area nearly every day and I've noticed that those guarding sensitive buildings make sure their bullet-proof-vested bodies are behind the heavy metal protective screens. The guards peer out over the top with their helmets securely on and their eyes follow you as you pass. They didn't do any of this with such assiduousness a few months ago. That's the problem with iron-fisted controls – you push the opposition underground and it bites you when you least expect it.

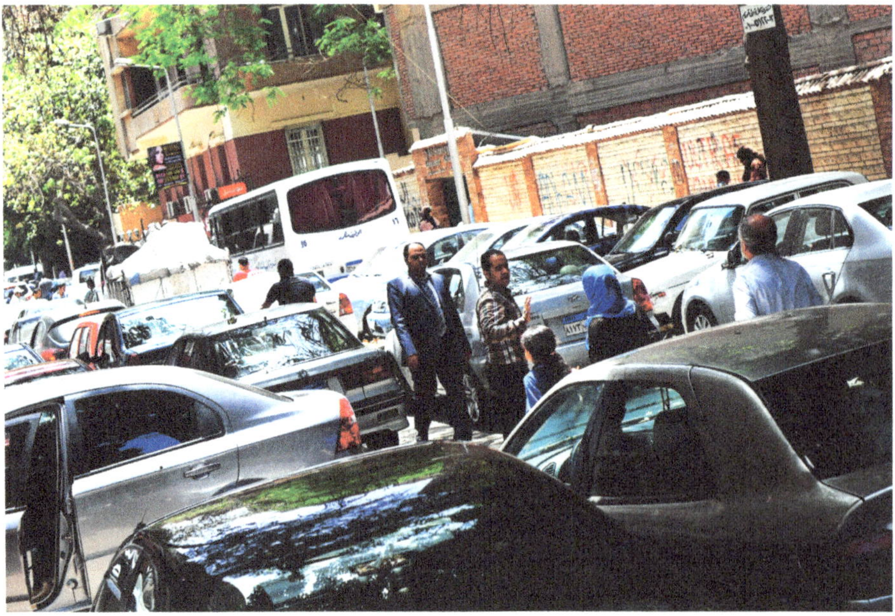

4 MAY 2014: MONDAY, MONDAY

Except it's Sunday, Sunday in the Middle East. Cars and people crowd the streets around the Cairo block on the first day of the week. It's worse today as all high-school students sit their biggest exam of the year. It's also oven hot today, touching 40°C!

I sat on the terrace of my usual coffee place and felt quite upbeat. The sun was out, the square animated, and everyone I've spoken to recently is hugely optimistic about the future of the country. Then I read the local press. After Syria and Iraq, Egypt is the country with the highest death rate among journalists in 2013. Over the weekend, two Mursi supporters were killed in Alexandria. Last Friday, five others were killed in various actions against the police in Cairo, including near the main Ramses railway station. Bail was denied the detained Al Jazeera journalists including the ex-BBC man, Peter Greste. One hundred and two people were sentenced to ten years-plus in prison for protesting last July when Mursi fell. Cairo University banned one hundred and seventy-three students from exams because of their protest activities. And so on, and so forth . . . not quite a settled peace then.

The presidential campaign also kicked off yesterday. I wonder how the two candidates will address these issues and what solutions they will propose.

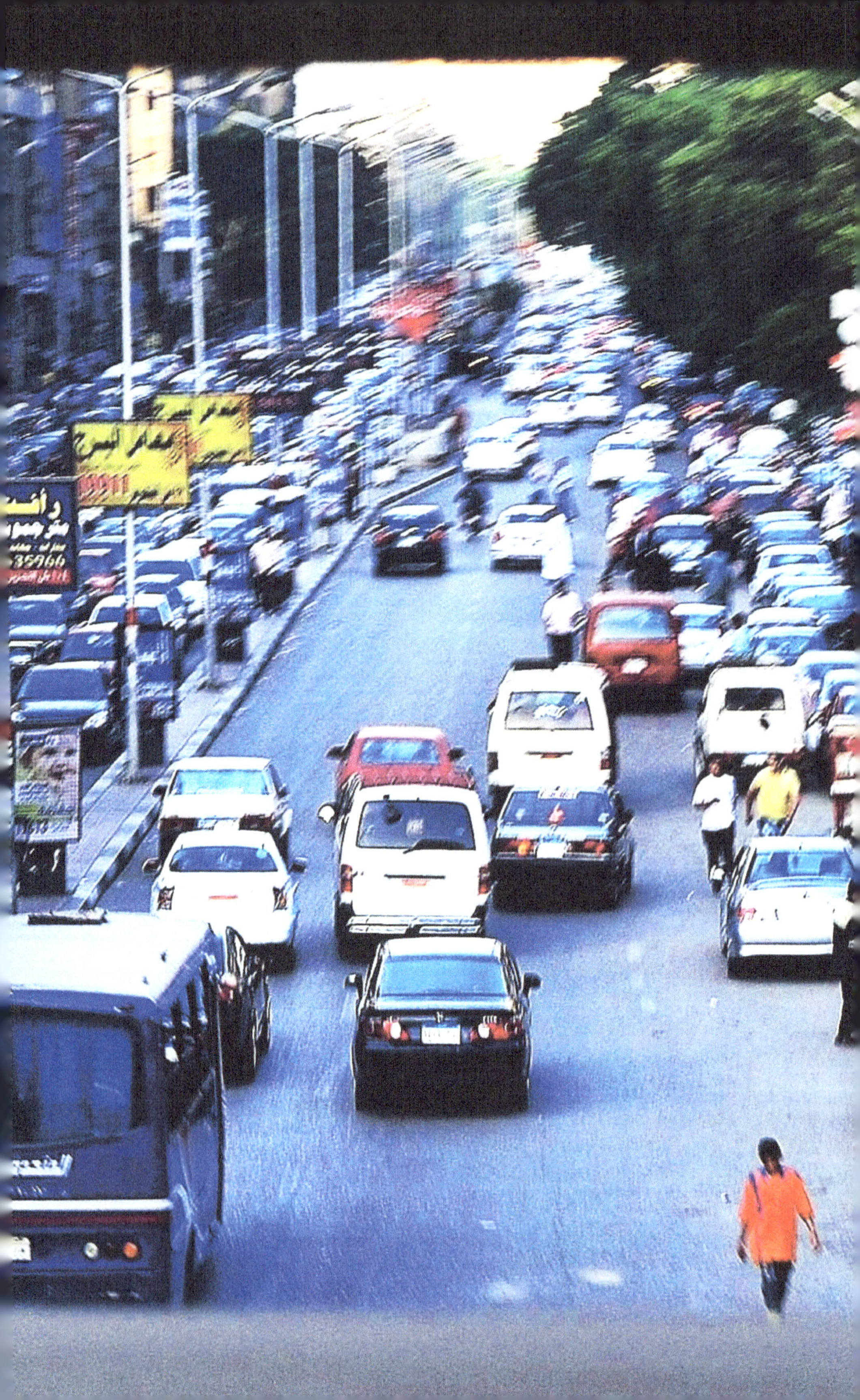

Chapter 9

The Parade Continues

18 MAY 2014: SISI FOR PRESIDENT

According to every prognosis, former General Sisi will be voted in overwhelmingly as president of Egypt in a week's time. The city bustles about its business as usual. Some billboards show Sisi dressed in an open-neck shirt and casual, beige-coloured sports jacket. He looks very relaxed and friendly. You could easily imagine having a glass of freshly squeezed guava juice with him in one of the private clubs on the banks of the Nile.

The army have provided the country's presidents for the last sixty years, apart from one year under Mursi, and it is little surprise that Sisi has put aside his uniform and presented himself in the coming election, confident in his standing as the country's saviour at the time of the coup last July. 'Just what we need!' encapsulates the popular sentiment among the older population, at least.

His path to the presidency looks straightforward. A number of factors help his cause. The Muslim Brotherhood is banned as a terrorist organisation. Only one other candidate, Hamoud Sabahy, has come forward but his standing with the young is not strong. Sabahy's a veteran politician who leans left in his views but, for some, carries political baggage such as his life-long support for the policies of the late President Nasser, one of the instigators of the 1952 military coup.

The liberal post-revolutionaries continue with a fragmented leadership unable or unwilling to put forward a candidate of their own. This reluctance to enter into the world of realpolitik will cost them. Democracy has to be learned first through the ballot box and then in the consensus building that follows. The line between idealism and political naivety is a fine one.

If ever there was a time for a young, civilian, engaging figure capable of uniting parties around the revolution's core aims of bread, freedom and social justice to step forward, then this is it.

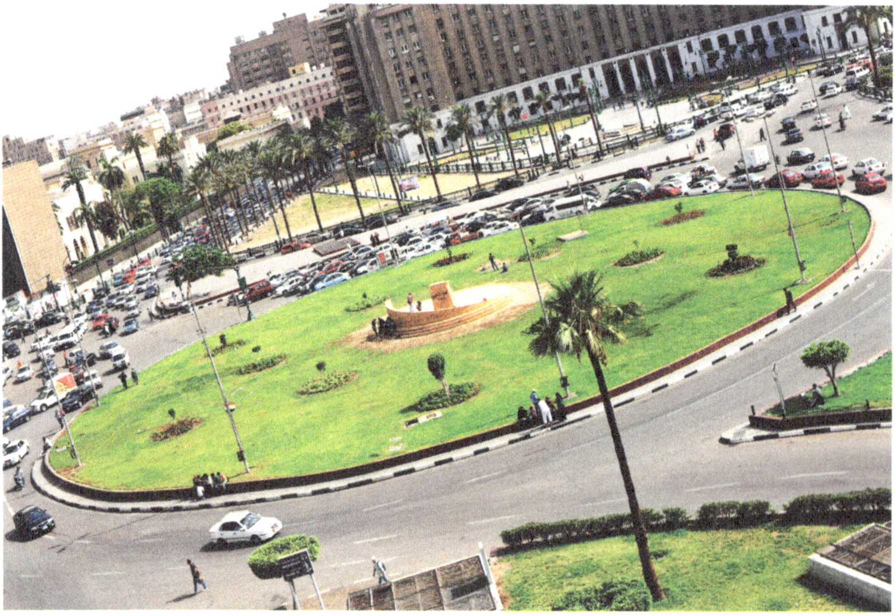

19 MAY 2014: TAHRIR REVISITED

'Where you go, sir?'

'The School . . .' I pause to steady my breathing, '. . . of Arabic.'

'Not far now . . . you're half way up!'

To be half way up is better than being all the way down, and that seemed to be my fate today as I tried without success to get past three doormen in my attempt to ascend a building, any building, overlooking Tahrir Square.

When I do get to the eighth floor of this one, flooded with light and crowded with dusty plants like a tiny oasis, I discover the language school is at the back of the building and there's no point going in. An old man inside sees me and comes out.

'What you looking for? Classes?'

'No, a photo of the square.'

'Why?'

'I'm interested in the election next week . . . and Sisi.'

'Ah, General Sisi!'

'Sisi, good?' I ask. I make a thumbs-up sign and rotate it down and back up.

'Sisi, not good.' He grins widely. 'Sisi, *excellent*!' His eyes sparkle as he sees I'm thrown for a second.

'Why?' I recover.

'We're like . . . what do you call a ship going under the water?'

'Sinking.'

'Yes, sinking . . . and here comes a man to . . .' He moves his hands as if raising a bucket from a well on the end of a rope.

'. . . to pull you up.'

'Yes, a great man. What we need.' He looks at my camera again.

'Your photo is downstairs at the accountant's.'

The young man at the front desk nods, signals me to follow him, and pulls aside a stack of chairs. He pushes open white-painted shutters and leads me onto a sunlit balcony. He raises his eyebrows.

'Perfect,' I say. I have the 50 mm lens on the camera and it feels right to use its very human width of vision for this place of courage and sacrifice. I try a few angles – there aren't many possible – leaning out and standing back as much as the space allows, and check and double check the aperture, speed, ISO, exposure and focus, as I don't fancy climbing the stairs again if I get it wrong.

That'll do, I think, before pausing to take in fully the scene below and the changes I've seen in it. The raised orbital walkway I walked round everyday many years ago has disappeared. The white Bedouin-like tents and tarpaulins from the summer of 2011, when the square was a hot bed of revolutionaries, are gone. The army have withdrawn the tanks that were ever present last year but the barbed-wire barricades still stand ready to be drawn across the entrances to the radial roads at a moment's notice. A new memorial, already daubed with graffiti, sits in the centre of the re-turfed roundabout edged by its pristine, newly painted black-and-white kerbstones. Traffic circulates peacefully on this May afternoon in 2014 as if the epicentre of the Arab Spring had never been here. It's hard to imagine the deadly mounted charges of the police – some on camels – or the stone-throwing ripostes of the various bands of brothers who fought ferociously to fulfil their hopes.

'You liked?' says the young man, as I step back into the office and close the shutters.

'Yes. Thank you. It's different from last year with Mursi, isn't it?'

'Yes, different, but Sisi is also no good.'

'Why?'

'You can't trust him. It's all, "The people asked me to do this." He's just manipulating us, taking power like Mubarak did . . . for himself. He cries crocodile tears on TV, talking in his soft voice, and comes up with things that won't work.'

'Like what?'

'Like his solution to the energy crisis. He says people, the poor people that is, should buy energy-saving bulbs! How can they afford them?'

'So, are you voting for the other guy?'

'I'm not voting for anyone. There's no one worth it, no one to trust.'

I had been up, but after many turns of the staircase descending into the gloom I'm very much down again. Opinions are divided about whether Egypt is up, down or neither up nor down. Time will tell very quickly who will lead it and in what direction.

Now, as I write in Café Riche, Sisi is on TV being interviewed live. His voice is deep and velvety and his hand movements assured as he makes his points with considerable ease and considered emphasis. He brooks no interruptions, his right hand sometimes resorting to the pointed finger. Three interviewers are ranged in front of him, including one woman. All appear overly respectful, allowing him to flow like the Nile in flood. The woman's eyes are slightly glazed over, and the man to her left twirls his pen nervously when he asks a question. There's no sign of the BBC's Jeremy Paxman's persistent and challenging interviewing technique here. But I don't speak the language. Maybe I should have asked for classes in The School of Arabic.

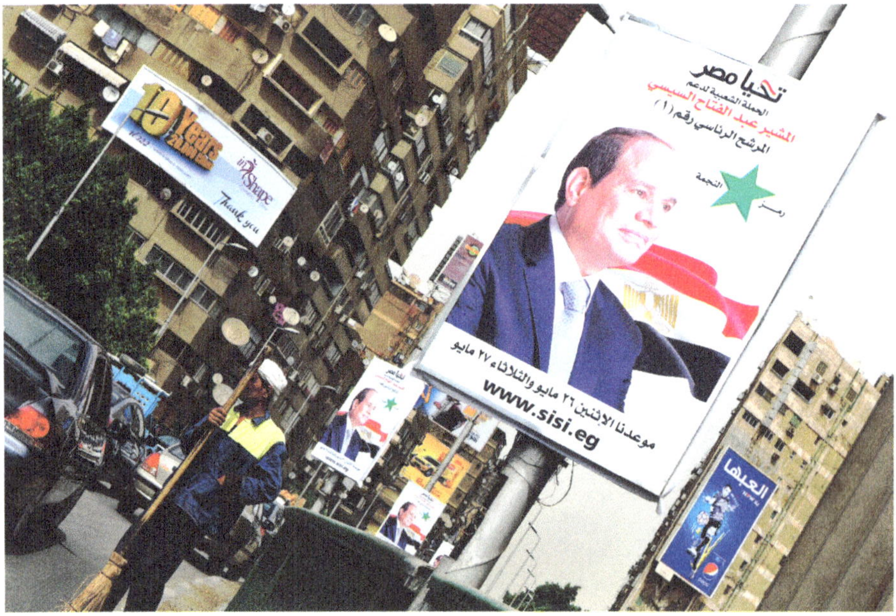
10 Years
in Shape
Thank you
تحيا مصر
الحملة الشعبية لدعم
المشير عبد الفتاح السيسي
المرشح الرئاسي رقم (١)
رمز
النجمة
موعدنا الإثنين ٢٦ مايو والثلاثاء ٢٧ مايو
www.sisi.eg
العبها

20 MAY 2014: MIXED MESSAGES

The election is close now. Candidate Sisi's latest posters show him wearing a suit and tie, his gaze towards a better future. 'The responsibility of every Egyptian is to work hard in times when there is no wealth to redistribute,' he says. I see Range Rover, Mercedes and BMW motorcars on my way to the five-star Marriott Hotel with its marbled pavilions. Every weekend exquisitely dressed brides and immaculate grooms hold elaborate wedding receptions there, all captured for posterity by multi-man film crews.

Yesterday Interim President Mansour issued an unchallengeable decree increasing the presidential salary twentyfold to take effect when the next incumbent is sworn in next month. I wonder what this road sweeper thinks of it all as he pockets his $2 a day.

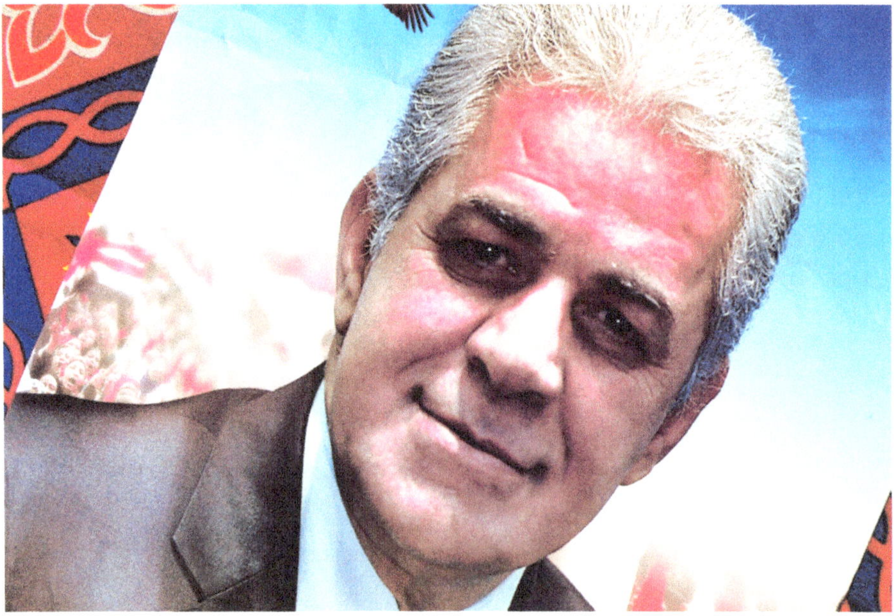

22 MAY 2014: THE ALSO-RAN

This is Hamoud Sabahy, the only other candidate in the presidential election. He's nowhere near as popular with Egyptians as Sisi and, barring miracles, he'll not win.

Sabahy is a journalist by first profession and poet who, through writing about politics, became a long-term opponent of the late President Sadat and then former President, now prisoner, Mubarak, being jailed seventeen times for his beliefs.

He subscribes to Nassercism, the ideology of Nasser, the driving force behind the Free Officer Movement that instigated the 1952 revolution. Sabahy's slogan is 'Bread, Freedom and Social Justice', which were among the aims of the 25 January revolution. He campaigns up and down the country while Sisi has yet to make any public appearance, apparently fearful of an assassination attempt.

Sabahy stood in the first knock-out round of the presidential election of 2012 against Mursi of the Muslim Brotherhood and Shafik, a former minister in Mubarak's regime. If Shafik had not split the anti-Brotherhood vote by capturing the support of Mubarak loyalists, Sabahy would have beaten Mursi and be Egypt's president today. Instead, Shafik edged Sabahy into third place and himself lost to Mursi in the run-off. There you have it . . . a coin lands on its edge and falls one way or another.

Would a Sabahy presidency have made any difference? I explore this with one of my Egyptian friends who has his finger on the political pulse.

'So, let's get this straight,' I begin. 'If Sisi wins and General Sobhi is the head of the army, and Sisi wants A and Sobhi wants B, what do we get?'

'A,' he says.

'And if Sabahy wins, and Sabahy wants A and Sobhi wants B, what do we get?'

'B.'

'Why's that?'

'It's what I've learned. I voted for Sabahy last time but he wouldn't have been powerful enough to be president.'

'But if you're the president, how much more powerful can you be?'

'Listen, what I've really learned is that the army is a country within a country and they decide everything.'

'So . . .'

'Only army presidents can do the job. They're strong and can control the armed forces. Mubarak lost it in the last few years when he put his own family first but before that he did a fine job. Military men are trained to put the country first. That's why you can trust them.'

'Therefore, should we expect Sisi to be president for the next thirty years?'

'The constitution says eight years maximum but people are already worried that this is too short and want to make it longer.'

So much for dignity, development and democracy. So much for bread, freedom and social justice. So much for the revolution.

At the moment, it seems that the only hope is for a future head of the army to genuinely let go of all its power for the long-term benefit of the country, as happened in Spain in the 1970s when King Juan Carlos I did just that when he superseded General Franco as head of state. Until then, the army will continue to subjugate the civilian outer country.

Shona has just phoned to say we've been put on alert for possible disturbances in our own area and on 6 October Bridge. This afternoon I saw a bridge lined with Sisi posters all defaced with graffiti saying in Arabic, 'Against you!'

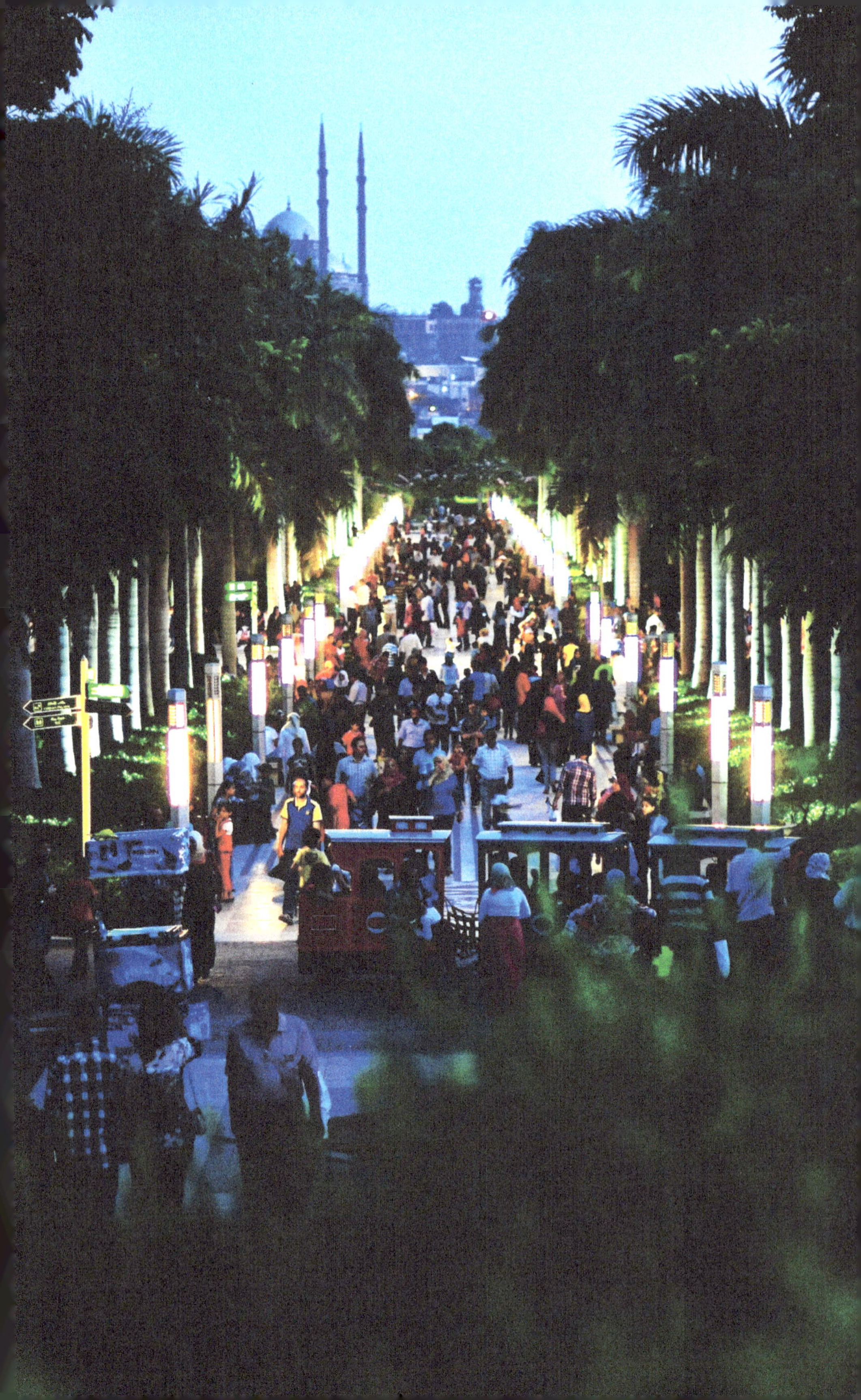

23 MAY 2014: AN UNEXPECTED PARTY

The blast rattles the windows and stops the conversation dead. We look at each other. Nahla's the first to react . . . 'That was a bomb!'

We're having lunch in her parents' apartment and, as one, we push our chairs back before crowding onto the balcony. There's a whiff of something burnt and bitter in the air. Smoke rises about eighty metres along the street to our left and a crowd of people press round the site of the detonation. Our taxi drove over the same spot when we arrived twenty minutes before.

Ambulances arrive and cut their sirens as police clear a way for them through the onlookers. Their blue lights continue to flash. A TV crew sets up a trailer-mounted satellite dish and soon we see the scene live on the set just inside the balcony doors. The reporter says it was a homemade device and no one's been injured.

Directly below us, police dogs with their handlers search the bushes for remnants of the device. Shrapnel has shattered the windows of parked cars and broken glass sparkles on the ground as policemen scuff it with their black-booted feet. One of the dogs backs out of the bushes with a piece of burnt metal in its mouth and an officer holds the object up to the cameras like a trophy.

I photograph the developing scene as best I can before we return inside as concerned relatives of Nahla's family phone to make sure they're OK and Shona goes to the toilet. Suddenly, there's a heavy-fisted battering on the front door and shouting in Arabic that clearly means 'Open up!'

Four heavily armed, plain-clothes secret service agents burst into the small apartment and the place becomes not only crowded but also tense. Shona gets a shock when she comes out of the bathroom to find so many people in the living room and at first thinks they're worried relatives. She's quickly caught up in the demands to show our IDs. I have my passport but Shona hasn't and I try to explain she's my wife. Our Egyptian hosts have to produce their identity cards, too.

'Who are these people?' asks the captain. Nahla's father takes his turn to explain.

'Where's the camera?' The captain turns to me, speaking in good English but with a lot of the bad cop in his attitude. I pause and swallow hard. Something flutters about inside me. I step over to the sofa and retrieve my camera from behind a cushion on the sofa where I had instinctively hidden it as soon as I heard the banging on the door. I wipe a sweaty thumb over the LCD screen on its back panel.

'Switch it on.'

I do.

'Give it to me.'

I do.

He slings his long double-barrelled pump-action rifle behind his back and clicks through the images stored in the memory card.

'What are these?' He points to the shots I took yesterday of Sabahy's election poster.

'Photos of Sabahy,' I say, stating the obvious.

'Why so many?'

I shrug, at a loss to explain why there are twenty shots from varying angles of such a prominent opposition figure's election poster in my camera.

'And these?' He scrolls further back through many shots of graffiti-damaged, Sisi posters taken on a bridge.

I shrug again. My forehead feels cold as perspiration evaporates.

'Wait,' he snaps, maintaining his command of the imperative, and disappears onto the balcony with both my camera and passport.

Two of the other agents go into the bedrooms and I see one kneel and poke his gun under a bed, moving boxes aside. Shona slips discreetly to my side and whispers, 'If they take the camera, let it go. Don't argue. It's better they take the camera than you.'

It's a very long ten minutes before the captain comes back in. He's worked through the entire back catalogue of photos and menus to reach the final stage in the deleting process but doesn't know the final sequence of buttons to press.

'Finish the delete,' he commands.

I do.

'Show me.'

I do, but there are some locked photos that can't be deleted. I try to explain. He points to one. 'Who's that?'

'My mother . . .'

He grunts and examines the other locked images. Another minute passes. My stomach muscles feel brick hard and I don't breathe.

'OK.' He thrusts the camera at me.

I cradle it as if catching a football. My muscles relax.

The other agents have completed their search of the flat and without warning they all troop out, walkie-talkies blaring.

'Can we have our IDs back?' Nahla runs after them. One of them turns in the doorway and obliges . . . the good cop. 'Don't worry. Welcome to Egypt,' he says.

In the evening, we escape to Al-Azhar Park above the city to calm our jangling nerves.

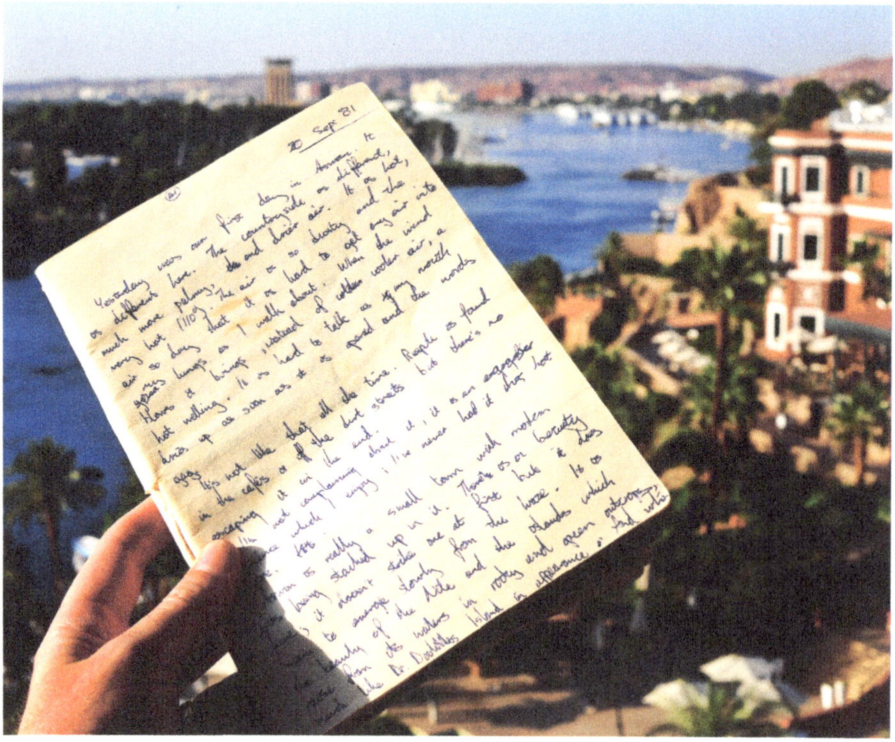

25 MAY 2014: SOME LIKE IT HOT!

'I've never had it so hot!' is one of the lines in my journal entry for 20 September 1981 pictured here, which describes my first arrival in Aswan. As I returned today it was again touching 43°C/110°F.

It's Shona first visit and she can't recall such heat. The annual precipitation is 1 mm, which equates to zero inches. Feeling the well of heat and seeing the desert stretch far away beyond the valley, that statistic doesn't surprise me at all.

It also emphasises the sheer life-giving force of the Nile as it runs its course – two miles at its broadest – through eleven countries from its furthest source in Lake Victoria in Tanzania to its outflow in the Mediterranean Sea, a distance of 4,200 miles.

Our hotel, The Old Cataract, is one of the most sumptuous we've ever stayed in. We arrived at 2 am and, from our high balcony, marvelled at the starry vista across Elephant Island including a very clear Plough or Big Dipper formed by the seven brightest stars of Ursa Major.

The assistant manager of the hotel claims to have thirty guests in residence but we have seen only six, apart from ourselves, and the prices are budget-level, driven down by dire need. It's more than worth a detour, and you couldn't feel safer than in these parts, as we discovered as we strolled into town along the Corniche and browsed in the old bazaar well past sundown. 'Welcome to Alaska,' was the most common cry. Some like it cold.

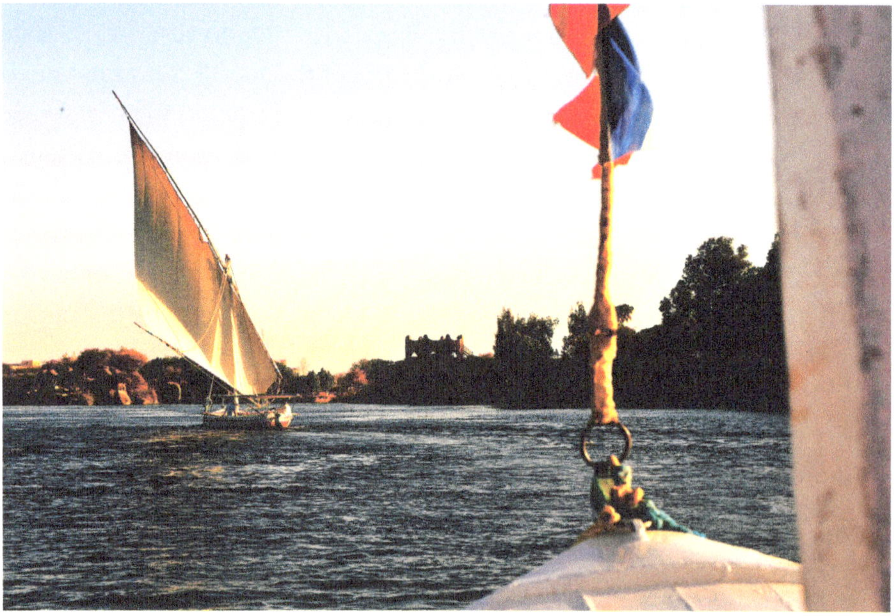

26 MAY 2014: PLACE OF MAGIC

I'm sitting now on the hotel verandah just as the sun slips behind the hill on which the Agha Khan's tomb stands. Wild dogs howl on the other side of the Nile. From the town, I hear a call to prayer signalling that the gates to paradise are open, yet again.

Paradise was the name of the felucca on which I sailed for three days and nights from Aswan to Luxor thirty-three years ago. Today we took a short sail on another felucca.

'Do you know the *Paradise*?' I ask our skipper Captain Mohammed as we tack gently south, passing Elephantine Island, to port with the Aswan Corniche to starboard.

'Oh, yes . . . she's an old boat. And Abdul, the skipper, is an old man. He now has a hotel over there.' He nods over his shoulder as he tugs a rope to make the wind play against the keel and keep us moving south.

'How much would it cost to hire you to take us on a three-day trip to Luxor?'

'Dinner and everything?'

'Dinner and everything.'

'Oh . . . let me see . . .' He looks anxious.

'Don't worry, I'm not going to do it. I just want to know the approximate price.'

He pauses some more. 'About 2,000 Egyptian pounds.'

'How much do you think it cost me with Abdul thirty years ago?'

He leans forward, all ears.

'Sixty Egyptian,' I say.

'Ha, ha, ha! Sixty? Really? How things have gone up!'

Or down, as the laid-up hulks of Nile cruise ships that line the Corniche, often three deep, testify. I count at least twenty large ones that would need hundreds of thousands of pounds sterling to make ship-shape again.

Now from the verandah I see the high sandy ridges to the west have turned inky black. The opalescent band above them has become a muted orange.

My thoughts return to Skipper Mohammed earlier today. He pulls up the keel as we round the southern tip of Elephantine Island. The swoop of swallow sail fills for the first time and the mast groans with pleasure as it braces itself against its old ally, the wind, to move us on at increasing pace.

And there it is from nowhere, the sudden rush of the breaking bow wave, dancing noisily and joyously at its momentary release from the body of the river. We tilt and fly as if for the very first time, but for this ancient design it's the millionth time.

After this spurt, the felucca enters the lee of Kitchener's Island, the home of the Botanic Gardens. We drift under low boughs, inhaling deeply the scents of rose, lotus, jasmine, narcissus, acacia, and chrysanthemum while we listen to another song of the Nile sung by kingfishers.

We complete the circumnavigation of Elephantine Island with the yolk of the late afternoon sun basting the tops of the date palms. Two boys on an old plank paddle furiously towards us, flip-flops in hand for added traction, before their small brown knuckles wrap over our gunwale. They sing to us like larks: 'Frère Jacques' and 'She'll be coming round the mountain when she comes'.

On the verandah, I lean back in my wicker chair and look up to the sky ablaze again with stars. I wrote in my older journal that here in Aswan 'I feel I'm in a place of magic'. It's good that some things in Egypt don't change.

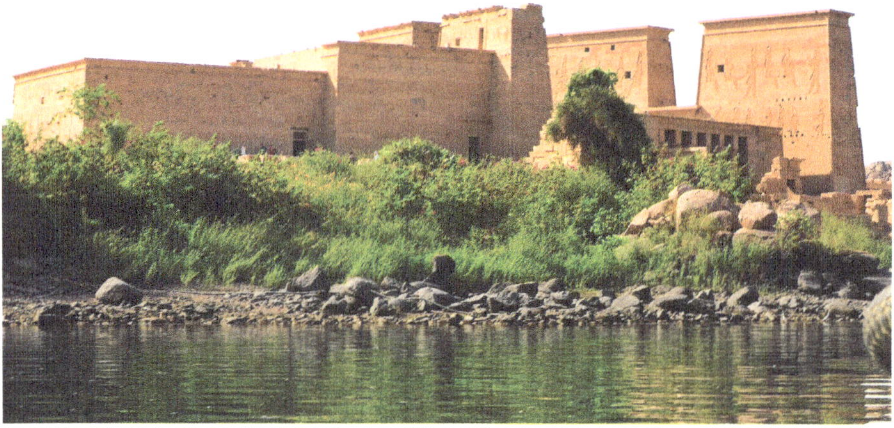

27 MAY 2014: THE TEMPLE OF ISIS: VISITS ACROSS THREE CENTURIES

Amelia Edwards, the British novelist, visited the Temple of Isis near Aswan in 1874. She wrote in her journal:

> *The approach by water is quite the most beautiful. Seen from the level of a small boat, the island, with its palms, its colonnades, its pylons, seems to rise out of the river like a mirage. Piled rocks frame it on either side, and the purple mountains close up the distance. As the boat glides nearer between glistening boulders, those sculptured towers rise higher and even higher against the sky. They show no sign of ruin or age. All looks solid, stately, and perfect. One forgets for the moment that anything is changed. If a sound of antique chanting were to be borne along the quiet air, if a procession of white-robed priests bearing aloft the veiled ark of the God were to come sweeping round between the palms and pylons, we should not think it strange.*

Twenty years later, an early-career Winston Churchill forced through a controversial structure for the new Aswan Low Dam. He insisted on a taller dam wall that would increase the capacity of the reservoir and irrigation possibilities. The downside was partly submerging the Temple of Isis. He clearly prioritised food for starving people over the interests of archaeologists and early tourists.

The dam opened in 1902 after a fourteen-year construction period. English writer R. Talbot Kelly visited the temple shortly after and gave an account in his book *Peeps Into Many Lands – Egypt*, published in 1908:

> *This is the greatest engineering work of its kind ever constructed, and spans the Nile Valley at the head of the cataract basin. It is a mile and a quarter in length, and the river which is raised in level about 66 feet, passes through a number of sluice gates which are opened or shut according to the season of the year and the necessity of irritation or navigation. Behind, the steep valley is filled, and forms a huge lake extending eighty miles to the south, and many pretty villages have been submerged, while of the date-groves which surrounded them the crests of the higher trees alone appear above water. The green island of Philae also is engulfed, and of the beautiful Temple of Isis built upon it only the upper portion is visible.*

In the 1960s, President Nasser was anxious to have more of the Nile's water stored in Egypt for political reasons. The alternative was further south in Sudan or Ethiopia where the evaporation rate is actually lower but he wanted control of this vital asset. He pressed ahead with plans to build the Aswan High Dam. Several ancient sites would be submerged completely and UNESCO intervened to move the Temple of Isis from the island of Philae to the island of Agilkia. Forty thousand individual blocks of stone were numbered, measured, dismantled, transported and re-erected in the operation. All is as it was except that the temple now points in another, less religiously significant, direction.

The high dam was opened in 1970 and I visited the relocated temple for the first time eleven years later.

> *Temple of Isis, Aswan, 21 September 1981*
>
> *It's the first Egyptian Temple I've visited and I was quite stunned. I walked about by myself. No one else was in view and suddenly I fell back into the ambience of this building, as it was originally intended, and not that of an historic site.*
>
> *Here I was at the far end of a pillared courtyard. In awesome splendour at the other end were the twin pylons of the temple. They were huge, and covered with hieroglyphics and frightening crow-faced bodies. I approached the entranceway. It was like being admitted to a great and secret place. I walked up a shallow ramp of stairs between two lions, feeling the whole weight of the masonry and faith press down. Each stage was only possible because I was being allowed to pass. I couldn't have done it by myself, there was too much power. I passed through a second courtyard and set of pylons. Through doorway after doorway I was drawn towards the innermost sanctuary with its stone altar.*
>
> *It was an hypnotic experience, a trance-like state was over me and the music of ancient Egypt sounded in my ears. I don't know where it came from but I was caught in its rhythms. As I exited along the processional path, I was met by electric air in the courtyard, a drumming, buzzing adulation. Bowed heads, gold and purple, chants of 'High Sun-Amun-Re.'*
>
> *The ferry broke down on the way back.*

Shona and I visited together today in this third decade of the twenty-first century. The ferry didn't break down but it was a very small and decrepit boat in which we glided through the floating graveyard of skeletal pleasure craft that were once employed to ferry tourists en masse to and from the temple island.

The sun was strong even at this early hour, bringing out sharply the reliefs on the pylons. The approach to the temple is exactly as Amelia Edwards described it a hundred and forty years ago. I note with pleasure that she and my younger self had the same musical antenna to detect chants and music in the air.

I did hear those sounds again today but it was more the sense of exalted gods admitting lowly mortals into their most holy sanctuary that came back to me. The architect of the temple was a master of staging. He created an unparalleled sense of unfolding drama that only the pharaoh and his high priests would ever have experienced fully as they processed from the outer courtyard to the inner sanctum. What a journey full of grandeur and mystery it must have been.

The essence of that sensed scene of a mass of worshippers kept in the outer courtyard, which I narrated in my older journal, found its echo today in the rows of stone seats built for the Son et Lumière show, the Ray-Bans and smart phones of their occupants being the new purple and gold.

In the boat on the way back, I clutched the second volume of my 1981 Egyptian journal and a first edition of Talbot's book *Peep into Egypt* that Teleri Williams's husband presented to me earlier this year. The bookmark in the latter is a photograph taken by Teleri of an olive branch. She would be pleased to know it was here in this land where peace is at a premium.

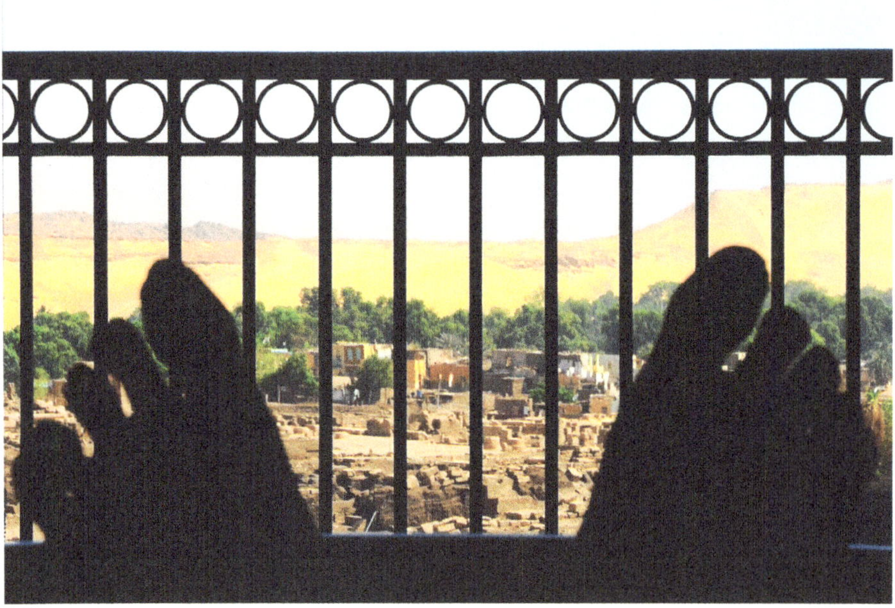

28 MAY 2014: THE FUNDAMENTAL THINGS APPLY

In the middle of this Aswanic oasis of calm, the only reminder that there is a presidential election going on in the country is the presence of European Union election observers at the breakfast tables neighbouring ours on the hotel verandah. An army helicopter occasionally batters overhead, circling the town, a subliminal message that Sisi has identified a severe security threat to the country and is the only man strong enough to deal with it on the people's behalf.

I look out over the First Cataract as a piano version of 'As Time Goes By' tinkles somewhere in the background. Motor craft ply their way up and round Elephantine Island, birds chirrup, and the ambient temperature is as agreeable and as relaxing as a hot bath. Everything is perfect, as it would be for anyone privileged enough to sit here this May morning.

The tune also makes me wonder about the fundamental things that apply to me; those things that give me energy, motivation and, ultimately, fulfilment. Being back in Aswan makes clear that travelling to very foreign places is important with all the exploration and excitement of discovery that goes with it and, also, translating the consequent sensations into words.

I used to lie soaking in the bath at home before going to Glasgow Central station to catch the sleeper train to London at the start of my long trips to Egypt or India or wherever. I let my arms float in the warm water, allowing the ripples to subside to an utter calm. I'd look down around the islands of my knees to my toes propped against the end of the tub, and enjoy the peace while I tried to imagine the unimaginable of what lay out there for me on the other side of the world in alien lands of which I knew nothing.

Then came that first great movement, which set the whole thing in motion as I heaved myself out of the bath, dried and dressed, strapped on my money belt, checked my passport, travellers cheques, notepad and pen and set off.

My shot above is taken from the bathtub of our room and shows my toes with Elephantine Island beyond. The view in Paisley was never like this.

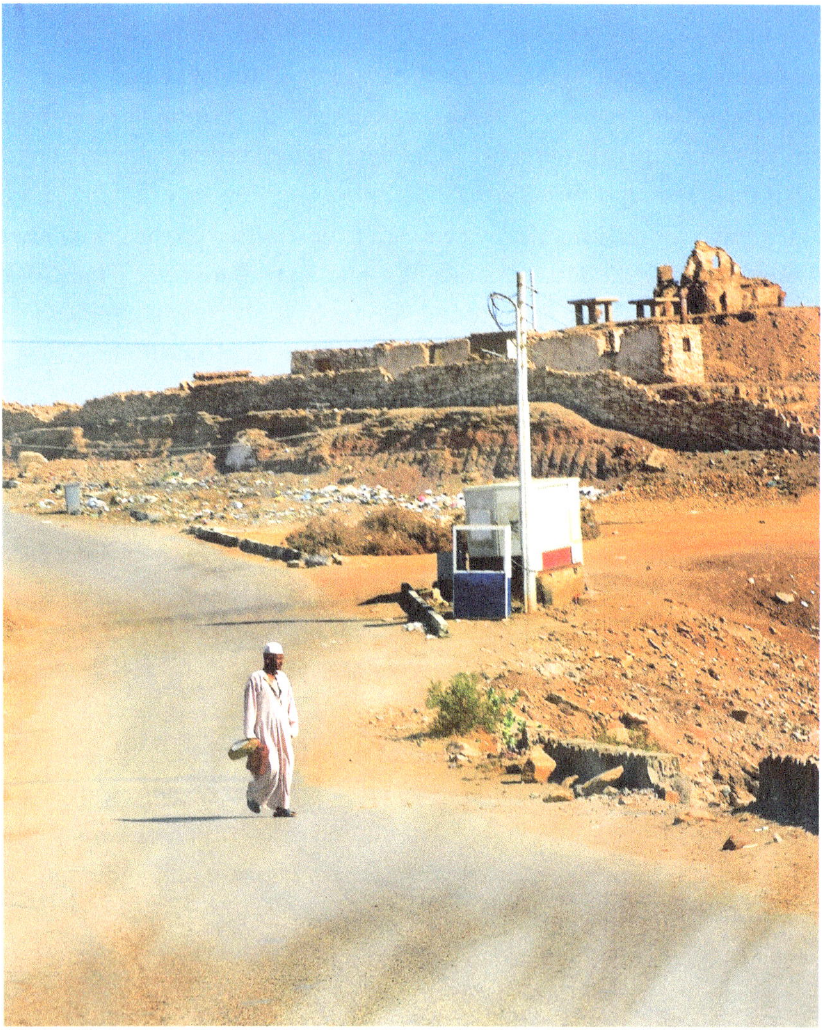

29 MAY 2014: THE VOTE

I wonder if this man in Aswan voted in the presidential election. It has not delivered the mandate General Sisi wanted. He had set a target of 75% turnout of the voting population; that would have made him a truly empowered president, but only 45% voted.

International observers reported a number of irregularities. Their principal concern was the extension of the voting period at the last minute from one to two days and the extension of the opening hours of the voting stations both days. The election authorities offered incentives of free transport and food to encourage people to attend and push the turnout figure up. 'This is unprecedented,' said the observers, but the efforts to encourage a greater turnout appear to have had little success.

The figure that will dominate national and international headlines is the 98% support the president-elect got from those who did vote. It shows that the Sisi constituency is substantial but still, in reality, a minority in the country.

The big question is when, how and where the 55% of the voting population who felt alienated in this election process, including the younger post-revolutionaries, have their say? Tahrir Square, perhaps?

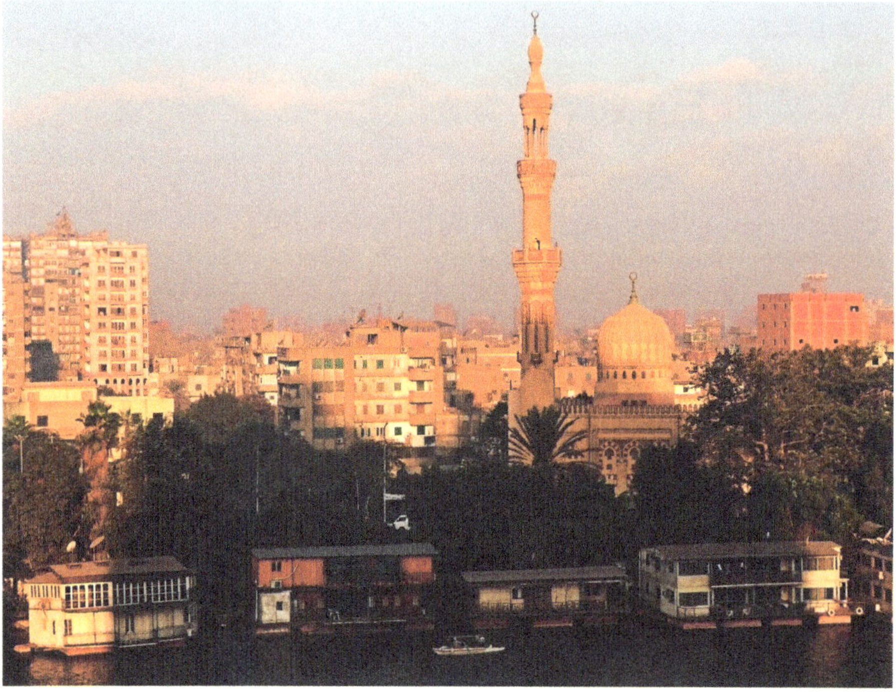

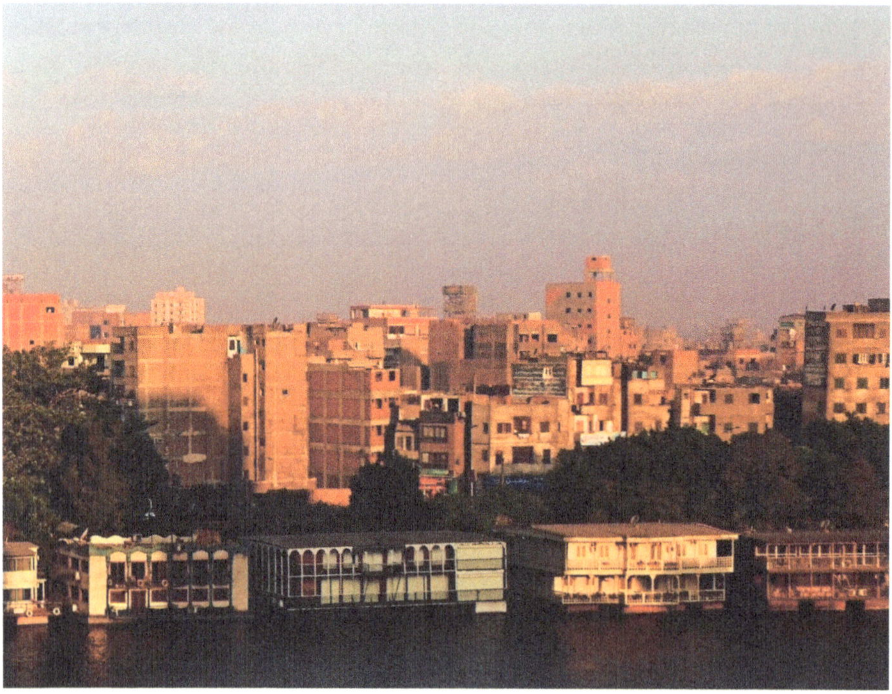

30 MAY 2014: STABILITY?

The leading state newspaper, *Al-Ahram*, ran a cartoon showing the sun rising above Cairo with the word 'stability' inscribed on it. It asserts a stable future for Egypt now that Sisi's victory at the polls has been confirmed. One would always wish a country stability but there is a doubt as to whether that can be achieved here and, if so, for how long and at what cost.

The scene is hardly set for tranquillity given that the Muslim Brotherhood has been pushed underground and its leader, the last president, may face the death penalty at the end of one of his four trials. Three or four policemen are killed every day in drive-by shootings around the country and there's practically a guerrilla war in the Sinai. The secular, liberal, young, rightly or wrongly, given that they had a chance to vote for a leftish upholder of the revolution's aims this week, feel excluded from how the country is run and sense their revolutionary hopes are dashed. The unemployed are likely to remain unemployed, the uneducated uneducated and the poor poor.

State censorship, imprisonment without charge, and a series of alleged breaches of civil rights are already the cost of that stability; a cost apparently accepted by a good proportion of the population, many of whom were out partying last night until the stability sun came up.

As I wrote in the early days of Mursi's term in office, 'Actions speak louder than words, Mr President!' The same applies to the now President-elect Sisi.

46°C in Cairo today.

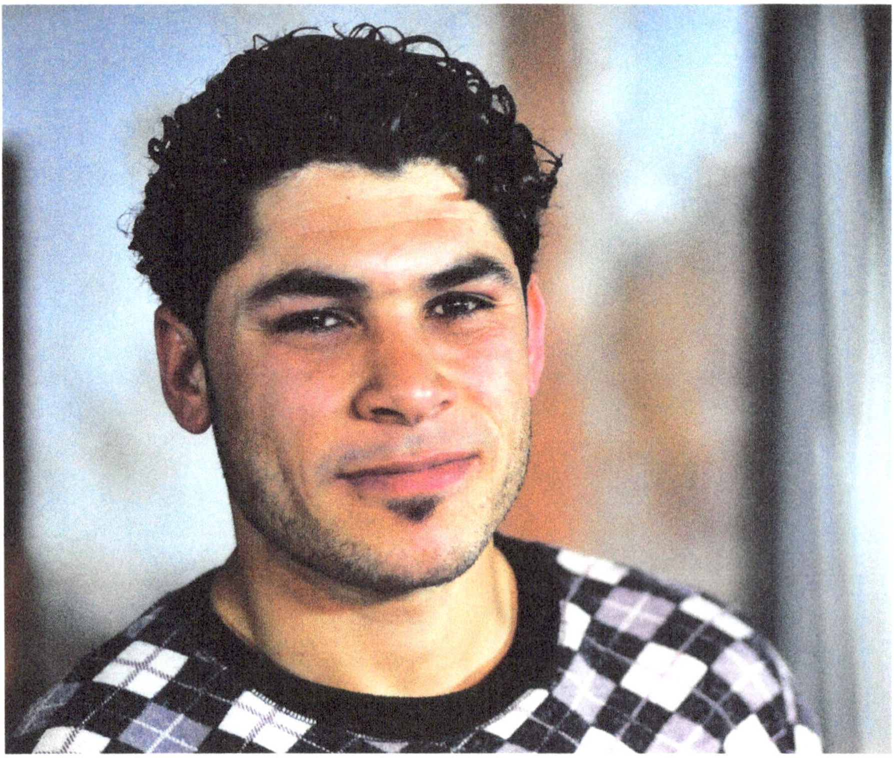

6 JUNE 2014: SAID

Said works at the parking lot in front of the building where the young, good-luck Su'ud lives. Said's a friendly and energetic youth like so many I've met on my visits. The recent election will have a huge bearing on his and all their futures. Let's hope it will be positive.

'Any news on Sisi yet?' I ask my elderly-gentleman friend, later.

'Yes, he's been confirmed officially as victor,' he says.

'Surprise, surprise.'

'Everyone loves Sisi.'

'Will he do well?'

'Let's see. But one thing you need to understand is that we're an army country. We love the army, and everyone has a family member in it, like me with my nephew. You can't have a non-army president until the people are all educated. And that will take years.'

'A hundred?' I proffer.

'Maybe fifty . . . let's see.'

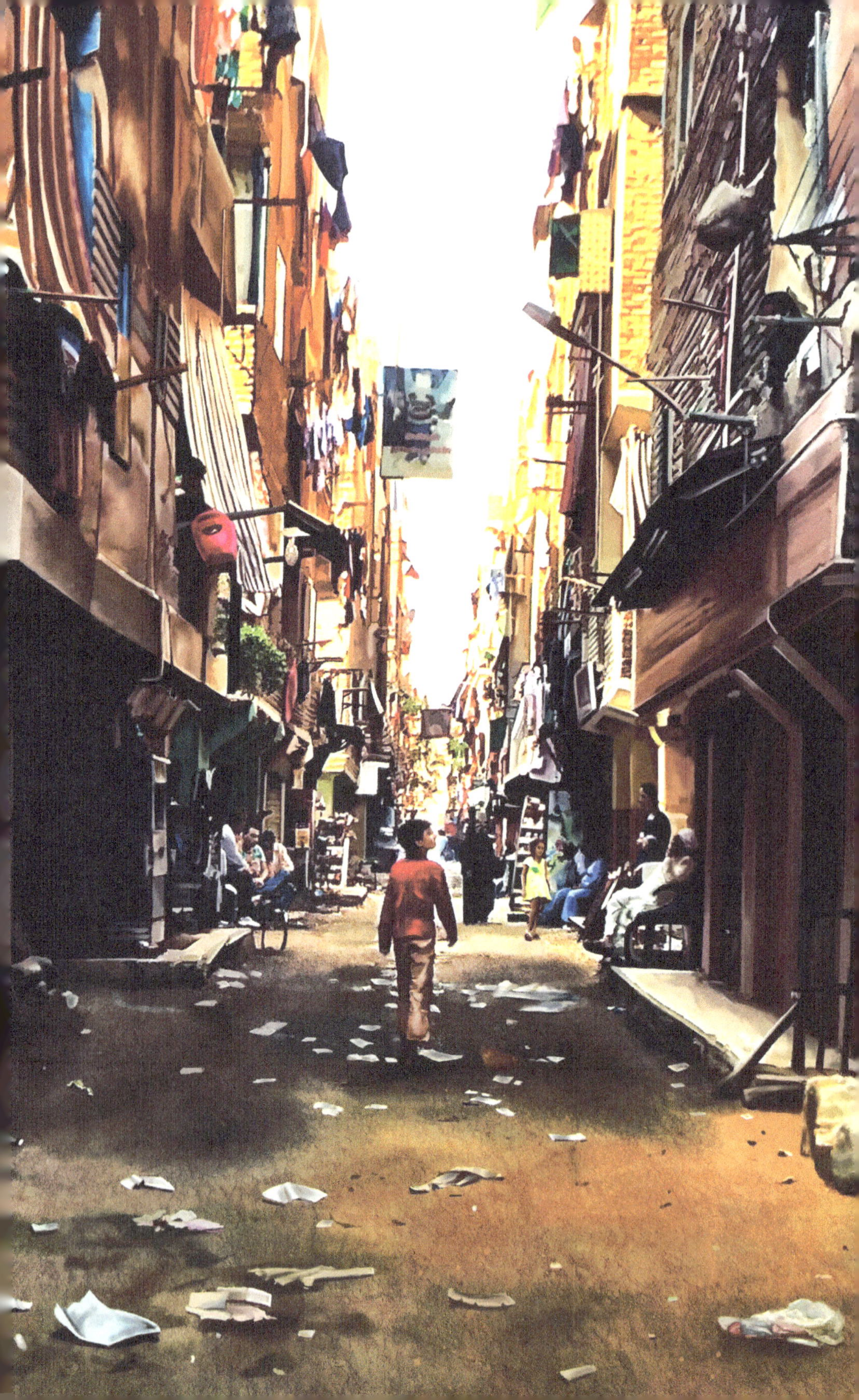

7 JUNE 2014: LET US GO THEN, YOU AND I . . .

. . . through streets that represent the reality of everyday life for over twenty million people in Cairo. They are located in the district of Imbaba and I went there today on a mission to visit Mohamed, an old man who used to work near our home. He's ill and I wanted to cheer him up.

Our car crawled along in a line of tuk-tuks passing within inches of fool stands, the laden platforms of delivery bicycles and men seated at tiny cafés, their chairs balanced on uneven kerbstones as they drew on shisha pipes. We'd phoned ahead for directions but still had to ask for help more than twenty times, each person repeating the address as they gazed along the street before waving their hand one way or another. I listened carefully to the degree of confidence in their voices to gauge how soon it would be before we'd have to stop again.

I don't know how but as we manoeuvred down the narrow earthen street you see to the left there was a tap on the glass beside my head. It was Mohamed with a thumbs-up sign and a broad smile on his lined face under his thin white hair. I lowered the window and he pushed his hand in to shake mine. His was cold and bony like a dead sparrow. 'Welcome. Come to my home,' Mohamed said, his voice weaker and more rasping than I remembered it.

He carried a large bottle of Sprite as I followed him around the corner and across a high threshold into a tight dark entranceway from which narrow stairs rose. The handrail was no higher than my knee. As we climbed, Mohamed paused several times to catch his breath and I caught glimpses of the interiors of shoe-box homes before entering one ourselves. The living space was just four feet by six and we sat squeezed together on faded-gilt upright chairs with stained cushions of maroon and cream stripes. A small marble-topped table held a vase of dusty dried flowers and a large flat-screen TV hung on the wall beside the front door which was made of unpainted planks and held shut by a simple bolt. One of Mohamed's five daughters served our Sprite in glasses on a tray.

Mohamed is struggling with angina and his spirits are low. He seemed pleased to see me and we caught up as best we could in his broken English and my four words of Arabic. It was all in the smiles and gestures. He touched my knee affectionately as he passed through to the kitchen cubicle.

This evening, a friend reminded me that sometimes hospitality is all people have to offer and that it's important to accept it. She also said connections like these 'will matter when all the goods that can be bought and sold have fallen to rot. That touch on the knee will be with you on your deathbed. It's that important.' I know it is . . . and it will be.

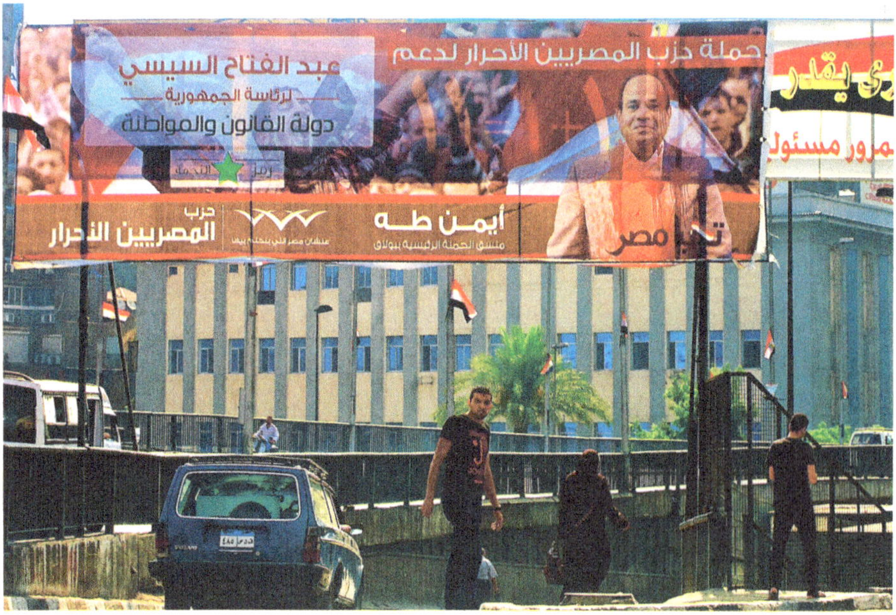
حملة حزب المصريين الأحرار لدعم
عبد الفتاح السيسي
لرئاسة الجمهورية
دولة القانون والمواطنة
حزب
المصريين الأحرار
أيمن طه
منسق الحملة الرئيسية ببولاق
مصر

8 JUNE 2014: A PARADE OF PRESIDENTS

There have been six presidents of Egypt in my lifetime: Nasser, Sadat, Mubarak, Mursi, Mansour and, being inaugurated a mile down the road from where I sit now in Cairo, Sisi.

It's been quite a parade over the years, with something of a slow-slow-quick-quick step to it, and some spectacular contretemps. Apart from Nasser, I've known them all. As I've recounted in this book, I was a mile from Sadat when he was gunned down at his own military parade on 6 October 1981, which was the day, in effect, when Mubarak took over. I walked through Tahrir Square in July 2011, shortly after the 25 January revolution, while Mubarak was being held in prison nearby, charged with murder. I was in Cairo when Mursi was elected, and across the city from him when, a year later, he gave his last televised address to the people before being toppled the next day by Sisi, on 3 July 2013. Today, Abdel Fattah Al-Sisi drops the 'elect' from his title following elections ten days ago, and is being proclaimed at this very moment president of Egypt. I can hear his audience in the Supreme Constitutional Court applaud with rhythmic unified clapping through a radio that is blaring from a taxi parked across the street and see fireworks fill the morning sky. A brass band with clashing cymbals strikes up as more marshal music is played for the continuation of this particular parade. 'Seesi, Seesi, in Para-deesi,' sings one supporter in the street beside me as he dances a jig and perhaps imagines the gates to Paradise will open more widely under Sisi.

The country awaits with unparalleled expectation for him to work miracles to rescue Egypt; miracles of the kind many feel were last seen when the pharaohs erected the pyramids.

What should Sisi's goals and priorities be? In whatever order necessary to start the causal chain to prosperity, they are: an equitable and effective tax system; a radically reduced administration infrastructure; transparent tendering for all government contracts; the elimination of nepotism and other types of corruption; a pluralistic parliament of peaceful, political parties; education on political process and the benefits of consensual problem solving; the upholding of the civil rights enshrined in the constitution; more jobs; an accessible-to-all health service and an effective education system.

Oh, and see that the army voluntarily gives up de facto control of the country, allowing voters to cast their ballot based on the premise that the government they elect will endure or fall on its own merits and not at the whim of the army.

Then, perhaps, Egypt will begin to modernise and build the dignity, rigour and resources to participate in the innovative world of the twenty-first and twenty-second centuries; in the pharaonic scheme of things, the latter is not that far away.

As we peruse the election poster of Sisi, here, depicting him in his disarmingly casual attire, we cannot fail to notice the blood-coloured paint splattered on his face.

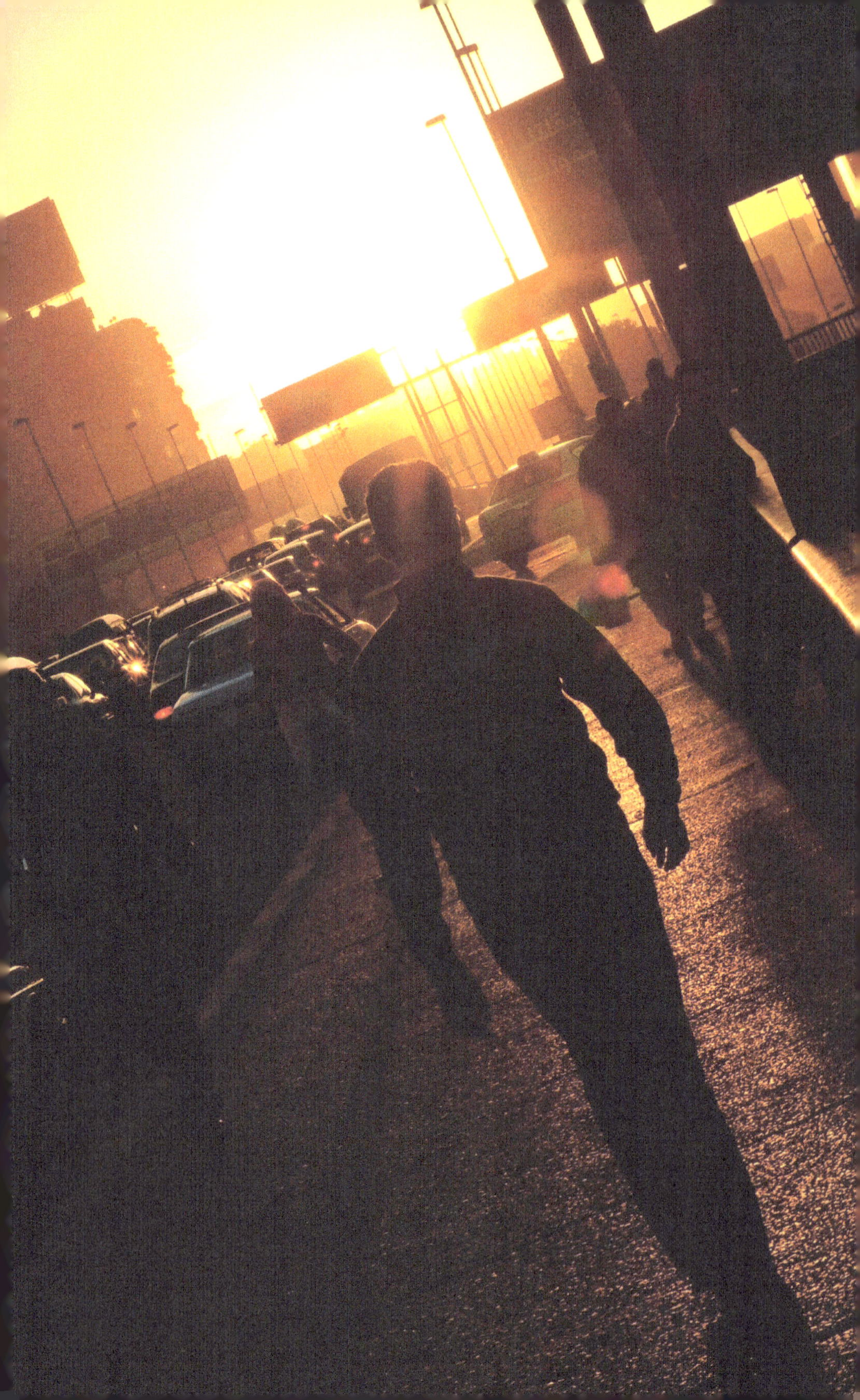

Epilogue

CAIRO, 25 JANUARY 2015

A young Alexandrian woman, Shaimaa Al-Sabbagh, was shot dead at point-blank range just off Tahrir Square last night. It was the eve of the fourth anniversary of the 2011 Egyptian revolution and she had gone to lay flowers to honour the martyrs who had lost their lives. Her husband and friends accuse the security forces of the crime and they, in turn, accuse the fundamentalists. The square is closed to the public today, in sharp contrast to its role as the crucible of the revolution when over a million people gathered to demand the resignation of President Mubarak.

The government has seemed ambivalent on how to mark those eighteen remarkable days that were meant to change Egypt forever. The death of King Abdullah in Saudi Arabia this week provided a solution to its dilemma. President Sisi cancelled all events related to the revolution as a sign of respect for the late king and declared a week of mourning. In Saudi Arabia no such mourning takes place under their customs, flags remain at full mast and government offices are open for business as usual.

I'm sitting on the same bench in Cairo where I wrote the prologue to this book seven months ago. I wish I could report that the revolution's aims of bread, freedom and social justice were nearer to fulfilment, but the current panorama is not hopeful.

Peter Greste and his Al Jazeera colleagues, Mohamed Fahmy and Baher Mohamed, remain in prison. A photo-journalist arrested at the Rabaa al-Adawiya Square protester clearances is still held without charge over five hundred days later. A young female human rights worker is serving three years for illegal assembly after buying a bottle of water near a street demonstration. Hundreds of students were fired on and many injured on their university campus for violations of the Protest Law. Foreign journalists and native English speakers have been detained after being overheard discussing politics and the revolution in public places. Former President Mubarak has been cleared of murder and corruption and may soon be a free man. Political parties will dispute less than a quarter of the seats in elections for the new parliament, if they are ever held; the rest are reserved for wealthy independents and presidential nominees. Six hundred minors are reportedly detained for protest activities in a government detention camp in the south of the country. Any civilian who damages state assets may now be court-martialled. Army generals sit on the boards of the major Suez Canal expansion and grain distribution projects. A whole stand of books on the revolution that was displayed prominently in one of the main bookshops has disappeared.

'What's happened to the revolution?' I ask the owner of a pharmacy I know.

'Look, there are three points here,' he starts. 'Why do you have a revolution? You need change. And the first revolution got that, got rid of Mubarak, who was part good, part not so good.' He pauses to sell someone nail clippers. 'And then you get another one like Mubarak, only with this . . .' He motions a beard on the end of his chin to conjure up the figure of former President Mursi, '. . . and he's no good either. People don't like the things he does, so we needed a second revolution to remove him.' Another person asks for cough medicine. 'Where was I?'

'Getting to the benefits under this latest president?' I prompt.

'It's too soon to say. The new system is not perfect and it will need time to work.'

'Can you see any economic improvement yet, anything for the man in the street?'

He gives me a long look before he answers. 'Give it a year . . . this is not a perfect system.'

President Sisi said this week in Abu Dhabi that there are more important issues than the Protest Law. He would argue that if the system is less than perfect then that's a necessary means to an end in a volatile, terrorist-filled world that threatens the country's national security. The underlying question concerns the true motivation of each president who has taken part in this sixty-year-long parade. Is it the protection of the homeland en route to a better place that all the people can enjoy, or the subjugation of the homeland to enable an elite circle of powerful men to maintain absolute control and prosper disproportionately to the rest of the population?

If it is the latter, then whatever is the most plausible threat in any particular period becomes the convenient narrative for the repression of the population, whether it be war with Israel in the sixties and seventies, the rise of the Muslim Brotherhood during the eighties or ISIS and the new caliphate today.

There is little evidence of fresh thinking or innovative actions being applied over the years. The presidents in our parade have employed measures like states of emergency, supreme-power decrees, curfews and protest laws for sixty years. It was left to the people to attempt to lead change through a revolution four years ago today. That initiative appears to have stalled and the realisation of Egypt's fullest opportunity in which dignity, development and democracy prevail is still some way off. Some would say it's a paradise lost.

Meanwhile people get on with their daily lives. Some enjoy more privileged positions than others. Beside me in the café, privately educated students pore over their English textbooks or review architectural drawings and electrical engineering diagrams in their study groups. Businessmen walk up and down with their hands in their trouser pockets, half-shouting down their mobile phones. Around the square, heavily built women in dust-covered black robes sit in gutters and hold their up-turned palms aloft for baksheesh. A shoeshine, dressed in a pencil-striped galabeya with thermals underneath, shuttles his brushes around the heel of his client's shoe. A boy sells packets of tissues on the street corner at a pound a time. A thirty-something mother sits cross-legged on the pavement and shouts, 'Mister! Mister!' at a passing foreigner. Her two young dirt-encrusted children scream and throw themselves across her breasts. She laughs and hugs them. Banana sellers stand with sharp knives in hand, ready to slice a bunch from the stems that hang on their rickety carts. Sweet-potato vendors trundle their mobile ovens into place and poke the embers to life in the small fires underneath. Rubbish collectors in open sandals bend double and use pieces of cardboard to scoop up piles of litter and muck. Taxi drivers in clapped-out vehicles toot their horns as they circle on the lookout for passengers. Above all, wails of sirens reach our ears from the direction of Tahrir Square.

And what of the youths we have met in these pages? The boy of the future with the bike is now an assistant in a pharmacy. Newborn Walid is two years older and has opened a small mobile-phone accessory shop across from his father's coffee stall. Good-luck Su'ud continues to live in his family's doorless quarters behind the parking lot and is no further along the path of my dreams for him, but he is as bright and cheery as ever. The fizzing young man with the tongue hanging out has yet to break into the world of politics. Yasheen/Hasim is at home for three weeks with a broken ankle after being hit by a car in the street. We've sent some books to him and are trying to set up private English classes for when he gets better. Some progress, but this country needs more. Will it come? Inshallah.

Alexander Murray 2015

Lightning Source UK Ltd.
Milton Keynes UK
UKOW07f0705031215

264030UK00015B/117/P